Jenny Dowling (June 2019)

£10

*Also by David Fowler*

God Bless the Prince of Wales
National Service, Elvis & Me!
Berby and Fuz
Why Should England Tremble?
The Clock Café Story
Scarborough Snippets
Don Robinson - Story of a High Flier

Copies are available direct from the publisher or through www.Lulu.com or www.Amazon.co.uk.

*

"'I've started, so I'll finish...' is an enjoyable, yet remarkable collation of a full and fulfilling life, so far.
I was intrigued how the author brought together into a flowing story his memories and observations, the observations of others, the passage of time and evolution of society and its behaviour, into a coherent whole that was a pleasure to read.
This book also has two other particularly pleasing features. It was written in bite sized pieces that I could readily pick up and read any time. The other feature that I greatly appreciated were the Brief Timelines at the start of each chapter. The content of those boxes of information were a constant source of interest, surprise and amazement - time flies by!'

**John M. Webster, BSc, PhD, DSc, FRSB,**
Professor Emeritus in Biological Sciences, at Simon Fraser University, British Columbia, Canada.

# 'I've started, so I'll finish...'

## A Memoir
### SECOND EDITION

## David Fowler

Copyright © David Fowler 2016-17

All rights reserved. No part of this publication may be reproduced, stored in a retrieval system, or transmitted, in any form or by any means, electronic, mechanical, photocopying, recording or otherwise, without the prior permission of both the copyright owner and the publisher.

David Fowler has asserted his right to be identified as the author of this work in accordance with the Copyright, Designs and Patents Act 1988.

If you are a copyright holder and feel your contribution has not been acknowledged, please advise the publisher and an acknowledgement will be placed in any future edition.

Where appropriate, extracts from David Fowler's previous books have been incorporated.

First published in Great Britain in 2016
by
Farthings Publishing
8 Christine House
Scarborough YO11 2QB
UK

http://www.farthings-publishing.com

E-mail: dgfowler@gmail.com

ISBN 978 – 1 – 326 – 38169 – 1

September 2017 (Cv)

# DEDICATION

- To Eileen, Phoebe, Sulyn, Mark and to all members of our family.

- To my good friend and partner in Farthings Publishing, Ren Yaldren, for her support and encouragement which have helped bring this book to fruition.

- To my late grandfather, author Tom Henry Fowler, who died aged only 41 in 1908, long before I was born, but whom I felt was always with me, looking over my shoulder and helping to steer me in the right direction.

- To the late Gerald Hinchliffe, for his encouragement and generous words over many years.

- And to Ella, Mia and Fern Lea Yaldren for their friendship and for giving me the opportunity to see what a joy being a grandfather could have been. Thank you very much girls.

\*

## ACKNOWLEDGEMENTS

- BBC Archives and Wikipedia for assistance in my research and use of extracts.
- John Nichol and Tony Bennell – 'The Untold Story of Allied POWs 1944-5'
- Rudolf Friml/ Brian Hooker 1925 'The Vagabond King'. 'Song of the Vagabonds'
- Rudolf Friml/Oscar Hammerstein II/Otto A Harbach 'Rose Marie'. 'Here come the Mounties'
- Robert Goddard, for the use of a short extract from 'Beyond Recall'
- Allen Ferguson, for providing photographs for Chapters 10, 11 and 14 and for his help in checking detail.
- Barrie Petterson, for the cover and title page cartoons.
- Sam Telfer for checking detail in Chapter 14.
- And to everyone who has helped in any way; including the following who all 'appear' in the book. These names were correct at the time the person entered the story.

Judith Abiss; Annie Aconley; Basil Aconley; Robin Aconley; Neil Aitchison; Howard Acklam; Geoff Aitken; Russ Allen; John Angell; Gee Armitage; Tony Atkins; Alan Ayckbourn; Heather Ayckbourn; 'Ayckbourn' & 'Todd'; 'Thomas'; Dick Baker; John Baker; Rachel Baker; Les Barker; Lofty Barnes; Irene Beagle; John Beagle; Dr. Beeching; Keith Beal; Peter Bell; Janice Bendell; Richard Benson; Brian Berryman; Frank 'Billy' Binder; Scouse Blinkhorn; Joe Boag, Ken Boden; Mr Borland; Marcus Whickam Boynton; Jack Bradley; Don Bradman; Sarah Beth Briggs; Phyllis Briscombe; Percy Briscombe; Barry Brookes; Gordon Brough; Les Brown; Stanley Brown; Deirdre Buchanan; Jean Bucknall (nee Taylor); Peter Bucknall; Graham Burnett; Rachel Carter; Arnold Catton; 'Chloe'; Winston Churchill; 'Bonn' Clarke; Brian Clayton; Dena Clayton; Emily Clayton; Lisa Clayton; Mark Clayton; Captain Coffey; The Lord Coggan; Eddie Colenut; Katie Colley; Ann Collins;

Ralph Connell; Angela Cooper; Bill Cooper; Letitia Cooper; Noel Cooper; Sir Edwin Cooper; Kath Coulson; Brandsby Croft; Mabel Cromack; Fred Coulthard; 'Darkie'; Rosemary Davies; Roy Day; Janie Dee; David Dennis; Paul Derek; Keith Dickinson; Margaret Dixon; John Douglas; The Duke of Devonshire; Bernard Durham; Tim Easterby; Dr Dorothy Ellison; Anne Elvy; Mike Elvy; Robert England; Veronica England; Charles Evans; John Fawbert; Margaret Fawbert: Peter Feather; Allen Ferguson; Angela Ferguson; William Fewlar; Barbara Fidler; Dorothy Fidler; Roy Field; Ron Firth; Ken Forrest; John Found; Eileen Fowler; Ella Fowler; Emma Fowler; Ena Fowler; John Fowler; Knapton Fowler; Neil Fowler; Phoebe Fowler; Susan Fowler; the late Tom H Fowler; Walter (Bill) Fowler; 'Pop' Francis; Clark Gable, Andrew Gibbs; Mr Giblett; Ken Gill; Linda Gillam; John Gledhill; Hermann Goering; Robert Goddard; Jane Goforth; Pancho Gonzales; Kenneth Goodall; Jim Goodman; Dr WG Grace; Roger Griffin; Russ Grimshaw: Mrs Grist; Anne Guest; PC David Haigh; Lilian Hainsworth; Louise Hall; Reginald Hall; Thelma Hammond; Mike Hanlon; Doris Harris; Tim Hartley; Trish Hartley; Brian Hawson, Dena Hebditch; Ken Herbert; Geoff Heselton; Margaret Hill; Gerald Hinchliffe; Adolf Hitler; Frank Hole; Bob Holmes; HM Princess Margaret; Annette Howard; Hon Simon Howard; Gill Hunt; Neil Hunt; HRH The Prince of Wales; Barry Ibbeson; Fay Jackson; Norman Jackson; Mary ('Lolly') James; Angela Jewitt; Maurice Johnson; Bernard Jones; Stephen Joseph; Igor Judge, Baron Judge PC QC; Helen Kirk; Frank Kitching; Julian Knowles; 2nd Lt Lacey 1 RHA; Chris Larwood; Miss Latham; Charles Laughton; Esme Laughton; Tom Laughton; John Lawrence; Doris Lawson; Edith Lawson; Robert Lawson; Chris Larwood; Ray Lazenby; Jean Lazenby; John Leadley; Vivien Leigh; David Lickess; Judith Lickess; Maureen Lipman; Janet Lisle; Roger Lisle; Susan Lisle; Albert Locke; Di Lowery; Tony Lowery; Archie Lowndes; Lord Lucan; George Luckett; Richard Lukey; Magnus Magnusson; Ana Marjanovic; HW Marsden; Ian Martin; James Martin; Charlotte Martin; Tom Martin; Hilda Mayes; Graham McCourt; Keith McFarlane; Eddie McGee; Ken McGregor; Julia McKenzie; Captain Turner McLardey; Jim McLenachan; Rudolf Metzig: Captain Hugh Miller MB; John Mills; Alan Milner; 'Mischief'; John Morley; Ann Morton; Mike Moses; Chris Munsch; Geoff Nalton; Peter Newham; Paul Newlove; John Nichol; Judy Nicholson; Joyce Noble; Dudley Ogley; Okasha; 'Oskar'; Bryan D. Overall; Linda Overall; Martin Oxby; David Paddon; 'Patch'; Fred Perry; Noel Pharaoh; Ted

Pickering; Sylvia Pinder; John Pitts; Libby Pobgee; Malcolm Pobgee; Robert Pollock; Eric Poppleton; Les Porritt; Colin Porter; Bill Potts; WF Potts; Elvis Presley; Angela Procter; Peter Prudom; David Puckering; Alexander Pushkin; Chitoor Rajaraman; Tony Rennell; Marjorie Rice; Susan Richards; Peter EW Richardson; 'Pike' Richardson; Sir Ralph Robins; David Robinson; Don Robinson; Mrs Robson; Peter Robson; Doug Ross; Lord Rowallen; Jock Roxburgh; Mike Sankey; Mike Saul; PEG Sayer; Jean Scarlet; Christine Scott, Francisco Segura; Pauline Shannon; Margaret Sharp; Nick Sheldon; 'Shimba'; Brian Shipley; Malcolm Bruce Smith; David Soul; Sylvia Spencer; WC Stainton; Gillian Stoddard; Ian Stoddard; Norman Stoddard; Peter Stoddard; Lesley Sturdy; Jill Sturgeon; Jeannie Swales; Alec Taylor; Jean Taylor; Jack Taylor; Colonel Teacher; Ernie Teal; Audrey Telfer; Sam Telfer; Christine Tomlinson; Nigel Tinkler; Steve Toal; Paul Todd; Christine Tomlinson; Fred Tomlinson; Margaret Thompson; Richard Toft; Debbie Towse; Freddie Trueman; 'Tschang'; Urs Umbricht; Pam Varlow; Elizabet van den Werve; Van Manstein: 'Lady W.'; Sulyn Waddon; Margaret Waddon; Mark Waddon; Basil Walker; Sqn Ldr J Walker; Frank Ward; Wilf Ward; Mrs Wastling; Eileen Watson; Heather Watson; Sarah Watson; John Weatherall; Miss Weathers; Andrew Lloyd Webber; Julian Lloyd Webber; John M. Webster; Albert Welburn; Alice Welburn; Annie Welburn; Edith Welburn; John Welburn; Maud Welburn; Robert Welburn; William Welburn; Linda Welsby; Peter West; JR Wilson; Geoff Winn; Alan Whicker; Arthur White; Sir Frank Whittle; Sam Wilberforce; William Wilberforce; The Rev'd Wilkes; Mrs Wilkes; Margaret Wilson; Police Sgt David Winter; Phil Woodcock; Mike Wrathall; Mark Wray-Mitchell; Ella Yaldren; Fern-Lea Yaldren; Mia Yaldren, Ren Yaldren; Roger Yaldren; Michael Yelland, Pat Yelland.

\*

# CONTENTS

| Chapter | Title | Page |
|---|---|---|
|  | FOREWORD | 15 |
| 1 | 'We've been swindled!' | 17 |
| 2 | Apples from Kent | 34 |
| 3 | Donkey droppings | 63 |
| 4 | An unsettling revelation | 81 |
| 5 | Freddie Trueman bowls a googly | 104 |
| 6 | National Service, Elvis Presley and Shivers up the spine | 129 |
| 7 | '…And DO watch the wallpaper!' | 159 |
| 8 | 'That might be fun' | 164 |
| 9 | Gliding high | 194 |
| 10 | Loitering on the docks | 205 |
| 11 | Our American dream | 214 |
| 12 | A lost bet | 224 |
| 13 | 'There's a rabbit in your room!' | 240 |
| 14 | 'Please drop the latch when you leave Castle Howard' | 272 |
| 15 | 'Damn protocol!' | 324 |
| 16 | 'A German shell is buried in your wall…' | 348 |
| 17 | Mark's 'No-brainer' | 372 |
| 18 | Stars & Stripes, Berlin, and a Celebration | 390 |
| 19 | Bodgit & Scarper | 409 |
|  | ENDPIECE | 417 |

# ANCESTORS OF DAVID GARDHAM FOWLER

**START HERE 1541**

- Willyam FEWLAR [1], b. abt 1541
- Marieraye CLAYE [2]
  - Thomas FEWLAR [3]
  - Elizabeth EAMISON [4]
    - Thomas FEWLER [7]
    - Elizabeth TAYLOR [8]
      - Robert FOWLER [13]
      - Margery WEBSTER [14]

**CONTINUE TO PAGE xi**

# CONTINUE HERE FROM PAGE x

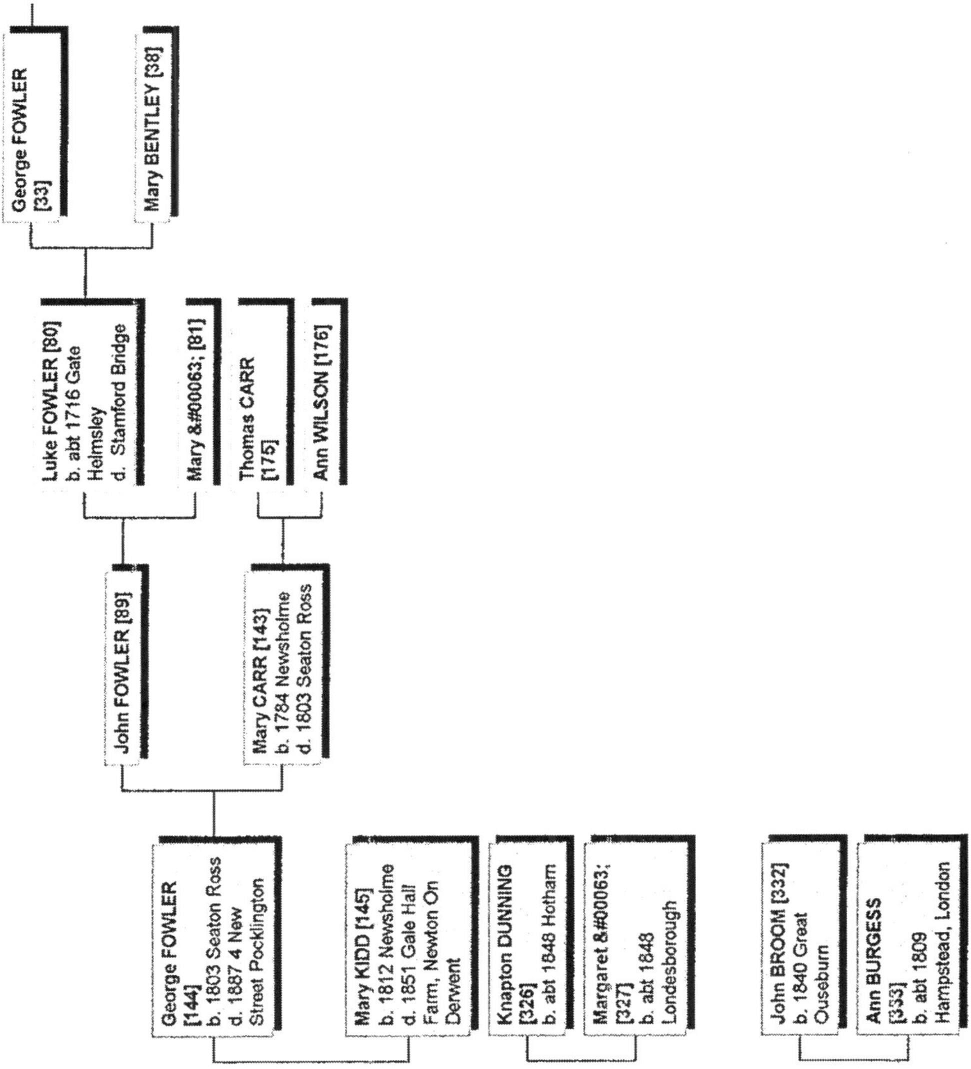

```
┌─ George FOWLER [33]
├─ Mary BENTLEY [38]
│
├─── Luke FOWLER [80]
│     b. abt 1716 Gate Helmsley
│     d. Stamford Bridge
├─── Mary &#00063; [81]
│
├─── Thomas CARR [175]
├─── Ann WILSON [176]
│
├── John FOWLER [89]
├── Mary CARR [143]
│    b. 1784 Newsholme
│    d. 1803 Seaton Ross
│
├── George FOWLER [144]
│    b. 1803 Seaton Ross
│    d. 1887 4 New Street Pocklington
├── Mary KIDD [145]
│    b. 1812 Newsholme
│    d. 1851 Gale Hall Farm, Newton On Derwent
├── Knapton DUNNING [326]
│    b. abt 1848 Hotham
├── Margaret &#00063; [327]
│    b. abt 1848 Londesborough
├── John BROOM [332]
│    b. 1840 Great Ouseburn
└── Ann BURGESS [333]
     b. 1809 Hampstead, London
```

# CONTINUE FROM HERE TO PAGE xii

**CONTINUE HERE FROM PAGE xi**

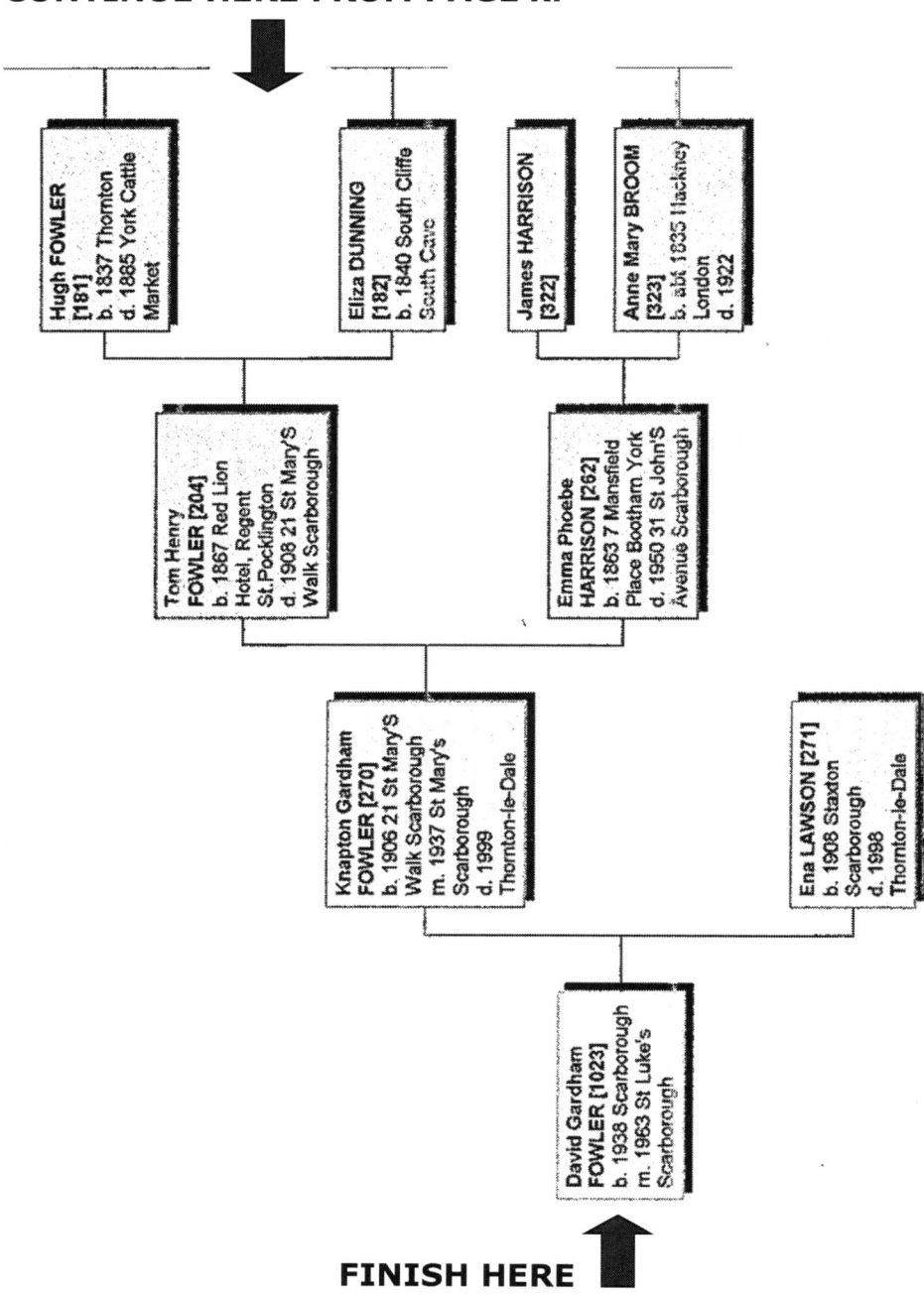

**FINISH HERE**

*'Living in the past. It's always said pejoratively, as if the past is necessarily inferior to the future, or at any rate less important; nobody's ever condemned for looking forward, only back. But the truth is that we live in the past, whether we like it or not. That's where our life takes shape. Somewhere ahead, however near or far, is the end. But behind, shrouded in clouds of forgetting, lies the beginning'.*

*Robert Goddard*
*('Beyond Recall')*

# FOREWORD

First, a word of warning! This book is not about the BBC TV show Mastermind, or the much-revered late Magnus Magnusson. However, his catchphrase, *'I've started so I'll finish...'* has been borrowed for which full credit is given.

This is the second edition of this book, which has been partly rewritten and brought up to date.

The story starts in 1545 which is as far back as I have been able to trace the Fowler family tree. It then moves swiftly forwards and weaves a fascinating web which includes World War II; The Long March (sometimes called The Death March); the first UK jet plane flight; wiping out very early TV programmes; building what was then probably the world's smallest radio; building a television set; National Service; Ouija boards; meeting Elvis Presley; meeting Freddie Trueman; banking anecdotes; using Royal Mail to send £15,000 to the Bank of England; visits to Egypt; Germany and the Berlin Wall, Italy, Russia, The Maldives, and the USA; Clubs and Associations in which I was involved; losing a bet and appearing in the ballet Sleeping Beauty; dropping the latch at Castle Howard; La Jurade de Saint–Emilion; meeting HRH Prince Charles; a holiday island in the middle of the Nile; a smiling camel; a Crown court case; meeting the Lord Chief Justice; and so on...

Banking in the second part of the last century is well covered and seems a world away from how banks operate today.

All the above and much more, is interwoven into this true story. Research started 23 years ago when I retired from Barclays Bank as a branch manager. I made jottings of events at the time they occurred and kept old diaries but then kept putting them to one side to accommodate other interests. I am after all a Gemini!

Then I would dust down the files and write a little more and so it went on over the years, until the title *'I've started so I'll finish...'* seemed very appropriate, particularly as I neared the end of the marathon.

The book is intended to be enjoyable, light hearted, informative and humorous as well as being a memoir of my life.

After school in Scarborough, I joined Barclays Bank before doing my 2 years National Service, following which I spent 39 years with the bank.

In retirement I took up writing, then publishing; initially to get my own books into print.

Each chapter of this book is preceded by a paragraph explaining what was happening in the world at the time of which I write.

If you do have any queries, comments or corrections; or you feel you should (or should not!) have been mentioned in the book, please do let me know, either by e-mail or through the contact page on Farthings Publishing web site.

David Fowler
Scarborough.
2017

dgfowler@gmail.com
http://www.farthings-publishing.com

*

# CHAPTER 1

# 'We've been swindled' 1541 to 1940

> **c.1541: Brief Timeline**
>
> Fall of Duke of Somerset; Duke of Northumberland succeeds as Protector; Archbishop Cranmer publishes Forty-two Articles of religion; On death of Edward VI, Lady Jane Grey proclaimed Queen of England by Duke of Northumberland, her reign lasts nine days; Execution of Lady Jane Grey; Mary Tudor ascends to the throne as England's first Queen; England returns to Roman Catholicism: Protestants are persecuted and about 300, including Cranmer, are burned at the stake; England loses Calais, last English possession in France; Death of Mary I; Elizabeth becomes Queen; Repeal of Catholic legislation in England; Treaty of Berwick between Elizabeth I and Scottish reformers; Treaty of Edinburgh among England, France, and Scotland; The Thirty-nine Articles, which complete establishment of the Anglican Church; Peace of Troyes between England and France; Mary Queen of Scots escapes to England and is imprisoned by Elizabeth I at Fotheringay Castle; Drake sails around the world.

It was January 1940. A lone Spitfire lazily looped the loop a few thousand feet above, its white vapour trail competing with the puffy, cotton wool, cumulus clouds in the sky.

World War II had started on 3rd September the previous year and the seaside town of Scarborough would take its share of punishment over the coming years.

The afternoon was bitterly cold; snow lay on the ground and an icy wind whistled through the bare branches of the trees. Darkness was gradually falling as three people and a dog stood at the open front door of 3 Throxenby Grove, Newby, about 3 miles from Scarborough. The lights from the house shone out, silhouetting them and casting shadows on to the snow covered front lawn.

I was one of the three. I was just 19 months old, and was standing there with my father, Knapton Fowler, my Great aunt Alice Welburn, and Patch, a rough haired terrier and the family pet.

A taxi pulled up to the open gate of No. 3 and the mellow light from the gas street lamp outside the house flickered as though in welcome and as if it also knew it would soon be extinguished for the remainder of the war. The driver got out and opened the back door and an attractive, dark-haired woman, slim and petite, and wearing a smart tailored suit and a Tyrolean style hat, stepped from the car. She was carrying a bundle wrapped in a white lace shawl. She glanced up at the Spitfire, before looking down at the bundle and smiling warmly. Carefully she walked up the drive, and was briefly illuminated by the soft yellow light from the street lamp. The waiting group welcomed her and her bundle into the warmth of the house and the door was closed.

It was my mother, Ena Fowler, bringing home my sister Phoebe who was about a week old. She had been born at the Dybdale Nursing Home in Avenue Victoria, Scarborough, on the 8th January 1940. I had been born at the Dybdale some 19 months earlier and I now live, and am writing this memoir, from our home in Avenue Victoria, only 50 yards from where the Dybdale Nursing Home stood.

My life has turned almost full circle.

The memory of me standing there and mother walking up the driveway with Phoebe in her arms as Patch barked his welcome, is as vivid to me today as it was seventy-seven years ago.

It is the first thing I remember.

Before moving forward in time, let me move backwards to sketch a very brief outline of my main ancestors, who all, until my grandfather's time, lived in, or within 30 miles of the City of York. An abbreviated ancestral chart appears in the early pages of this book.

The earliest ancestor I have been able to trace is one Willyam Fewlar. He was born 'about 1541' and he married Marieraye Claye at St Martin & St Gregory's Church in the City of York on 20th January 1561.

They had one son, Thomas, who married Elizabeth Eamison at Holy Trinity Church, Goodramgate, York, on 19th February 1585. Thomas and Elizabeth went on to have three daughters – Elizabeth, Anne and Margaret, and two sons, Thomas and Reynold.

Thomas is our link and he married Elizabeth Taylor on 11th June, 1609. She produced daughters Ellene and Elizabeth, and sons, Robert, Ralph, John and Jhon. Our link is Robert Fowler (by now the spelling had changed from Fewlar) and he married Margery Webster at Holy Trinity Church, York on 2nd January 1639. Margery gave birth to Robert, Willm, (not a misspelling), Richard and George.

Our line follows through the youngest son George, who was christened on 25th October 1650 at St Michael le Belfry Church in York. He was 45 years old before he married Sarah and she gave him a son, Leonard, in 1697. Sarah died in 1713 but George outlived her and he didn't die until 1727 – aged 77 – which was a good age in the early 18th century.

George must have been a randy old goat. In 1716, three years after Sarah died, he married again – this time to Mary Bentley and whilst, by then, George was 66, they went on to have six children, Luke, Sarah, Mary, Elizabeth John and Jane.

Of these, Luke is our next link. Born in 1716 at Gate Helmsley – the year George and Mary married – Luke grew up and became the butcher at Stamford Bridge, near

York. He married (another) Mary in 1745.

Two years later in 1747 Luke Jnr was born with other sons being Matthew and John.

John continues our line and he became a farm labourer and married yet another Mary on 29th November 1774 at Seaton Ross – this time it was Mary Kemp, who gave birth to Sarah, Ann, Mary, Luke and Francis. But Mary, John's wife, died on 24th April 1796 and in October 1803 John remarried – this time to Mary Carr, having first had a son with her – another George, who was born on 21st July 1803.

Our line then follows this George from John's second marriage and he eventually became a Yeoman Farmer at the 154 acre, Gale Hall Farm in Newton on Derwent. I visited the farm around 45 years ago when the then farmers were customers of the bank in York. I then visited again about 20 years ago and it was a strange feeling, walking on land my ancestors had farmed nearly two centuries previously.

On 27th May 1833, George married, yes – another Mary; Mary Kidd, and she and George went on to have Hugh, born 8th October 1837, Mark and Sarah.

When George senior died on 16th June 1887, family folklore suggests there was a dispute with his will which was changed in favour of a nurse who had looked after him until his death. My late Aunt Phyllis, (Briscombe née Fowler) had done what research she could in the pre-computer days and she passed down the story to me. She certainly felt very strongly that 'our line of the family had been swindled!'

However, I have a certified copy of George's will dated 19th December 1885, and probate indicated that George left a net estate of £3,070.19.7. Inflation alone would have taken its value to £353,000 today, and invested wisely, indications are that, this could even be worth around £4 million; hence Aunt Phyllis's concern! [www.calculator.net]

George was very specific in his will that his estate be left entirely to members of his direct family; sons, daughter, grandchildren and his widow. He also instructed that any balance was to be held in trust for his widow for her lifetime benefit.

This proved will was written eighteen months before George's death and we know that in the last months of his life he needed nursing care at home. His nurse was said to have persuaded him to write a new will in her favour and she was said to have 'made off with a large majority of his estate'. This obviously seems untrue.

He could, of course, have gifted her money or assets before his death and outside the will; he could have made a new will in her favour which he subsequently destroyed; or the new will could have stood, but then been contested by the family at probate stage. However, whatever the circumstances, and we shall now never know, the will he made some two years before his death stood and was proved, leaving all his assets to his family.

To move on, George and Mary's son, Hugh was born at Gale Hall Farm and attended the village school at Newton upon Derwent. Eventually he took over the farm from his father George, but after a few years he decided farming was a lonely existence and he hankered after brighter lights. On 9th April 1863 he married Eliza Dunning of South Cliffe, South Cave, near Hull, the daughter of wealthy landowners Knapton and Margaret Dunning.

The newly married couple, Hugh and Eliza Fowler, moved to Pocklington, a small market town equidistant between York and South Cave, some 14 miles from each. There, they took over the Red Lion, a coaching inn in the town's Regent Street and it was in Pocklington that Eliza gave birth to George Knapton, Walter Gardham, Tom Henry, Herbert Hugh and John William.

So, my father's two forenames, Knapton (coming from Knapton Dunning) and Gardham from Tom Henry's bachelor brother's second forename, came into the story at this stage. Gardham has been one forename of various male members of the family since then.

Here arises an interesting aside. John, (son of Luke born in 1716) also had a younger brother, also called Luke, born c.1747. This Luke married Elizabeth Nottingham at Aughton in 1776. This Luke's mother-in-law was Elizabeth Nottingham née Wilberfoss, daughter of William Wilberfoss. The Wilberfoss family had been Lords of the Manor of the village of Wilberfoss for centuries and subsequently changed the spelling of their surname to Wilberforce. Elizabeth Wilberfoss who became Elizabeth Nottingham on marriage, and husband John Nottingham left the village by c.1750, the Wilberfoss descendants already having left the village for Beverley, and, later, Hull.

There is therefore a relationship between the Fowlers and the Nottinghams through whom there appears to be a tentative relationship with the Wilberforce family and thus William Wilberforce (1759-1833).

There are two further points of interest. Hugh Fowler, my great grandfather, married Eliza Dunning, the parents of whom (Knapton and Margaret Dunning) were wealthy and owned and farmed the large South Cliffe Estate near South Cave, the estate being advertised as 'containing an area of '2 miles by 1 mile". We also understand that at one time William Wilberforce might have had an interest in this estate, possibly at the same time, and maybe in partnership with Eliza's parents.

However, Sam Wilberforce, William's descendant who looks after the family website but stressed he is not a genealogist, told me he knew nothing of any past involvement by his family in the South Cliffe Estate.

The story goes further in that there was a suggestion that William Wilberforce was a direct descendant of King Henry II, but again, Sam Wilberforce told me that he had heard of no royal connections in the family.

I am indebted to Sam for his courtesy and assistance and if any reader can add anything as to whether or not we might be related to William Wilberforce, whether he might have been connected to the South Cliffe estate or even to royalty, I would very much like to know.

William Wilberforce

*'William Wilberforce was born on 24th August 1759. He was descended from a Yorkshire family which possessed the Manor of Wilberfoss in the East Riding of Yorkshire from the time of King Henry II until the middle of the 18th century. He was an English politician, philanthropist, and a leader of the movement to eradicate the slave trade. A native of Kingston upon Hull, Yorkshire, he was educated at Pocklington School and St. John's College, Cambridge University. He married Barbara Ann Wilberforce (nee Spooner) and began his political career in 1780, eventually becoming an independent Member of Parliament for Yorkshire.*

*In 1785, he became an Evangelical Christian, which resulted in major changes to his lifestyle and a lifelong concern for reform. He founded the Royal Society for the Prevention of Cruelty to Animals, the Anti-Slavery Society, and the Church Mission Society*

*He and his wife had 6 children: William Wilberforce (b.1798), Barbara Wilberforce (b.1799), Elizabeth Wilberforce (b.1801), Robert Isaac Wilberforce (b.1802), Samuel Wilberforce (b.1805), and Henry William Wilberforce (b.1807)'.*

William Wilberforce died on 29th July 1933 aged 73.

Returning to our family tree, and with Tom Henry Fowler being my paternal grandfather we are nearly home.

Tom was born on the 21st July 1867 at the Red Lion Inn, Pocklington. He was the youngest son and not a strong child, having frequent bronchial complaints. His mother died when he was only 13 and his father Hugh died 5 years later at York Cattle Market on 10th November 1885, although Hugh, as a publican, was said to have liked his drink which possibly had a bearing on his death.

When his father died Tom Henry was only 18 years old, and was apprenticed as a compositor to a Wolverhampton newspaper. There he spent time learning his trade and he also played football for Wolverhampton Football Club. His first sport, however, was cricket and after returning to York to work as a journalist for the York Herald in Coney Street, he regularly visited Scarborough for the cricket festival which started in 1876 and which attracted such well known players as Dr WG Grace.

Tom Henry Fowler married Emma Phoebe Harrison at St Thomas's Church, York on 5th January 1889 and they subsequently had children – Phyllis Phoebe (my aunt) and Ella Violet, (another aunt). The family initially lived at 21 White Rose Street in York but Tom Henry's chest and bronchial problems persisted, possibly aggravated by his work as compositor in Wolverhampton in earlier years.

In 1902 the family moved to Scarborough on doctor's advice, for Tom 'to seek the sea air'. They took this advice very literally as their Scarborough home – also at number 21 but this time at St Mary's Walk, was in the old part of the town, perched on Castle Hill just below the Castle and St Mary's Church, and overlooking the harbour and Scarborough's South Bay. Tom was an avid sportsman and his interviews were frequently with famous sportsmen of the time. One notable interview was with cricketer Dr WG Grace and Tom might even have played football with Dr Grace as they both played for Wolverhampton

Wanderers although Tom was a number of years younger than the doctor.

Tom's 'office', where he wrote, (using a steel dip–in pen and writing in tiny well–formed characters), was in one of the sea–facing upper rooms overlooking the harbour. By this time he made his living by writing free–lance; many short stories, serialised stories, reports and sports interviews for various periodicals, newspapers and magazines of the day, such as Cassells and Chums.

*Tom Henry Fowler*

## 1897.

### Sixty, Not Out
### Vivat Victoria
### A Record Performance.

Sixty up, & still the wicket
   Stands erect with untouched bails
Though perhaps you're fond of cricket
   Wait a bit, Monsieur of Wales
George of York, & little Edward
   Put your pads & gloves away,
For, be sure they'll not be wanted
   Let us hope for many a day

Sixty up, & still her people
   Watch her play, applaud & shout
Rising now from tower & steeple —
   Sixty up & still not out!
May she yet prolong her innings,
   And augment her mighty score,
Batting at Britannia's wicket
   Stoutly, blithely, as before.

                      Diamond Jublee
                            1897

*In 1897 – then aged 30 and before his marriage or move to Scarborough – Tom wrote the above poem for his younger cousins to commemorate Queen Victoria's Diamond Jubilee. His poem is based on his love of cricket.*

*Emma Phoebe Fowler in her later years. Tom Henry's wife, mother of Knapton Gardham Fowler, and grandmother to myself and Phoebe.*

Scarborough was where Walter William Hugh, (my uncle), and Knapton Gardham, the baby of the family and subsequently my father, were born. Tom Henry and Emma also adopted Margaret Elizabeth Sharp who is buried with them both in Scarborough's Dean Road cemetery.

Tom's poor health took its toll and he died on 5$^{th}$ October 1908 aged only 41. Father was only 2 years old at the time so never really knew his own father. As I was born 30 years after Tom Henry's death, I never knew my grandfather and the facts I include here have been passed down the family.

Tom's widow Emma was 45 at the time of his death and she subsequently left St Mary's Walk and moved to a newly built property, 31 St John's Avenue, then on the fringe of the town and in an area called Falsgrave. The house became her family home. A terraced property, it was large having a sizeable dining room, large quarry tiled kitchen and separate walk–in pantry, good sized lounge, and three double bedrooms, a bathroom and separate toilet. There were steps up to the front door but the back entrance was almost level, with entry from a private lane.

The house had a back yard which was a real suntrap where numerous plants flourished in pots. This yard had a sitting out area, and a deep outbuilding which housed an additional toilet, but this was never used as Phyllis used the space to store her bicycle, and much other paraphernalia. At that stage Phyllis had not married and she lived at home, moving with her mother to St John's Avenue and looking after Emma. But on 23$^{rd}$ January 1941 Phyllis married Percival Briscoe Briscombe (known as 'Percy' by everyone), on a snatched leave of his, at All Saints Church, Falsgrave, Scarborough. That church has long since gone and now comprises a furniture store and flats.

Percy came from a large family in Ripon and worked in Scarborough before, then after the war, for GW Moore & Sons, radio and cycle retailers who moved into the TV market when it was first possible to receive television transmissions in Scarborough in the early 1950s. He became a director of this then thriving family firm and also had financial interests in his family's Ripon businesses.

*Phyllis Fowler marries Percy Briscombe 23rd January 1941. My mother Ena, is front row left. Father was in the RAF and could not obtain leave.*

For many years, if anyone left food on their plate Percy would gently remonstrate with them and it was only much later he explained that food was so scarce whilst he was a prisoner–of–war that it upset him to see it wasted. He was a keen radio 'ham' and would smuggle pieces for bread up to his radio room at the top of the house as if he needed to keep a private emergency stockpile in case he was again without food. In later years these pieces for bread were upgraded to a stock of Kit Kat chocolate bars.

My grandmother Emma Phoebe Fowler died on 20th December 1950 and is buried with Tom Henry in the town's Dean Road cemetery.

Some months after Emma had died Phyllis and Percy decided to sell the house in St John's Avenue and move out to the village of Irton some 5 miles from the centre of Scarborough.

Percy died suddenly on 22nd March 1977 aged only 68. He had been waiting for a bus to take him home after leaving his car at a garage for a service, when he collapsed. A post–mortem showed his heart to be in very poor condition and his war time experiences were likely to have had a bearing. Even though Phyllis was 9 years older, she outlived him, dying herself on 1st June 1991 aged 91.

Tom and Phoebe's second daughter Ella, had been born on the 16th December 1901, and she moved to Burnt Oak, Edgware after she married Edward Kelly Richardson (Ted) on the 2nd October 1926 at Scarborough Register Office. They had one son, Peter Edward William who rose to senior level at Barclays Bank's head office, then at 54 Lombard Street, London.

Walter William Hugh (Willie) was born on 15th September 1904. He and his first wife Hilda Mayes had two sons, Neil Malcolm and John Michael Gardham – both of them my cousins. Willie and Hilda divorced, and both Willie later remarried, Willie to Doris Harris on 13th February 1948. His second marriage was childless and Willie died in hospital on the 3rd June 1974.

My parents Knapton Gardham Fowler and Ena Lawson married just before Christmas on 19th December 1937. I came into the world on 18th June 1938 and Phoebe arrived 18 months later on January 8th 1940. Phoebe and I are therefore twelfth great grandson and granddaughter descendants of Willyam Fewlar, born in 1561.

*Knapton Gardham Fowler married Ena Lawson on 19th December 1937.*

24 years later Phoebe married Peter Ernest Brian Clayton (Brian). Their first child was a son, Mark Anthony Clayton, who was born on the 23rd June 1965 in Nottingham, UK.

Shortly afterwards, Phoebe and Brian and their family moved to Canada where their daughter Dena Hannah Clayton was born in Montreal on 21st July 1967. Coincidentally, this would have been the centenary of the birth of her great grandfather Tom Henry Fowler. From Canada, Phoebe's family moved to the USA, settling in Las Vegas where Mark Clayton married Lisa Wilson on 28th April 1991. They had Emily Blanch Wilson Clayton who was born in Carson City, Nevada USA on 19th December 1994.

Phoebe and Brian Clayton later divorced and Phoebe remarried another Brian – Brian Hawson – whom I nicknamed 'Brian 2'. He was a lovely man and sadly died very prematurely in Paris on February 16th 2008.

To move on, Eileen Watson and I married on 27th March 1963 at St Luke's Church Scarborough, where Phoebe and I had attended Sunday school so many years earlier. Our daughter Susan Lynne Fowler was born in Scarborough almost a year later on 3rd March 1964 and christened at the same church.

*We married on a very showery day, 27th March 1963*

Mother's Lawson family tree is much less complicated; but only because we haven't been successful in tracing details.

My maternal great grandparents were called John William and Annie Welburn although we have no maiden name for Annie. Annie gave birth to Alice (my great aunt who was standing with me on the door step when Phoebe arrived home), to Albert, who was born on 19th December 1908 and who later married Maud Beatrice Hall on October 11th 1941, and to my grandmother to be, Edith Mary Welburn.

Edith married Robert Atkinson Lawson, a 'Farm Servant', on 28th December 1907 when the couple were aged 23 and 26 respectively.

Albert served in World War I and his forces records indicate him as being in the Army Service Corps in 1915, and I understand he was gassed during the conflict.

I vaguely recall hearing that he had a brother who was killed in the same war and who is commemorated on the Menin Gate monument. I could trace nothing, then, amongst Albert's papers I found a few picture postcards of the Thiepval monument in France. It seemed probable that if Albert had a brother he could be commemorated there. An online search reveals one Welburn who died and was commemorated at Thiepval; 'Lance Corporal George William Welburn, c/1097, 16th Battalion Kings Royal Rifle Corps, died 15th July 1916'. Whether he was the brother of Albert we shall probably never know, but may he rest in peace whether he was related or not.

Robert and Edith Lawson went on to have 5 daughters of whom three died. Their mother Edith (my maternal grandmother) also died – all during the 1918 Spanish 'flu pandemic.

Family folklore indicates that after losing his wife and 3 daughters, Robert could not cope with looking after the remaining two daughters so, rather than manage himself or find another wife to help bring up his existing family, he moved out and made his life elsewhere, taking on responsibility for that lady's existing family.

Albert and Alice were left to bring up the two surviving daughters, Doris Lawson, my Aunt, who married Jack Taylor and who gave birth to my cousin Jean Barbara, and my Mother Ena Lawson who was born on 6th December 1908. Ena married Knapton Gardham Fowler on 19th December 1937 and their children were me and my sister Phoebe – the bundle who arrived home to 3, Throxenby Grove, Newby, by taxi, with her mother.

*

# CHAPTER 2

# Apples from Kent
# 1938–1945

> **1938: Brief Timeline**
>
> An underground explosion at Markham Colliery, near Staveley, Derbyshire, killed 79; The Bren light machine gun came into service with the British Army; The London and North Eastern Railway's streamlined Class A4 4468 *Mallard* reached a speed of 126 mph (203 km/h), the highest certified speed for a steam locomotive; Gas masks were issued to the civilian population; Test cricket was televised for the first time; *The Beano* comic went on sale featuring the character Lord Snooty; English cricketer Len Hutton scored a record Test score of 364 runs in a match against Australia; Prime Minister Neville Chamberlain met German Chancellor Adolf Hitler in an attempt to negotiate an end to German expansionist policies; RMS *Queen Elizabeth* is launched at Clydebank – the largest ship in the world at this time; Neville Chamberlain returns to the UK from Munich, memorably waving the resolution signed the day earlier with Germany, and later in Downing Street giving his famous *Peace for our time* speech.

Having been born on 18th June 1938, and being only 7 years old at the end of the war, I remember little of those wartime years, but I did discover much from research for my book *'God Bless the Prince of Wales'*.

World War II started on 3rd September 1939 with Chamberlain's radio broadcast and whilst the first months were called 'the phoney war', frantic activity was taking place all over Britain.

Numerous airfields were being built, munitions were being manufactured and stockpiled, and war planes – Spitfires, Hurricanes, Whitleys, Halifaxes, Wellingtons, Lancasters, to name but a few, would be built in ever increasing numbers.

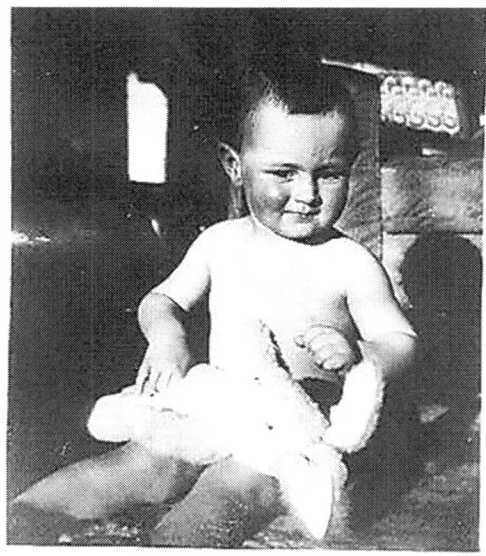

*Left: A young me.*

*Above: Patch the family pet, dad and me*

Shelters to protect the population against enemy bombs were not built in Scarborough until after the 'March Blitz' in 1941 when the authorities had to accept that Scarborough appeared to be an enemy target. In all, 1,500 shelters were then built in the town. Civilians were called up to the Army, RAF or Navy to train for the expected long conflict.

Women were called up in increasing numbers, to join the forces; to replace men in teaching, in the Civil Service, and in medicine; or to join the Women's Land Army which was reformed in 1939. Their involvement was vital as so many men were being called up into the forces.

Beaches, at what were thought to be vulnerable invasion areas were protected with barbed wire and anti-tank barriers; pillboxes were built on the approaches to strategic towns – including Scarborough – yet children from the cities considered to be in danger were evacuated to what were thought to be safer areas – Scarborough being one of these.

But was it? We shall see.

*Above: Phoebe and me, both a little older, with bluebells*

Before Phoebe had been born, father had sold his little Austin Ruby car as Mother didn't drive, petrol would be rationed and scarce and he would have little use of a car when he was called up for the services. Patch was also found a new home.

*A similar Austin 7 Ruby – but not father's actual car.*

Dad was naturally concerned for the safety of his family as he knew would shortly be called-up for military service. The house at Newby was a conventional 3 bedroom semi-detached built in 1936 with a central staircase to the upper floor. Under the staircase was the usual 'under stairs' cupboard.

It was decided that this cupboard would be the family's refuge in case of attack, so he decided to reinforce the hall ceiling and one Saturday around March 1940 a lorry arrived bearing planks of wood and sacks of sand. Supply had been easy as Uncle Bill – dad's brother – worked in the office of Sinclair's, a large local form of joiners and builders.

A framework of wood was built across the hall to give

additional support to the ceiling, then, sacks of sand were placed on top of this and to the sides, to absorb any blast.

Was the house to take a hit and the family was sheltering at the time in the under stairs cupboard, there would be a small degree of protection.

I don't know whether there had been any government advice on the best place to situate an indoor air raid shelter, but whilst preparing this book it struck me that the under stairs cupboard, with gas and electric meters and main service supply taps, must have come pretty low down on the list!

Whilst dad and some friends were undertaking this work he was put in charge of Phoebe and I, while mother took herself off to the Odeon in Scarborough to see the epic film Gone with the Wind, with Clark Gable and Vivien Leigh. This had been released the previous December.

On January 8th 1940, my sister Phoebe had been born and on the 19th October that year father was called up into the RAF. His peacetime job was working for wholesale tobacconists Youngman's in Sales and obtaining and delivering orders to their customers. Youngman's would have to cope without him for 5 years

Scarborough, a well-known seaside town and acknowledged to be the first British seaside resort, had apparently been thought not to be of interest to our enemies. The powers-that-be felt it would continue very much as a backwater, but without the usual hordes of holiday makers who, until the war started, had flocked into the town each summer.

*Scarborough*

However, the town had been bombarded from the sea by the German Fleet during World War I. Hadn't this rung bells about its possible vulnerability?

In 1940, agreement was reached that the majority of large hotels in Scarborough, (and other seaside towns, as they all had promenades and beaches which were excellent for PE and marching), be requisitioned by the military. The town then became one of the main training centres for RAF aircrew. This was for their initial training, PE, marching, endurance skills, navigation training and all necessary book work in which trainees had to qualify before they were let loose anywhere near a plane.

On March 18th 1941, when I was nearly 3 years old and Phoebe was just 14 months, Scarborough received its most serious bombing raid of the war. The German Luftwaffe either confused Scarborough with Hull, or decided the town was important enough in its own right to bomb.

Whilst we were relatively safe out at Newby some 3 miles from the centre of the town, we used the reinforced hallway and under-stairs cupboard and were usually joined by spinster Miss Weathers who lived on her own next door. Gas and electric were all turned off and we took flasks of tea and Camp coffee (which was the only coffee available unless you had black market contacts!) to the 'shelter'. We even took the galvanised dustbin lid! Phoebe reminded me recently that this was included to protect her – then still a baby – from falling masonry should the house be hit.

After Scarborough was declared a restricted area, the threat of invasion was on everyone's minds in the town. Troops started pouring into Scarborough and the RAF took over many hotels as Initial Training Wings. The Grand and The Prince of Wales hotels and Scarborough College became respectively 10 ITW, 11 ITW and 17 ITW.

The town's second railway station, Londesborough Road, was taken over by the military when war broke out and it was not until May, 1946 that this was returned to LNER. (Railways were later nationalised from 1st January 1948).

Defences were erected very quickly in and around the town; barbed wire and posts were installed on slipways leading to the beach and some of the South Cliff Gardens were barricaded, as were the North Side gardens and promenade.

Concrete anti-tank blocks were erected along the Royal Albert Drive and on the piers. Barriers were erected at all entrances to the town – Stepney Road, Scalby Road, Seamer Road (near to the then football ground), Spa Bridge, Corner Café, Chain Hill, and Stepney, (near to what was the Girls High school and is now the 6th Form College). All these areas were guarded by soldiers.

Concrete Pill Boxes were erected all over the town and the surrounding district in places such as Springhill Lane, Sandybed, Scalby Mills, Cornelian Bay, and Cayton Bay. The cliffs above Scalby Mills were used for bomb and rifle training by the Home Guard and the pits they used could still be seen up to a few years ago.

Large water tanks, or static tanks as they were called, were constructed at various places in the town for use in case of fires caused by incendiary bombs.

Initially, cinemas and entertainment centres were closed but were soon re-opened to the public with restricted hours. A few months later they reverted back to their former opening hours of 2.00pm until 10.15pm although no one was allowed in without their gas mask.

The Pavilion Hotel, Scarborough, was the first in the provinces since the outbreak of the war to be granted an extension of the music and dancing licence from 11.00pm until midnight. This was granted because the hotel had an air raid shelter in its basement, which could accommodate the guests.

During the permanent blackout and for the duration of the war, all street lights and traffic lights were turned off and no premises had to have any lights showing. To help pedestrians get around, kerb edges, trees and other obstacles were painted with white bands.

The beaches, cliffs and promenades resembled battlefields as barbed wire was laid in case of an invasion. On the outer harbour wall and at the South Bay pool there were machine gun posts and at the bottom of Wheatcroft Avenue overlooking the sea, a heavy naval gun salvaged from World War I, was installed in case of invasion. The harbour was mined and the plunger to detonate the mines was placed in a fake ice cream kiosk, at the bottom of Bland's Cliff, manned by the Army 24 hours a day.

Summer 1939 had seen the resort packed with holidaymakers. The same could not be said of 1940. The sands were bare of holidaymakers and were restricted areas. Anyone venturing onto them stood the risk of being shot. Indeed, one young lady did lose her life one night when a sentry shot her after she ignored his challenge.

The hotels and boarding houses had been full of visitors on the first Christmas of the war but this was all to change as one by one they were taken over by the military for the billeting of the armed forces. Because of Scarborough's restricted status it was difficult for anyone who didn't have the appropriate papers, to enter the town.

As, elsewhere throughout the country, shop and house owners taped up their windows to stop glass damage in case of air raids.

The Villa Esplanade, Dorchester, Southlands and the Red Lea hotels were used to house Leeds Training College students. The Red Lea still has a wooden seat today within the hotel's porch, which was donated by 'ex-students of Leeds Training College' who used to hold annual reunions at the hotel.

Scarborough's first air raid warning sounded at 9.25am on 29th January 1940 following German planes being spotted flying over Cayton Bay. On that occasion nothing occurred but the following months saw the town subjected to 'tip–and–run' raids which caused considerable damage to property. However, much worse was to come as Scarborough had too many important targets, including the Admiralty Wireless Station (now GCHQ), the Army barracks, the harbour, and of course, the RAF Initial Training Wings and other military presence in the town.

On 10th October 1940, a lone raider swooped over Castle Hill and dropped a landmine on the densely populated old town. The crater in Potter Lane measured 60ft across and 30ft deep. Four people died in this raid and around 500 houses were either damaged or destroyed.

The result of another raid on Scarborough on March 18th 1941 – which became known locally as the March Blitz – was that 1,378 buildings were either destroyed or damaged and there were 29 fatalities – civilians and military. A further 45 people were recorded as being badly injured. The raiders closed in on Scarborough about 9.00pm and subjected the town to hours of heavy bombing with high explosives, parachute mines and thousands of incendiary bombs. The incendiaries showered down on all parts of the town and surrounding area and people in the streets attempted to put them out. They bounced down Castle Hill in thousands and burnt themselves out on Marine Drive, much lower and just above sea level.

At the printing firm of ETW Dennis and Sons in Melrose Street, incendiaries first fell at about 9.15pm. The staff had only left at 9.00pm and the building soon became a blazing inferno. The lead print-type melted in the composing room heat and made a river of molten metal.

*ETW Dennis print works in Melrose Street, Scarborough, well alight and almost a shell when this photo was taken, March 18th 1941.*

That raid was the worst Scarborough suffered during the war. It started at 8.00pm when ninety eight planes flew over Flixton, Folkton and the Carrs dropping large numbers of incendiary bombs. The raiders closed in on Scarborough about 9.00pm and subjected the town to hours of heavy bombing with high explosives, parachute mines and thousands of incendiary bombs.

The old Waddingtons Warehouse near the Mere on Seamer Road was bombed. It had been taken over by Tonks and Sons as a repository and all the furniture that had been stored there was destroyed.

An unexploded bomb fell outside Westborough Methodist Church, and several incendiaries set the stage alight and damaged woodwork at the Opera House in St Thomas Street.

Incendiary bombs also fell on St Peter's Church, and on Queen Street Central Hall. 40 Moorland Road was demolished by a bomb as were 3 houses in Langdale Road. High explosive bombs damaged 3 houses in Trafalgar Road and Tennyson Avenue. In Victoria Park Avenue a house was set on fire by incendiaries, as were houses in Woodall Avenue. The Floral Hall Café was destroyed after being hit with incendiaries.

A parachute mine damaged Red House, Springhill Lane and the town's reservoir was cracked by the blast from a parachute mine which fell on what is now the Sandybed estate. Oak Road and surrounding streets suffered blast damage from a parachute mine which fell at the top of Falsgrave Park. At Queen Margaret's School, the gym was destroyed by a parachute mine. The girls had been evacuated to Castle Howard and whilst soldiers had then been billeted in the school, luckily they had left the day before. Roland Sheard was killed by bomb blast as he cycled down Filey Road at the junction with Queen Margaret's Road, to go on duty as a member of the Home Guard.

On that night Jean Scarlet of Row Brow Court, Scarborough was a bus conductress working on the South Cliff route from the old Court House in Castle Road, to the Cornelian Drive area. Her bus was in Ramshill Road when a parachute mine landed on Queen Margaret's School gymnasium. She remembers that the bus 'lurched' and at one time the road surface was on fire from all the incendiaries which had fallen.

Also badly damaged from bomb or incendiary damage were numerous properties throughout the town. This included Boots Chemists, then on the corner of St Nicholas Street opposite Barclays Bank.

It was 4.30am the following morning before the all-clear sounded.

The George Medal was later awarded to Captain Hugh Davidson Miller MB of the Royal Army Medical Corps who had displayed 'conspicuous courage' in attending to casualties both military and civilian during the raid. He had crawled under the wreckage of 1 Queens Terrace which had received a direct hit with high explosive bombs. Another bomb which was of the delayed action type lay within 10 yards of him as he carried out his rescues. They included a Royal Signals soldier who was trapped by a beam. Captain Miller administered morphine and stimulants and comforted the victims although the house was in a dangerous state and other bombs were falling nearby.

Squadron Leader J. Walker, a Canadian, and his wife died in their home from gas and were not found until two days later. Their baby was unharmed. Evidently during the raid an incendiary bomb had hit the house and the resultant fire had burned through a gas pipe.

The bus service continued to run throughout the raid and one particular bus travelling up Dean Road was stopped as an incendiary bomb fell in front of it. The driver calmly got out of his cab and covered it with a sandbag and then drove the bus over it.

Many people were at the cinema that night and the films kept showing throughout the raid. When the audiences did leave they came out to a very battered town with a blood red sky which reflected the many fires which were still burning.

*

RAF records only give brief details of father's wartime service and in later years, like so many servicemen, he was evasive about what he did. His service records indicate he was trained as a 'Clerk–provisioning'. However, we do know that after training he was transferred to Kent and he spent much of his service involved in organising barrage balloon crews in the Kent area.

It was in 1938 that Balloon Command was set up with the job of creating a barrage of huge balloons aimed at protecting our towns and cities, and key targets such as industrial areas, ports and harbours. They were intended to protect everything at ground level from the terror of the time – low–flying dive–bombers and, later, V1 rockets.

Barrage balloons, which were set at heights of up to 5,000 feet, made enemy planes fly higher. This, in turn made bombing less accurate and brought the planes within range of the anti–aircraft guns.

Balloon crews, which could be as many as 16 strong, came mainly from the Women's Auxiliary Air Force. The working conditions could be difficult and dangerous.

By 1944 the number of balloons had risen to nearly 3,000 and many were moved to make up a ring around south London to combat the V1 'flying bomb' menace. This met with a fair degree of success and as many as 100 V1s snagged themselves on the balloons' cables.

It was not all plain sailing, however. The balloons were filled with hydrogen and some were struck by lightning while others were shot down.

Smaller balloons were suspended low, tethered by cable, over the landing craft on D–Day, protecting the allied troops from low–flying enemy aircraft which attempted to attack the men and ships. A barrage balloon was on average about 62 feet long and 25 feet in diameter.

There was another, more secret kind of balloon, which was used as a weapon. These were smaller and ninety thousand of them were launched and left to float with the wind across the North Sea. Some contained propaganda leaflets, some strips of metal which, it was hoped, would land on power cables, and some carried incendiary chemicals.

Whilst in Kent, dad sent us large boxes of apples, (through his role as 'clerk, provisioning'?) delivered, by what to Phoebe and myself seemed to be a weird 3 wheeler motorised railway wagon. These boxes arrived once or twice a year. Mother used to lay these apples out on the top of a wardrobe to ripen.

Dad also mentioned on one occasion that he had 'guarded the first Allied jet plane'.

*The Gloster E28/39*

On 8th April 1941 a top–secret event which was to revolutionize world aviation took place at Brockworth in the county of Gloucestershire.

To avoid the possibility of bomb damage at Brockworth, a likely Luftwaffe target, this diminutive aircraft had been fitted with Frank (later Sir Frank) Whittle's revolutionary gas turbine engine at Regent Motors in Cheltenham. During these initial trials the E28/39, (or Gloster Whittle) made three hops reaching a height of only 1.8m. This was sufficient to distinguish the Brockworth airfield as the site of the first allied jet flight and it therefore became an international aviation heritage site.

According to Sir Ralph Robins, the Chairman of Rolls–Royce, 'Frank Whittle's pioneering work on the turbojet engine is probably the most important mechanical invention this century. Certainly there can be few, if any, in the world whose lives have not been affected by it'. An official contract was issued on the 3rd February 1940 by the British Air Ministry for two prototype aircraft stipulating 'that the aircraft must have provision for two .303 machine guns in each wing.' Construction started right away.

The first prototype was finished by April 1941 and on the 7th April 1941 was moved to Hucclecote for ground testing, some of which was done by Frank Whittle himself. By the end of April the aircraft was moved to the Gloster site at Cheltenham for some modifications; then in early May 1941 it was moved to Cranwell (as it had a hard runway) and on 15th May 1941 at 7.45pm test pilot PEG Slayer lined the aircraft up on the runway.

After a run of about 1800 feet, Sayer felt sufficient control response to attempt lift–off, and the E.28/39 climbed into the early evening sky. Sayer found the control responses light and responsive during the 17-minute first flight.

Fourteen test flights were carried out over the next 13 days, with the E.28/39 being flown to 25,000 feet and achieving an indicated airspeed of 300 mph.

The Gloster E.28/39 was the first British aircraft to be powered by a jet engine. It would eventually lead to the development of the Gloster Meteor, the first operational British jet aircraft.

An early memory of mine was when dad was due to come home on leave. Mother walked up the hill near our home to Hutton's farm where she asked to buy an egg. This might sound incredible today but in wartime fresh eggs were extremely hard to get and most egg needed for baking and so on was the powdered variety.

She came home clutching this precious egg and the following day father arrived home in uniform, complete with kitbag.

The morning after he arrived he had his boiled egg with toast and I remember part of the toast being cut into 'soldiers' then being dipped into the egg and me getting a treat.

Whenever he came on leave he always brought home presents made by himself and his RAF colleagues. I can recall a miniature barrage balloon made of actual balloon fabric which had an unusual smell. He also brought shopping bags made of balloon fabric which he and his colleagues had made. These were silver and thin but very hard wearing and lasted for years after the war. He had filled a couple with ripe plums – a real treat in wartime. Plums were apparently just allowed to rot on the trees in Kent as there was no one available to pick them. He also brought bangles made from Perspex from broken plane windscreens. These were often in the style of a circular snake with coloured markings indicating the head and eyes.

It would probably have been around 1943 when we were allocated, and forced to take, two evacuees from the east end of London. They were two brothers, much older than us – they would be around 9 and 10 – and much rougher and tougher. Mother must have been pulling her hair out as they were reported to her by neighbours for defecating in an air raid shelter not far from the house. In the house they swung on curtains, had very poor cleanliness habits and tried to encourage Phoebe and me to follow their bad examples. Eventually Mother persuaded the authorities that they must be found other accommodation. They were. But we were then allocated a woman with a parrot!

When dad was home on leave he had to do a certain number of overnight ARP stints based at Scalby Parish Hall. His ARP badge reads 'Scalby UDC Reg. No. 105'.

*'In April 1937, an Air Raid Wardens' Service was created. By the middle of 1938 about 200,000 people were involved, with another half a million enrolling during the*

Munich Crisis of September 1938. By the outbreak of war there were more than 1.5 million in the ARP (Air Raid Precautions), or Civil Defence as it was later re-named.

The most visible members of the ARP were the air raid wardens. Each ARP post covered a certain area, varying across the country, but with about ten to the square mile in London. Each post was divided into sectors, with perhaps three to six wardens in each sector. An ARP warden was almost always local – it was essential that he or she knew their sector and the people living there.

Since no significant German air raids followed immediately after the outbreak of war in September 1939, the main duties of the ARP wardens in the early months were to register everyone in their sector and enforce the 'blackout'. This meant making sure that no lights were visible which could be used by enemy planes to help locate bombing targets. These activities led to some ARP wardens being regarded as interfering and nosy.

However, during the Blitz of 1940–1 wardens and other civil defence personnel proved themselves indispensable and heroic. Whenever the air raid sirens sounded, the wardens would help people into the nearest shelter and then tour their sector, at considerable risk from bombs, shrapnel and falling masonry. They would also check regularly on those in the air raid shelters.

In the aftermath of a raid, ARP wardens would often be first on the scene, carrying out first-aid if there were minor casualties, putting out any small fires and helping to organise the emergency response. Other members of the Civil Defence services included rescue and stretcher (or first-aid) parties, the staff of control centres and messenger boys. Their work often overlapped with the fire and medical services and the WVS (Women's Voluntary Service)'.

With dad away for most of the time, the remaining family members – mother, myself and Phoebe – had a routine, often on a Sunday when we visited Aunt Phyllis and granny at 31, St John's Avenue for lunch. From Newby this was a walk of about 2 miles each way so mother took the pram for Phoebe and I walked.

Being granny's, the St John's Avenue house was somewhat Victorian in outlook – heavy embroidered brocade cloths on the round walnut dining table; hoop back chairs with similar embroidered panels; a very large fireplace with two white china dogs sitting in the hearth; a tall bookcase and china cabinet which contained bound copies of the books containing grandfather's stories – he having died in 1908 long before Phoebe and I were born.

The dining room was quite dark as the one small window overlooked the rear yard, and whilst the wall had been whitewashed to reflect light and the yard held an abundance of colourful pots of flowers and plants, not a lot of light got into that room.

Around teatime – or earlier in winter, we started off on the journey back to Newby. Little did Phoebe and I know what was happening in Scarborough, or, in fact how it was being 'invaded' by the military who were training there to protect the country's population. In fact at that age I had no idea what had happened in Scarborough before the war – so all happenings were treated by a 4 year old as being the norm.

One persistent memory of that time was, when walking back home in the late afternoon, being overtaken by convoys of tanks and tracked vehicles on their way to or from the training ranges at Harwood Dale, north of Scarborough. On the tarmac roads these monsters cannot have been easy to control and they constantly slithered this way and that, regularly chipping the kerb stones. To my young eyes they were coming perilously close to demolishing mother, myself, and Phoebe in the pram.

A second memory was of Sunday school, and probably took place some two years later. Both Phoebe and I and a few other neighbours' children attended St Luke's Church Sunday school near Scarborough Hospital – a half mile walk from Throxenby Grove.

After the service one Sunday a few of us were 'exploring' and discovered a rope had fallen from its normally secure home on a hook much higher up the wall than we would have been able to reach. We decided to haul on the rope and see what happened. A wonderful melodious sound rang throughout the neighbourhood and this led to many further 'pulls'. We didn't know of course, as no one had had reason to tell us, that it was not allowed to ring church bells in war time, as the ringing signified an impending invasion.

In fact, within minutes there was an invasion of sorts when a very irate and flustered Mrs Wilkes, the Vicar's wife, came scurrying across Scalby Road from the vicarage, then up the steep path to the church, complete with apron as she had been cooking Sunday lunch. She was completely out of breath, but nevertheless I still remember her wagging finger as she remonstrated with us.

During those war–time years with father away, and money tight, mother did a marvellous job of bringing up Phoebe and myself.

Much later she told us that shortly after father had been called up, the pay allotment he had arranged to send had not arrived. She made enquiries but still it did not come and she was getting desperate and just about to approach Phyllis to see if she could provide a temporary loan – as she willingly would have done. However mother first decided to go through clothing in the wardrobe to see if any coppers had been left in anything.

She got to dad's dinner suit and there in the breast pocket found a neatly folded, large, old style white £5 note. It was his emergency money and was worth a mint in those days being more than an average week's wage of four pounds, ten shillings (£4.50). We were able to eat without troubling Phyllis.

Mother took us on picnics to Raincliffe Woods and to gather tadpoles from Throxenby Mere. Other neighbours' children whose fathers were away at the war were invited, as well as some whose fathers were in reserved occupations so were at home, but didn't seem to bother with such outings.

On one occasion when we were all playing hide and seek along Lady Edith's Drive on the way from Raincliffe Woods, I hid within the lower branches of a large bushy conifer and sat down – on to a nest of complaining wasps. Ouch!

Mother also took us to the beach – normally the South Bay when we caught a bus to Scarborough, walked from the then bus station, down Vernon Road and along the Foreshore to the small area of beach still available for use by families. Most of the beach was barricaded with barbed wire and tank traps to disrupt the expected invasion. Whilst we didn't know it at the time, cables ran from an 'ice–cream kiosk' at the foot of Blands Cliff, under Foreshore Road, and under the sands to the South Bay where they were connected to mines which had been installed in the harbour area to delay invasion. The plunger, in the 'ice cream kiosk' was manned by the army 24 hours a day.

On another occasion mother made Phoebe and I a kite. She had no proper kite material but in those war time years it was a matter of 'make do and mend'. She stitched part of an old sheet into a diamond shape, then made pockets at each corner; cut, then split pieces of garden bamboo cane and slotted these into the pockets as supports. She then knotted string round the bamboo supports where they crossed and tied the kite to a large ball of string.

And it flew! The kite zoomed and twirled in the breeze, with a backdrop above of a single Spitfire doing aerobatics. It was maybe the same 'plane we had spotted when she brought Phoebe home in 1940.

One night we were in the shelter under the stairs when a number of loud 'crumps' were heard. The following day we learned that bombs had been jettisoned on farmland near Moor Lane – then known as the Roman Road at the top of Throxenby Lane and no more than ¼ mile from the house. This happened occasionally and was officially put down to enemy planes ditching their bombs before turning for home, or, as one story went, enemy planes mistaking Scarborough for Hull and thinking they were over their target.

At the end of our garden was a field about half the size of a football pitch. This was part of a property on Throxenby Lane to which Throxenby Grove ran at right angles. This field was owned by a Mr Reveley and contained a very large shed which, at a guess, must have been at least 30 yards long and 10 yards wide and before the war had been used to rear chickens. This shed and its roof were clad entirely in corrugated steel sheeting and, from the air, on a moonlit night, it possibly looked like a small factory building. The nearest we got to being bombed or shot at was when a wayward enemy plane – reputedly a Heinkel – flew very low over the houses, spraying all before it with machine gun fire. Imagine the din as many of these bullets hit this metal shed.

Many years later when I was gardening I dug up a bullet, and whilst it wasn't engraved 'Hergestellt in Deutschland', it can only have come from that enemy plane.

Even in what was then an almost rural environment, the 'black–out' was strictly enforced. Father had worked for a wholesale tobacconist before being called up so the Fowler blackout consisted of large, thick cardboard panels cut from packing cases – with 'H.O. Wills', and 'Passing Clouds' printed boldly upon them. They were cut to fit within each window frame thus ensuring a near light–tight fit. The normal curtains were then drawn and from the inside of the house all appeared normal.

Over the road Mr Catton, a school teacher, kept a stirrup pump and a bucket of water and another bucket of sand near to his front door in case incendiary bombs rained down on us. Remembering the size of the buckets I often wondered what good they would have been had his house caught fire.

Great Aunt Alice – mother's aunt – visited us fairly regularly during the war years. She worked in a factory making munitions and towards the end of the war I recall her saying she had 'got the sack as there was no more work'. It took me years to fathom out what 'getting the sack' meant.

One of her visits coincided with Phoebe's serious illness when she would be 3 or 4. I got measles, then chicken pox, and Phoebe then got them the other way round – but ended up with pneumonia and was in a coma for days. Neighbour Miss Weathers, had always said, 'Phoebe is a weak child and will not last through childhood', but now, well over 70 years later she has, thankfully, been proved wrong. It was only Dr Dorothy Ellison managing to get early samples of M+B tablets – the early version of penicillin – that saved her life. Coincidentally, Phoebe's illness could have been around the same time as that of Winston Churchill:

*'The very nature of warfare between 1939 and 1945 forced the medical world to rush forward the pace of advance in medicine. Advances in the treatment of infection had occurred pre–war but with the turmoil of war, research pioneers pushed forward to find solutions to very pressing problems. In 1936, 'M+B' was produced by the firm May and Baker – the first effective sulphonamides that could be used for a variety of infections. Called 'M+B 693' it was*

*used as a treatment for sore throats, pneumonia and gonorrhoea. A development of 'M+B 693' was 'M+B 760'. Both proved very effective as treatments against infections. However, the very nature of war meant that both treatments were needed in far greater quantities than during peace time. Therefore, probably for the first time since World War One, medical production was put onto a war footing so that the supplies that were required were produced'.*

In 1943, Winston Churchill was given 'M+B 693' as a treatment for pneumonia and on December 29th, 1943, he told the nation:

*'This admirable 'M+B' from which I did not suffer any inconvenience, was used at the earliest moment and after a week's fever the intruders were repulsed'.*

Further memories of those early days are sparse. A family's laundry was done by hand, the only washing machines being large commercial models. Mother washed the previous week's dirty clothes every Monday in a 'Peggy tub' (a drum about 2½ feet in diameter and 3 feet high which bellied in the middle and was ribbed from top to bottom for strength). She filled this with hot water which had to be boiled in pans and the kettle on the gas cooker, then added soap powder into the tub. Into this went the weekly wash which was then manually pummelled about. Initially she used a 'Peggy stick' – like a round milk maid's stool with legs, but with a tall vertical stem coming up from the middle of the 'stool' with a crossbar towards the top. This enabled her to give the dirty clothes a good vigorous pounding in the water.

Later, she acquired a 'Posher' – made of copper and funnel shaped, with its widest part at the base and its narrowest part fixed to a stout upright wooden stem with a handle at right angles towards the top. The copper funnel had holes round it and as it was thrust up and down on to the clothes in the tub it made a 'poshing' noise – which was probably where the name came from. The action of 'poshing' and the holes in the base, caused suction which helped clean the clothes. The tub was then emptied and the dirty water replaced with clean to rinse everything before they were put through a hand operated mangle with two large rollers which squeezed out much of the water.

One day I was trying to help dry some clothes through the mangle and Phoebe, always inquisitive, put her finger on the back side of the roller. When I turned the handle the pressure of the two rollers trapped her finger and the first I knew that something was wrong was when I heard a loud squeal. Her finger was extricated but I think she still has one finger a little flatter than the others.

On fine days the 'wash' was then hung out on a line in the garden to dry, but in winter or on wet days a clothes horse round the coal fire had to suffice. This left a damp and not unpleasant smell in the room which I still remember.

Other random memories of those days were of the small United buses which plied the route between Scarborough and Scalby and back again every 15 minutes. As fuel was so scarce they had large rubber containers strapped to their roofs which, it was said, contained gas.

Buses also had no individual bells to warn the driver if you wanted to get off, as do present day buses. There was just one long string stretched from back to front below the ceiling and you pulled on that; presumably the string was attached to a bell in the driver's closed compartment. All buses in those days carried conductors to issue and check the tickets. However, all buses had conductors as well as drivers.

I was always puzzled by a warehouse on Falsgrave Road with a tin sign on the door which proclaimed 'Fyffes

Bananas'. What were bananas? I always pondered what these funny shaped things could be and how they tasted. I never did find out until after the war.

When the war ended and VE day was announced there was great jubilation and Aunt Alice took us to Woolworths and bought us an ice cream each. That was something else we had never seen or tasted and whilst the first post war ice creams were somewhat custardy in taste and appearance they soon improved.

Starting on Sunday May 13th 1945 Scarborough held a week of thanksgiving following the end of the war in Europe.

A Spitfire, (above) thought to be a Mk XVI with the characteristic bubble canopy and four bladed propeller distinguishing it, formed part of the display, and it certainly attracted attention in its prominent position on what is now St Nicholas Cliff car park between the Grand Hotel and what was the St Nicholas Hotel (now the Travelodge).

Both hotels, together with the Prince of Wales, The Crown, The Weston and the Waldorf and many others were used for RAF pre–flying training during the war years so the appearance of a Spitfire in the town was very appropriate. A VE [Victory in Europe] Thanksgiving Service took place outside the Railway Station in pouring rain on Sunday, 13th May, 1945. Three thousand members of HM Forces took part in it, and there were probably even more civilians. Aged nearly 7, I was one of them!

*VE Day Thanksgiving Service, Scarborough. The old Odeon cinema appears on the right; the railway station entrance on the left*

I also remember the following year, a Victory Celebration party in Newby, held on a field where Highfield Estate stands today. There was a massive bonfire and fireworks and food and something that sticks in my mind – very large animal shapes made of coloured tissue paper, which, when held over the heat of the fire, ballooned out and floated off into the dark night sky. Later that year on VJ Day, [Victory over Japan] on 15th August 1945, bands played, signal flares were lit and bonfires burned brightly to celebrate the end of the war in the east.

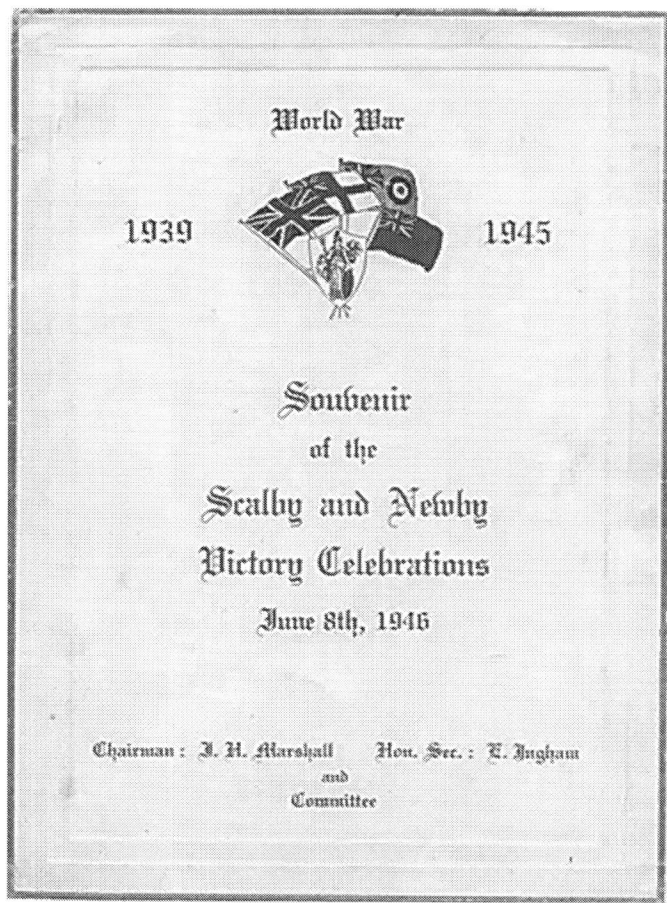

*Phoebe's Invitation and Souvenir of the Scalby & Newby Victory party on June 8th 1946*

Many years after the war had ended, Roy Day, who had trained as aircrew at the Prince of Wales Hotel on Esplanade, Scarborough during the war years, recounted his memories of the end of the war for my book, *'God Bless the Prince of Wales'*.

'After training as aircrew at the Prince of Wales Hotel I went on to fly Lancaster bombers and carried out many bombing raids against Germany.

I am now 92 and in 2012 still flying as the oldest flying member of Perranporth Flying club. Whilst VE day had effectively finished the war in Europe, my crew and I had not completed the necessary 30 operations which were needed to count as a tour of duty, so we were sent to train on the North Sea ranges for Tiger Force – the offensive against Japan. This was boring work and after one training session, instead of flying back to our base in Lincolnshire I decided to divert, to look at my old Training Wing, the Prince of Wales Hotel, from the air.

I did a few very low passes over the hotel and you can imagine the noise and reverberation from 4 Merlin aero engines.

I then flew back to base in Lincolnshire thinking little about my escapade but on landing I was immediately put on a charge and later court martialled.

It transpired that on the day of my flight – just after VE Day – the RAF band was performing at the Spa in Scarborough, being attended by the Mayor, and an Air Vice Marshall. The event was effectively drowned out by my unscheduled fly–past.

At my court martial I was 'Dismissed the Service', even though by then the war was over. The authorities thought my display might encourage more low flying and admitted they wanted to make an example of me'.

Only later was Roy to realise that this had been the best possible outcome for which he could have hoped. The RAF was downsizing, but it might have been some months before he was demobbed. And at the end of the war when civilian airlines were expanding rapidly and clamouring for qualified pilots Roy got in on the ground floor and spent the rest of his working life flying commercially and for pleasure.

Foreign prisoner–of–war labour was being used to build prefabs at Sandybed, Scarborough, for the troops who would shortly return home, and to replace the many properties bombed and subsequently demolished. The

RAF and the military and all their equipment were moving out, hotels were handed back to their owners, who were finding many pieces of ammunition had been left behind, some even under floorboards, and the Spa and other public places which had been requisitioned by the military were handed back. The owners of the Prince of Wales hotel found many floorboards missing as the RAF airmen billeted there had burnt them in the fireplaces in the hotel's bedrooms, in an effort to keep warm. The Spa re-opened for the 1945 season. The lighthouse's warning beam of light to safeguard shipping recommenced. Traffic lights and street lights were switched back on and Londesborough Road railway station, used by the military for troop trains and to bring in vehicles and tanks for training purposes, was handed back to the LNER.

By October, 1945 the many servicemen and prisoners of war were starting to arrive home and the town was slowly recovering and starting to get back to normal although some rationing remained until as late as 1954.

Dad was demobbed from the RAF on 1st October 1945 and returned home.

Shortly afterwards, a gasman on a bicycle visited Throxenby Grove. He was wobbling somewhat precariously, as he was riding with one hand and carrying a ladder with the other. Then aged 7, I watched him from my bedroom window in excitement. He dismounted, placed the ladder against the lamp post, carried out some maintenance, and then, 5 years after we had last seen the mellow yellow light, we had back our gas lamp. This had shone on mother when she brought Phoebe back from the Dybdale Nursing Home and being only 15 yards from my bedroom had shone into my window each night until it had been extinguished shortly after the start of the war.

The country was again at peace.

*

# CHAPTER 3

# Donkey droppings
# 1943–1949

> ### 1943: Brief Timeline
>
> Panic at the sound of new anti–aircraft rockets leads to a crush at Bethnal Green tube station, killing 183 people; The Gloster Meteor, the first operational military jet aircraft for the Allies, has its first test flight, at RAF Cranwell in Lincolnshire; Capture of Tunis ends the campaign in North Africa; Operation Chastise (the 'Dambuster Raid') takes place: No. 617 Squadron RAF use bouncing bombs to breach German dams in the Ruhr Valley; World War II: Allied invasion of Italy: Allied forces under General Sir Bernard Montgomery land in mainland Italy; The Salerno Mutiny occurred when soldiers of the British Army's X Corps refused postings to new units; First 'Bevin Boys' selected from conscripts to work in the coal mines; Construction of prototype Mark I Colossus computer, the world's first totally *electronic* programmable computing device, at the Post Office Research Station, Dollis Hill, to assist in cryptanalysis at Bletchley Park, was completed.

I first attended Gladstone Road Infants School in September 1943, my 5th birthday having been on 18th June that year.

Why Gladstone Road school I don't know as we had a school at Scalby, much nearer than Gladstone Road which was over 2 miles from home. But Gladstone Road School had (and still has) an excellent reputation so that might have had a bearing. And my aunt's address was 31 St John's Avenue – ¼ mile from the school which was the address registered for me – presumably to put me within the catchment area if bureaucracy had invented such things in those far off days. Also I had my lunch with her rather than stay for school dinners so that maybe legitimised using her address.

However, the St John's Avenue address caused all sorts of problems.

One incident occurred when, for some reason, the school bank needed the signature of one of my parents. It must have seemed urgent at the time as I was sent 'home' to obtain it. When I returned to school well over an hour later, there were suggestions that I had been malingering – but an hour to Throxenby Grove and back in those days was not bad going, despite the teacher thinking I had only had to go to St John's Avenue.

A few weeks later, teacher Mrs Grist told me I was to be moved to a higher class, so effectively I was transferred to join the previous year's intake.

I don't remember much about the Infants years – except school milk! It put me off milk for life – especially when it arrived frozen in winter so was put on radiators to thaw out.

On the beach once in summer with mother and Phoebe we children had donkey rides and who should the donkey stop in front of to relieve himself, than Miss Dena Hebditch, one of my teachers.

The following Monday she mentioned in class that 'David's donkey stopped in front of me and left me a pile of donkey droppings'.

Incidentally, Dena Hebditch now lives in Montrosa, run by the Soroptomist Housing Association. This backs onto the property we now own. It's a small world.

On one occasion the teacher told us there would be a knitting lesson. The boys in the class laughed but she said, 'I mean you lot as well!' and she did! So we knitted dishcloths and similar items and I remember even knitting myself a scarf at home.

Subsequently, we moved up to the Junior School from the Infants. Both on the same site but I only clearly remember two staff members from Gladstone Road Juniors – Headmaster Reginald Hall, known as 'Pop' to everyone and Margaret Hill, who later became our form teacher.

The school put on a play each Christmas to which parents were invited. One year this play was about the story of King Midas and I was asked to take the part of the King. I wore father's maroon silk dressing gown which was so long it nearly tripped me up on a number of occasions, and a hand-made crown. I can still recall my opening words, 'I am Midas, King of the underworld. Everything I touch will turn to gold....' I'm still waiting!

The address problems continued!

In the winter of 1947, myself aged 9, my sister Phoebe then 7, and 3 other children who also went to 'Glaggo Road', set off from Throxenby Lane at around twenty past eight, our usual time to catch the bus on Scalby Road. Snow was already about 2 feet deep, and it was still snowing and laying. As it was apparent there were no buses, we set off to walk to school. There was no thought of closing schools in those days because of wintry weather and the present 'Health and Safety' industry hadn't been invented.

It must have been after 10.00am when we trooped in to our different classes, and later in the morning 'Pop' Hall, the headmaster, called into our classroom and gave me a mild ticking off for being late arriving. He had apparently thought I had walked from St John's Avenue – all of ¼ mile from school – rather than from Newby! To give him credit, he must have spoken with the other late arrivals, and realised we had all walked to school together. Later on, he returned to our classroom and, in front of everyone, described the five of us as a being, 'a good example of commitment to the school' on making the effort to get there in the snow.

What always puzzled me was that the others who lived at Newby also went to Gladstone Road school but were registered at their Newby addresses. Maybe my parents had been ultra–cautious to make sure I got a place?

Shortly afterwards they decided to buy me a bike on which to get to school and back. The only problem was that they opted for a girl's bike without a cross–bar as they said I could pass it on to Phoebe when I outgrew it. I accepted it a little begrudgingly but passed on my misgivings. 'Me? Ride a girl's bike?' and shortly afterwards I was provided with a proper boy's bike and Phoebe took over the girl's version.

That enabled us both to cycle happily to and from school together and it also provided flexibility and gave us confidence on the roads – much quieter roads, I hasten to add, than today's.

When we had moved up to the higher classes at the junior school, teacher Margaret Hill (or Miss Hill, or 'Miss' as we had to call her), took us on nature walks and on a visit to Scarborough Castle. She was a wonderful teacher, if a strict disciplinarian and she had previously taught at the adjoining Gladstone Road Senior School.

The photo on the next page shows part of her class returning from a nature ramble to Throxenby Mere, all complete with jars of tadpoles. This photograph appeared in the press at that time and over intervening years has frequently been republished as people have tried to trace all the names of those present. I appear 2nd from the left.

*From left: Ken Herbert, David Fowler, Ann Collins, Angela Procter, Gordon Brough, Joyce Noble, Frank Hole, Peter Feather, Sylvia Spencer and Pauline Shannon.*

The schools all ran 'Hip & Haw' collections 'to help the war effort' and we were all encouraged to go out and pick them at weekends. There were small prizes for those who collected the most. We also collected blackberries and bilberries but they were for home consumption.

I also inwardly smile when I hear anyone use the word 'nice'. I remember someone using it in Pop Hall's hearing. 'Don't use that word,' he said, 'It means nothing and is not descriptive. There are a lot more suitable words you can use.' And there are! I remember his advice vividly to this day and think of him if I'm ever tempted to say 'nice'.

One day, during a lesson in Margaret Hill's class, I felt something wet and sticky on my neck. I didn't know what it was and instinctively called out. She asked what was wrong and I said I had something sticky on my neck. It transpired that friend David Lickess, who was sitting directly behind me, – and who, incidentally, became a

Canon in the Church of England – had finished sucking a piece of chewing gum and had stuck it on my neck.

'Come out here Lickess,' she said. She was the first teacher to use our surnames and this was probably linked to her previous senior school experience. She slowly walked across the room and picked up her cane. 'Hold out your hand Lickess'. And she gave him 3 strokes of the cane across the palm of each hand for chewing gum in class.

During my time in the Juniors I went to Aunt Phyllis's for lunch instead of having school dinners. It was a walk of about ¼ mile and sometimes she met me mid–way. Her semolina pudding always had a face on it in jam!

I knew, of course, that Percy was a prisoner of war and Phyllis told me years afterwards that I used to listen attentively to the radio news while she was preparing lunch and if there was anything of interest such as the war going in our favour, or prisoners being repatriated, I would let her know.

Only very recently Phoebe managed to get details of the camp in Poland where Percy was imprisoned and that led on to further information:

Percy had been called up at the start of the war and because of his interest in amateur radio and his ability in using the Morse code he was posted to the Navy as a radio telegraphist. Official records say he was 'a Telegraphist, Naval Forces – Officers and Ratings' and his Military number was C/WRX/683.

Later, his vessel was torpedoed and the only communication Phyllis received was to the effect that he had probably been lost when the ship was torpedoed and had sunk. That must have been a terrible time for her.

However, amongst her papers I came across an actual letter she had sent to Percy on 28th February 1942 at 'Dulag Nord' and which she had copied to the Agence

Centrale des Prisioniers de Guerre, in Geneva, when she learnt that he had been taken prisoner and could possibly be in Dulag Nord. He obviously received and cherished her letter and brought it home with him when he was released as it is stamped with an official German POW stamp.

He ended up as Prisoner of War number 448, in Stalag 344, Lamsdorf (Oberschlesein) Poland. Whilst he never mentioned the camp but simply that he had been a prisoner of war he did say that he, and others, had suffered much deprivation. He mentioned 'lack of food', 'a long walk' and 'scavenging for food from waste bins' during this walk.

'The Long March' (sometimes called 'The Long Walk', or 'The Death March') took place from Lamsdorf, Poland, to Goerlitz, Germany, when the Russian Army was advancing. The facts fit the little that Percy told me a number of years before his death – although like so many ex-servicemen he would not talk specifics.

I strongly suspect he was involved and if any reader can shed light either way, proving, or disproving Percy's involvement I would be very pleased to hear from them. (His full name was Percival Briscoe Briscombe C/WRX/683, and his UK short-wave radio call-sign was G8KU)

The March is covered in detail in the book 'The Last Escape – The Untold Story Of Allied POWs 1944–45' by John Nichol and Tony Rennell and a very brief extract follows:

*'In January 1945, as the Soviet armies resumed their offensive and advanced into Germany, many of the prisoners were marched westward in groups of 200 to 300. Many of them died from the bitter cold and exhaustion. The lucky ones got far enough to the west to be liberated by the American army. The unlucky ones got 'liberated' by the Soviets, who instead of turning them over quickly to the*

*western allies, held them as virtual hostages for several more months. Many of them were finally repatriated towards the end of 1945 through the port of Odessa on the Black Sea.*

*The Long March took place during the final months of the Second World War in Europe. About 30,000 Allied PoWs were force-marched westward across Poland and Germany in appalling winter conditions, lasting about four months from January to April 1945. It has been called various names: 'The Great March West', 'The Long March', 'The Long Walk', 'The Long Trek', 'The Black March', 'The Bread March', but most survivors just called it 'The March'. It has also been called 'The Lamsdorf Death March".*

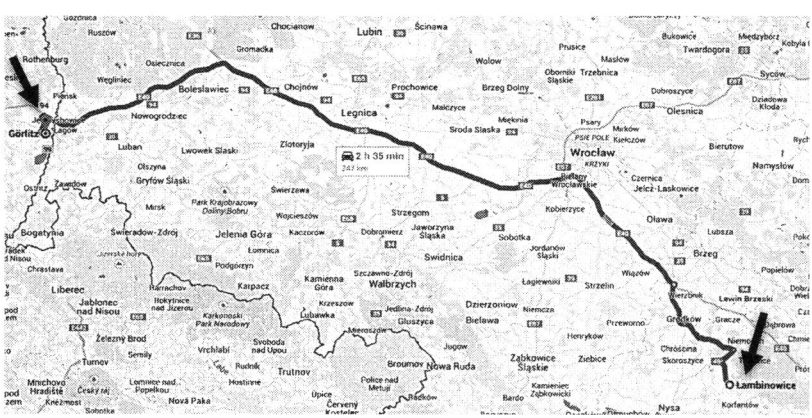

*The arrows indicate the start point, Lamsdorf, bottom right, to Goerlitz, Germany, top left.*

'As the Soviet army was advancing on Poland, the Nazis made the decision to evacuate the PoW camps to prevent the liberation of the prisoners by the Russians. During this period, also hundreds of thousands of German civilians, most of them women and children, as well as civilians of other nationalities, were making their way westward in the snow and freezing weather and many died. January and February 1945 were among the coldest winter months of the twentieth century, with blizzards and temperatures as *low as –25 °C. Even until the middle of March temperatures were well below –18 °C. Most of the PoWs were ill–prepared for the evacuation, having suffered years of poor rations and wearing clothing ill–suited to the appalling winter conditions......'*

Whilst an indication of the route of the forced march is shown on map on the previous page, that main road was not built until after the war so the actual route of the march zigzagged between towns, villages and hamlets and was much longer and could have extended to 500km or even more. About 30,000 Allied PoWs were involved.

*

Back to Gladstone Road Junior School and a somewhat unusual, but regular, pastime at playtime was to play at 'Weddings'.

We would probably be around 8 or 9 years old at this time, and how the roles were picked I cannot now recall but for some reason I was always the groom and a classmate called Ann Collins was always the bride. David Lickess, of chewing gum fame, was always the Vicar – which turned out to be very appropriate as he looked the part even in those days – he was tall with well-groomed hair always neatly parted, combed and Brylcreemed – and went on to become a Canon in the Church of England.

In the space of one playtime Ann and I had the time to arrive at church, have the service, get married, then parade round the playground. I don't know if Ann had a bouquet she threw to the 'guests' but I do recall that we didn't have time for a honeymoon! However I suppose I can legitimately claim that Ann was my first girlfriend – and my first wife!

It is funny how things happen. I was writing this book when my wife Eileen and I decided to walk down to Clock Cafe, on the cliffs beyond Scarborough's Spa. It was Saturday 22nd August 2015.

We found a seat on the terrace overlooking the harbour

but I took little notice of the other people at adjoining tables. However, suddenly a tall, attractive lady appeared before me smiling, and said a little hesitantly,

'Err, I'm sorry to interrupt and you probably aren't, but could you by any chance be David Fowler?'

I knew instantly it was Ann. She had the same voice, the same smile and the persona I remembered from so long ago and I just said, 'Ann? Is it really you? After 66 years!'

We had a hug and reminisced for a good half hour about Gladstone Road School and its pupils and teachers and what each of us had done since those long ago school days. After leaving Gladstone Road School Ann had moved to the Girls' High school but there was little contact between the three grammar schools in town so we hadn't met since each of us had left Gladstone Road school and moved on to our respective High Schools.

Ann Hunt (nee Collins) had moved away from Scarborough and married but kept on the house her parents had lived in at Scarborough which she now uses for family breaks and holidays. She had with her, her son, daughter–in–law and grandson.

In those far off days she was taller than me but I've caught up in the intervening years and at 6ft 2" am now a few inches taller than her. Strangely, after meeting Ann for the first time for 66 years on the Saturday, the following Tuesday Ren and I (Ren comes into the story later on but is my partner in Farthings Publishing and we give talks together on books we have written), were giving a talk to a retired group in the Concert Hall at Scarborough Library. After the talk had finished one of the members came up to me and said, 'You don't recognise me do you?' I told her I felt there was some vague recognition but I couldn't really place her so it must have been a long time ago. 'It was', she replied. 'We were in the same class together at Gladstone Road Junior School 66 years ago. I am Angela Procter'.

That name triggered my hazy recollection into full-blown

recognition and I recalled Angela had appeared in the nature walk photograph next to Ann Collins. I told her Ann was in Scarborough and I'd met her on Saturday although she didn't now live here.

Angela replied that she and Ann had been best friends at school and had kept in touch over the intervening years.

It really can be a very small world.

*Left: Me, Ann and Angela, all aged around 9, after gathering tadpoles on a nature walk to Throxenby Mere as part of Miss Hill's class at Gladstone Road Junior School.*

To return to our school days we all reached 11 plus exam time and sat the first part of the exam at Gladstone Road School and the second part in the High School. A few days after sitting the first part 'Pop' Hall said I looked worried. I told him I was worried I had not passed so would not go to the High School.

'I wouldn't worry,' he said, 'I'm sure you've passed. And he was proved right when the results came out.

Away from school, life went on despite there being a war on. Before she married, mother had been a companion to members of the well-known local Quaker family, the Rowntrees, who had then lived at Endcliffe,

Granville Road, Scarborough. During the war years mother had received an invitation to visit Mrs Robson (née Rowntree) at her Scalby home and Phoebe and I were included. To the two of us it was a completely different world. We were used to a 3 bedroomed semi–detached house. This was a much larger, older, detached property – and a maid came with it!

We had been instructed before we set off what to do and what not to do, 'or there will be trouble'! The afternoon went well and we were served tea and cakes by a maid, through the serving hatch between the kitchen and the dining room – something we had never come across before.

Many, many years later I was invited for lunch at the same house by the same couple whose son was then a bank client. Again, it is a small world but I'm sure Mrs Robson didn't connect the two visits and I didn't enlighten her.

When we had health ailments we went to Dr Ellison, a Scottish spinster lady who had her surgery along Scalby Road, about half a mile walk from home. She was a delightful white haired lady with a sparkle in her eye and I always remember, when I had suspected appendicitis, she told me, 'make sure you always chew your 'fud".

By today's standards the surgery was somewhat old fashioned. It had green baize covering all the doors and when Dr. Ellison prescribed she got out her mortar and pestle and proceeded to make the pills herself there and then.

When we had to go to the dentist it was the school dentist. I can remember us both needing treatment and mother took us into town, then after the gas, with its almost suffocating sensation, and extractions, we went back home again and got the rest of the day off school. I never had any faith in that dentist from the following morning when I discovered that instead of taking out the bad tooth he had taken out the perfectly healthy one next door. I still have that annoying gap in my lower set of teeth, and the 'bad' one was subsequently sorted with a simple filling.

Late in 1945 dad had been demobbed and was now home from the RAF and back working with Youngmans. Each Saturday he started to bring sweets home for Phoebe and me and whilst the gesture was appreciated they were always Spangles, Polo mints, Rowntree's fruit gums and Rowntree's fruit pastilles, and oh, what we would have given to have chosen what we wanted ourselves. We had a meeting and I was deputed to have a word with dad. He agreed that we should have our own sweet coupons (rationing was still in force) and pocket money, so we could buy what we wanted. We already received 6d a week each (2½p) so presumably sweet money came on top. Youngman's, dad's employers, had recently started their own confectionary department to supplement the existing tobacco business, so dad would probably have been entitled to discount on the sweets he bought from the firm. This discount could have helped strained family finances but at that stage it was way above our understanding and we were just delighted our approach had been successful.

In the school summer holidays we went and 'helped' with the harvesting in fields then surrounding Throxenby Grove. We even took packed lunches so we could eat with the farm hands at lunchtime. That land is now a large housing estate.

At 3, Throxenby Grove we had a small rear vegetable garden and grew peas, potatoes, carrots, potatoes gooseberries, raspberries and strawberries. There were also two apple trees, the sturdier one being great to climb. In front of the house and to the rear, there were small lawned areas and on the back lawn we put up a tent in which we slept occasionally in summer. When not being used as a tent the waterproof tent material was used to cover the three family bikes in case of rain as there was nowhere to store them under cover. Later, a garage was built at the end of the drive.

During the school summer holidays, cousin Jean (Taylor) used to visit us and she, Phoebe and I usually played quite well together although sometimes two of us ganged up on the other one. From memory it was usually the girls who ganged up on me.

Sadly, Jean died on 18th September 2016 and after her funeral her husband, Peter Bucknall, recalled that she had often talked of the telephones, she, Phoebe and I made and used to call each other. These consisted of two empty tin cans with a tight piece of string knotted through the base of each. The string was then pulled tight and even many yards, with one of us at each end they worked!

There were a number of other children living nearby with whom we played. Traffic was not a problem and in summer we would be out from around 9.00am until teatime often taking packed lunches with us. After the war the fields which had almost surrounded us slowly gave way to the large Lady Edith's housing development and the even larger Highfield estate, so playing amongst the stacks of timber, and bricks and part built houses was a wonderful way to spend our time.

Members of 'our' group consisted of John Mills – who later went on to work at the Fylingdales Early Warning station; 3 of the 4 Lisle children – Janet, Roger & Susan, (Roderick was too young to join us); Tony Atkins; Dorothy and Barbara Fidler; John Leadley; and Gillian, Ian and Peter Stoddard.

Janet Lisle was the eldest of all of us so she was responsible to make sure we all caught the service bus to school. There were no special school buses in those days. Occasionally Mr Lisle gave us a lift in his car. He was in a 'reserved' occupation – probably insurance – so he needed a car and was allowed a petrol allowance. One day we asked him how fast the car would go. He wound it up to 50 mph for a few yards and that was our talking point for weeks afterwards. We'd been driven at 50 miles an hour!

Bill Potts was a couple of years older than me and his sister Mary 5 years older. Bill often joined us for rambles to Throxenby Mere to collect tadpoles or for the occasional picnic mother arranged. They were living nearby with their aunt, Mabel Cromack, while their father, WF Potts, and in peacetime physics master at the High School and later senior science master, was away helping the war effort. He worked on degaussing allied ships to reduce or eliminate their magnetic field and prevent them being 'seen' by the enemy.

*Degaussing is the process of decreasing or eliminating a remnant magnetic field. It is named after the gauss, a unit of magnetism, which in turn was named after Carl Friedrich Gauss. Due to magnetic hysteresis, it is generally not possible to reduce a magnetic field completely to zero, so degaussing typically induces a very small "known" field referred to as bias. Degaussing was originally applied to reduce ships' magnetic signatures during the Second World War.*

One scrape which caused parents to get very het–up – remember it was the '40's – was when John Leadley asked one of the Fidler girls, 'Will you show me yours if I show you mine?' There is no record of what reply he received.

Also one day, John who was older than the rest of us, got into some scrape which could have had serious consequences. Mr Borland had a bakery about a half a mile away and he delivered bread and cakes regularly each week. He was a rather sad looking character with a moustache and he always wore a trilby hat and a sand coloured warehouse coat. He might have also had a speech impediment as his speech was not clear and he seemed to tilt his head to one side all the time. His bakery was on Scalby Road and he ran a very small brown 3 wheeled van. One day he left this at the top of a hill whilst delivering. John Leadley climbed in and released the hand brake. The van started moving slowly backwards and John was able to jump out before the van rolled faster and faster down the hill, eventually leaving the road, passing over a grass verge and ending up in someone's front hedge. Luckily there was no other traffic or the 'accident' could have been even worse. We all played dumb and when Mr Borland reappeared he looked astonished when he could not see his van where he had left it. He eventually spotted it and we never knew whether he discovered what had happened.

Another friend was Peter Newham who lived further up Throxenby Lane and near to the Fidler sisters. However, Peter was not really part of our group as we were all much of an age whilst he was a few years younger.

However, he followed me to the High School and did well, becoming solicitor for Northampton Borough Council. We are still regularly in touch as he is editor of 'Summer Times', the Old Scarborians' Magazine (members are ex–pupil and masters of the long gone Scarborough High School for Boys). For a number of years I edited the magazine then persuaded Peter to take over the role which I now publish it for the Association.

Model theatres of one sort or another always seemed to be on my agenda and I was always, and still am interested in the technical side of theatre. We set up a 'stage' on our back lawn and, for lighting I rigged up a bulb holder and bulb within the silvered inside of an old tea chest and spread the cable to reach a socket in the kitchen of the house. We had a stage and we had light. This was of course, on a bright sunny summer day so why we actually needed light is another question.

As a performer we 'borrowed' a neighbour's dog called 'Darkie'. He was a small energetic black dog, very friendly and he loved chasing balls and he played his part perfectly – even though I doubt he was a member of equity. David Lickess had a model theatre with lighting and that gave us both hours of enjoyment during winter. On wet days in summer when cousin Jean was visiting us, mother would send the three of us off on the bus to Gala Land, then an underground entertainment complex built on a Turkish theme, and near to the South bay. There were slot machines, cranes where you tried to fish out prizes, talent competitions, (I seem to remember cousin Jean getting onto the stage to sing), Thelma Hammond and her All Girls Band, fish tanks and virtually anything which would satisfy three youngsters for a few hours on a wet day.

*Above: Thelma Hammond and her All Girls Band at Gala Land. But isn't it a man near the microphone?*

*Left: Gala Land was a delight to young and old. Nicknamed 'The Scarborough Umbrella' it could accommodate 5000 people.*
*It started life as 'The People's Palace and Aquarium' in 1877, the Corporation took it over in 1921 and it was demolished c.1968 to make way for a large underground car park.*

Around this time – just before moving to the High School, John Mills and I joined the 38th Scarborough Cub Scouts which met at a building called Claremont on Castle Road. We needed to get the bus into town and back again, then had a fairly lengthy walk from, and to, the bus station. Afterwards we usually bought some chips from a fish and chip shop near to the meeting hall and to do so we walked past the town's fire station. What excitement when there was a call–out and we saw the firemen dash into their vehicles and career off up the road to wherever the fire or incident was taking place.

Being members of the cub scouts we attended a Scout Jamboree one weekend. It was held at the Knavesmire, York and many scouts and cubs were there as well as the chief Scout – then Lord Rowallen. Afterwards there was a competition when all those who had attended were invited to write about their impressions of the day.

What a surprise, when, at a future Cub meeting I was taken to one side and was told I would be receiving an inscribed book for my essay which had been judged the best of those entered. That was probably my first literary success.

*

# CHAPTER 4

# An unsettling revelation 1949–1955

### 1949: Brief Timeline

Peacetime conscription requires men aged 18–26 in England, Scotland and Wales to serve full-time in the armed forces for 18 months; Post-War rationing of clothes ends; Royal Navy frigate HMS *Amethyst* goes up the Yangtze River to evacuate British Commonwealth refugees escaping the advance of the Mao's communist forces; Wolverhampton Wanderers F.C. win the FA Cup; First women appointed King's Counsel; Manchester Mark 1 computer operable at the University of Manchester; First self-service launderette opens; The gas industry is nationalised; Dock strike forces the government to use troops to unload goods; Maiden flight of the British–built de Havilland Comet, the world's first passenger jet; Old Trafford football stadium, home of Manchester United F.C., is re-opened following a comprehensive rebuild due to bomb damage; The pound was devalued by 30% against the US dollar; The first comprehensive school in Wales is opened in Holyhead, Anglesey; The Berlin Airlift comes to an end, during which 17 American and 7 British planes have crashed delivering supplies to Soviet blockaded Berlin; Sutton Coldfield transmitting station begins transmitting BBC Television to the English Midlands, the first broadcasts to be seen outside the London area.

In 1949, passing the '11 plus' exam was required in order to get into grammar school. This exam consisted of 2 parts. We sat the first exam in our junior schools. If we passed, the second part was taken in the Scarborough High School for Boys'; the girls took theirs at the then Girls' High School or at Scarborough Convent – also a grammar school - in St. Thomas Street.

*Scarborough High School for Boys – Westwood site until September 1959 when the school moved to a new building*

*at Woodlands*

In the middle of that year a letter dropped through our parent's letter boxes – some envelopes were long and some were larger and square. From memory I think the long ones were used if you had failed, but the larger square ones informed the proud parents that their son had passed his 11 plus examination and was due to start at Scarborough High School for Boys on a given date in September that year. The title was quite a mouthful but it was stressed to us once we arrived at the school that only the full title would do. But then, the note which follows, from HW (Joey) Marsden, the nail–biting Lancastrian headmaster, who, incidentally, was superb at his job, was merely headed 'Scarborough High School'. Maybe the education authority was saving money and using the same letterhead for the Girls' High School? Or maybe they had one rule for themselves and another for the pupils, in those far off days. We shall never know.

The letter telling us we had been successful was followed on July 21st 1949 by a further letter, barely legible and duplicated in blue ink on an old hand duplicator – photocopy machines and computers and printers were then just a twinkle in some engineer's eye – advising our parents:

### SCARBOROUGH HIGH SCHOOL
*Valley Bridge Parade*
*Scarborough*

- **School Hours** *are from 8.50am to 12 noon and from 1.35pm to 3.45pm.*
- **Dinners:** *It is hoped that all who wish may have school dinners but at the moment the number of meals which can be supplied from the Dining Centre is limited.*
- **Clothing:** *The School Uniform consists of Cap, Blazer and grey shorts. For Physical Training, vest, shorts, gym shoes and towel are required. For Games, Football Boots and Jersey are necessary; for cricket a white shirt.*
- **All clothing** *should be plainly marked with initials and name.*
- **Books and stationary** *are provided free of charge. A satchel or case is needed for carrying books.*
- **Games** *are compulsory unless a boy is excused by a Doctor for health reasons.*
- **Cycles:** *As there is only limited shed accommodation, boys living furthest from school will have priority for shed places.*
- **Absences:** *Punctual and regular attendance is essential. If leave of absence is desired, application must be made by letter to the Head Master stating the reason. A boy returning to school after absence through illness must bring a*

> note from his parents. It is helpful if parents will notify the school at once, by letter or by telephone, if a boy is unable to come to school.
> o **Reports** are sent out at the end of each term. A letter of acknowledgement is required at the beginning of the following term.

*Yours sincerely*
*HW Marsden,*
*Headmaster*

Our first day at the High School dawned on a fine autumnal morning in September 1949, and whilst excited, most new boys were also somewhat apprehensive eleven year olds. Each was in new uniform consisting of short grey trousers, school socks, black shoes, grey shirt, tie, sweater, blazer and cap – and most of us carried a very new, very stiff leather satchel.

No–one else from our group at Throxenby was starting at that time so I was on my own. I had been issued with monthly bus tickets printed on blue card, with the dates of the month round the edge and these gained punch holes round the edges as the month progressed.

We didn't know it at that time, but there was a custom to 'bush' new boys as a sort of initiation ceremony. This involved two older boys picking up a newcomer and literally throwing him into a line of gorse bushes bordering one of the playgrounds. I was lucky and managed to keep away from this activity; in fact a year or so later it was stopped when a boy who was thrown into the bushes badly damaged his elbow.

For the first year I found myself in Form 1A (maybe A stood for 'assessment') but after the first form we were transferred into one of three streams, 'A', 'Upper', and 'L'. Throughout the High School, I was in the 'L' stream, and whilst I cannot recall that we took a lot of notice of the different streams, I do remember that some of us felt that with there being an 'Upper' stream, it seemed logical that the 'L' stream stood for 'Lower'.

It was years after leaving school that a then retired master explained that 'L' stood for languages so the brightest pupils were in the 'L' stream. All streams took French but in the second year the 'L' stream had also to choose between Latin and German. I opted for German but it was with some foreboding as the German master, Mr Clarke, nicknamed 'Bonn', came with quite a reputation. There was some doubt about the spelling of his nickname as he had taught both French and German at different times so 'Bon' would have been correct for the French pupils whilst Bonn (the city) appropriate for the German learners.

When we were due for a lesson with him there was no sitting with friends – he wanted us all in alphabetical order. After a lesson or two with him most of us were terrified. Each week he would set a test of 4 questions based on extensive homework we had been given during the preceding week. Woe betide anyone who got less than 3 answers correct.

Bonn was a really hard task master. He taught from a German grammar book he had written and had published some years previously. He called this the 'Mudpie'; published through at least six editions, and was used by many leading schools.

What I certainly never knew at the time was that he was a Quaker who refused to fight in the Great War, but did act as a stretcher bearer and had apparently served with distinction. He was severely wounded and won the Military Cross. His injuries left him with what he described as a cork leg, a steel plate in his skull and a damaged right hand. He taught himself not only to write with his left hand but was also said to be unbeatable at table tennis. We were told that right into the 1930s he was still going to hospital in the school summer holidays to have bits of shrapnel removed.

We never knew this at the time of course, but one day

there was an altercation between him and one of our fellow pupils, John Pitts. Pitts was an excellent boxer and Bonn called him out to settle the dispute and asked Pitts to punch him in the stomach as hard as he could.

What an opportunity! Pitts did just that and it would have floored most men but Bonn just relaxed, stood there and took the punch. He didn't move, flinch, or change his facial expression. Then he said, 'You didn't know I wore a leather corset did you? Now, back to work bad boys.'

'Bad boys' was a favourite expression of Bonn's, but we got back to work, Pitts nursing his bruised knuckles.

Much, much later, whilst doing my two years national service I had very good reason to be grateful to Bonn as I shall mention later.

In 1951 when we were in the 2nd form we were having a Physics lesson when one of the class let out a 'whoop' and said the Pavilion Hotel on Valley Bridge Parade was on fire. And so it was. The southern end of the building had been under scaffolding for renovation work and possibly a blow torch had set fire to the fabric. Physics took a back seat while we glued our noses to the classroom windows to see what we could of what was going on.

Academically, I usually languished somewhere in the lower half of the class, but I blame this on Percy who was a very keen 'radio ham' with the call sign G8KU, and had returned from being a prisoner of war since my earlier 'Glaggo Road' days. I think the attraction of 'helping' him contact people in far off lands through the air waves, was of much more geographical usefulness than Mr Giblett's geography homework.

In those days I was the second smallest boy in the class. Brian Berryman being the smallest, and in all school photographs I look like a pixie with sticking out ears. It was only during my national service that I shot up to 6' 2" inches within a very short time.

A close friend at this time was Graham Burnett who

also attended the High School. Whilst Graham lived at 134, Prospect Road where his mother ran a guest house, he had an aunt and uncle who lived 2 doors from us in Throxenby Grove.

Graham and I got on well and he later became interested in short wave radio having got the bug from me and my uncle.

Whilst we were in the second form at the High School in 1950 and around 12 years old, we both went to the Open Air theatre to see the musical by Rudolf Friml, *The Vagabond King*. I don't know whether we went with his family, my family or possibly with a school party or even alone together but we both much enjoyed the production which had a cast of over 200. The lighting, costumes and sets were colourful and impressive; it was a superb production and the music was really lively and particularly rousing; especially the *Song of the Vagabonds*. Graham and I could really see ourselves as Vagabonds! The libretto follows together with a picture postcard showing the last night of the Scarborough production.

SONG OF THE VAGABONDS

*From the Scarborough Open Air Theatre production 1950 (1925) (Rudolf Friml / Brian Hooker)*

*Come, all you Beggars of Paris town,*
*You lousy rabble of low degree*
*(Chorus: You rabble of low degree!)*
*We'll spare King Louis to keep his crown*
*And save our city from Burgundy*
*(Chorus: Our city from Burgundy)*
*You and I are good for nothing but to die*
*We can die for Liberty.*

*Sons of toil and danger,*
*Will you serve a stranger*
*And bow down to Burgundy*
*Sons of shame and sorrow,*
*Will you cheer tomorrow*
*For the crown of Burgundy?*

*Onward! Onward!*
*Swords against the Foe*
*Forward! Forward the lily banners go!*
*Sons of France around us,*
*Break the chain that bound us,*
*And to Hell with Burgundy!*

*The last performance of The Vagabond King at the Open Air Theatre Scarborough, September 1950. In front of the stage is the illuminated glass raft on which the ballet performed*

The following day, probably a Tuesday or Friday as the shows took place each Monday and Thursday, Graham and I had agreed to 'play golf' on the miniature golf course adjoining Peasholm Park. This must have been during the school summer holidays.

We met, paid our fees and collected our clubs and

balls. We started paying the course and before long were enthusing about the Open Air Theatre show the night before, how good it had been, and how we should be Vagabonds. We then started singing the song of the Vagabonds at full throttle as we went round the course, throwing our clubs around as we gave it all we had but I don't think we got the same applause as had the chorus the evening before.

I don't know who won the golf, or whether there were any holes-in-one but we certainly gave Rudolf Friml's operetta all we had and the music and most of the words of that one song have stayed with me to this day.

*Gerald Hinchliffe*

Back to the High School and Gerald Hinchliffe who was an excellent master, and taught us English and English Literature.

A highlight in the Third Form in 1951 was when Gerald encouraged us to write and put together a magazine called 'The Third Former'. He told me many years later that everyone in the class had contributed in one way or another. I still possess a rather inky copy of contributors with even inkier autographs.

Someone unkindly commented that the magazine was 'badly typed, badly printed, and it was poorly bound.' On looking at those areas I see I was involved in each one!

Gerald subsequently moved to Nottingham University but for the last 25 years he and I kept in touch a few times a year and on the 13th February 2012 it gave me great pleasure to arrange a 90th birthday lunch for him at Hart's Restaurant in Nottingham. 26 Scarborough High School old boys attended. Gerald had been quite ill and the event was in some doubt but two days before the agreed date he rallied. He recognised most old boys by name and spoke eloquently without notes for half an hour, insisting on standing. That was a real achievement at 90.

Sadly, Gerald died in 2013 but his son remarked that the lunch we had arranged for him had really perked him up and probably given him an extra year of life.

After the lunch Gerald had sent me a handwritten greetings card thanking me for arranging the event. It was a magnificent photograph of Whitby's 199 steps with the town in the background.

An extract follows:

*'I am now 90. It is time for reflection. The first thought that came to my mind concerned that wonderful occasion on February 13th. In particular I was aware of the fact that it happened and was superbly organised by yourself. So much imagination. So much work. So much devotion to making it a success and the determination to ensure, despite the weather, that it occurred.*

*You were at your best. The flair that has characterised your many enterprises was so apparent. You have my eternal gratitude and I am sure that everyone who was present would share it. The growing swell of excitement, the flow of reminiscences from chaps who had maybe not seen each other for nigh on 60 years will always remain in my mind, as well as your kind words which made the occasion so memorable for me.*

*When I tell friends about this event, they are amazed. They use the word 'unique'...*

*Thank you for the beautiful framed print of Scarborough;*

*a reminder for me of the happy days I spent there. It hangs in my study. I look at it and smile. When I tell people that a bunch of 70 year olds came from all over the UK, and many more wrote to me, they say, 'They must have liked you'. I reply, 'I loved them. It was a great privilege to teach them.'*

Gerald passed away just over a year later but I was proud to have known him, to have had him as my friend; and to have his encouragement, enthusiasm and support.

Probably in our third form days in 1951, when we would be 13 years old, I had a discussion with Brian Berryman on the puzzling topic, 'where do babies come from'. A very erudite discussion it was too, I recall, with us coming to a unanimous decision that it must be from the belly button! Sex education was then non-existent. The language stream did not even study biology!

After University at Durham, Brian became Scarborough Library's Reference Librarian, later writing illustrated books about Scarborough over the years.

I still have many memories of the school and a few follow:

- The Westwood School building; the smell of it – especially at the start of a term when floors had been varnished and black boards blackened.
- The bike sheds – always overcrowded – and, looking upwards, the beams and floor boards of the classroom above.
- The smell in the chemistry labs – a mixture of experimental leftovers from the last 50 years.
- The steep rake in the lecture theatre. And the tinny loudspeakers and music system Arthur Costain had to use when teaching us about classical music

- 'Bonn' Clarke, and his weekly German tests where you had to get at least 3 out of 4 answers correct. And everyone had to sit in alphabetical order.

- And Bonn again, when he was taking me for GCE German oral. He played it 99% impartially but nevertheless encouraged me by nods, a raised eyebrow, a smile and so on. I was grateful to him many years later as I shall mention in the national service chapter.

- Language teacher 'Billy' Binder's ginger coloured suit. And his Chess club. At the time we thought Binder was an eccentric master, but in our retirement we realised what an intellectual he really was, and there is circumstantial evidence that he had been a British spy in the 1930's in Germany.

- In form 3L, the magazine The Third Former we produced under Gerald Hinchliffe's guidance. And particularly, the smell of duplicating ink we used for the hand operated duplicator.

- Maths teacher 'Pike' Richardson's gown which always appeared to me to be a dark, drab, olive green – rather than black.

- And Pike's regular instruction, 'Watch the board while I go through it!' We waited patiently but he never did.

- Chalk dust and blackboards. (Whiteboards were then unknown).

- French master Les Brown, sweeping into a room to start a lesson – then realising it was the wrong room, doing a wide U–turn and sweeping out again, his gown billowing behind him.

- Cycling to and from Oliver's Mount – uphill all the way there – to the school playing fields for rugby and shinty in winter. We were exhausted before we even started games. The only blessing was that afterwards, we could freewheel all the way back to school.

- Showers after PT with Jock Roxburgh (sports master) – particularly the last cold shower he insisted we take. And the strict time limit he gave us to get dressed.
- The strict stair code in the school building – up one set and down another.
- Headmaster 'Joey' Marsden biting his nails and in his broad Lancastrian accent, 'Eeh lad. I think you ought to go into teaching.' Many took his advice and did well.
- One morning, and most unusually, 4 boys being publicly caned in Assembly for stealing.
- School master Eddie Colenutt's Lambretta scooter – one of the first, if not the first, in Scarborough and with what appeared to be ivory brake handles.

- The School library – where pupils at least pretended they were being quiet and industrious. I was a librarian and am seated at the left of the middle row in the photo above; not in school uniform as, by then, I had left school.

- Religious teacher Pop Francis's abundance of hair sprouting from his ears – and his nick-name 'Fungus lugs'.

- Not being able to go on annual school camps as my parents could not afford it. But they made it up for me by letting me go to London with the school for the Festival of Britain.

- The Festival of Britain School trip; staying in the dormitories deep beneath Clapham Common – resurrected from the war days. Getting fellow pupil Arthur White up to the surface when he had an asthma attack. And the Skylon at the Festival.

- The annual Scarborough Cricket Festival and getting autographs. Meeting BBC commentator Peter West, and seeing the BBC 'transmitter room'. It had been a small coalhouse under the grandstand and had great glowing glass valves at least a foot each in height. Then getting free entry tickets for the next day, by helping clean rubbish from the ground after the day's play.

*I am centre row far right (arrowed) where my 'sticking-out' ears are evident.*

- The school choir (above) attending the Eskdale Tournament of Song, by train – and winning. And ex–

professional singer Brandsby Croft's mother, who travelled with the choir and bought us all ice creams on Scarborough Station platform to 'relax your larynxes'.

o   As soon as TV did reach Scarborough, many fellow pupils talked about the programmes they had seen. Every evening when I was approaching home after school, I crossed my fingers hoping our roof had sprouted an aerial. It never did until years later when Percy and Phyllis bought a TV for my parents for their 25th Wedding anniversary.

Around 1953 I had an older friend called Nick Sheldon. He was not an SBHS pupil but had been to Ackworth School in Pontefract and one day we cycled through to his old school. Nick had already left school and was training to be a radio and television engineer. This involved part-college and part practical – working in a radio and TV repair shop to gain practical experience. He did that alright! War surplus was still reaching the market and one day he told me he could get us ex-army 'walkie-talkie' sets for around £2 each. Each was about the size of a medium sized suitcase. We got one each with mine being located at my home in Newby and Nick's at his home in Seamer - a distance of about 4 miles as the crow flies.

We worked out how to tune them to the same frequency and decided on call signs and on a time to try to contact each other over the air. This was long before mobile phones, home computers, laptops, tablets and so on and we felt we were broaching the outer limits of communications and technology. My set was in my bedroom and at the appointed hour I switched it on, twiddled the knobs, picked up the microphone and launched into, 'Radio Nick, Radio Nick, are you receiving me?' There was a deathly silence and, if he was, I wasn't getting any reply. I tried a few times with no success until there was a loud knocking on the front door from a neighbour who asked my father, 'Is your David doing anything to affect my TV?'

This was at the time when TVs in the area were very new and very few people had them. This neighbour, however, did have one and often invited us in to view sporting events, and so on – maybe a dozen of us – all watching a 12" screen. Mind you, it did have a goldfish bowl type magnifier in front of the screen. This made the screen seem a little larger but also made the people on screen look distorted, just like those curved 'magic' mirrors in amusement arcades where you appeared either very fat or very thin.

Of course I denied doing anything to affect his TV, but hastily dismantled my rig and pushed it under the bed.

The following morning at the bus stop there was much discussion about 'Radio Nick', and whatever could it have been that had had wiped out the TV signal for over a ½ mile?

I kept very quiet, got rid of my set as soon as possible but was quite concerned on returning home from school for the next few days, expecting to find a Radio Detector van outside the house together with the police! I never did find out why our 'network' didn't connect.

Between 'mock' O-levels and the real things a year later, friend Peter Robson suggested we do a little family tree research in the Scarborough Room – the reference section of Scarborough Library.

We started by looking at old copies of the local newspaper and reading reports of his parent's wedding, and then mine. Then we looked for his birth and sure enough it was there. But where was mine?

My parents' wedding on 19th December 1937 was recorded in the paper and we looked for a few weeks either side of my birthday the following June 18th, but could find nothing. We were extremely puzzled.

A few weeks, or even a couple of months later, the

penny dropped – hard. My parents had married in December 1937. I had been born in June 1938 about 6 months later. They had married because of me.

At that time in the first half of the 1950's I assumed I was illegitimate, although my parents had married long before I was born. In today's very relaxed climate this news would have meant nothing at all but to an impressionable 15 year old I felt the floor had opened up beneath me.

It also explained a few previously unexplained facts. I had always got the impression that Phoebe, my sister, was treated by our parents better than me. Yes, her health had caused problems but... (I did discuss this with her recently and she thought the opposite – that I had been the favoured one!)

My view seemed to be supported by aunt Phyllis who was always encouraging me – almost as if she too felt Phoebe was the preferred child – giving me regular pocket money, (which I shared with Phoebe), lending me her portable typewriter and buying me paper and typewriter ribbons to enable me to write my first book. Actually it was a story I wrote for a competition run by Collins Publishers for teenagers, (although I cannot recollect that the word 'teenager' had been coined at that time). I didn't win a prize but my story did get an extract printed in a future issue of the magazine. That was my second literary effort, the award from the Wolf Cubs being the first.

Anyway, GCE time came and I didn't do as well as I had hoped or had been expected to do and to this day I feel the revelation Peter and I discovered – or actually didn't discover, in the newspaper birth announcements in Scarborough Library that afternoon, was the main cause.

However, hindsight is a wonderful thing. To be fair to my parents, I do feel that revelation shared the blame for my poor results with the other reason being the influence of Uncle Percy.

For Christmas he had built me a crystal set, and, with a pair of earphones I could listen to the BBC Home Service which was re-broadcast from a booster station in Dean

Road, Scarborough. He also gave me a small toolkit and an electric soldering iron and taught me how to solder.

For many years Percy had been secretary of Scarborough Amateur Radio Society and I joined as their youngest member and was given the position of librarian. This merely involved keeping radio magazines in order, discarding old copies and highlighting items which might be of interest to the members. And, after all, I was a librarian at school! Once a month members had an auction of their surplus equipment and having saved up diligently from weekend jobs, I bid and obtained an Eddystone S640 short wave receiver. A short wave receiver then needed a lengthy aerial and someone produced an old telephone pole which we erected at the end of our garden, supporting the base in a big pit of concrete. With the receiver and the aerial I was able to tune in to other local amateurs, as well as Percy, and stations much further afield in many, many countries. Using the Eddystone and as an established 'listener' I had my own shortwave QSL cards printed which I could send to stations I had logged, reporting such things as date, time, my position, signal strength, clarity and so on and frequently the recipients would return their own cards in acknowledgement.

*Left: I look to be in somewhat of a trance but here I am with my Eddystone S640 short–wave radio receiver. On the back wall are QSL cards from stations I had listened to and reported on, and my Short Wave Listener number G6142.*

Possibly my newspaper discovery had led to me 'burying my head' in another pursuit instead of concentrating solely on examination revision.

A few times a year the Radio club entered 'mobile' competitions with other clubs, each trying to get the most distant contacts. This involved being under canvas, and using very bulky equipment and power generators. Aerials, of course were needed and the camp needed to be on as high ground as possible. Contests lasted for variable lengths of time but probably a continuous 48 hours was the norm.

Today someone would probably just e-mail or pull a mobile phone from their pocket to make a call to the other side of the world but transistors were then unknown and people could only dream of the small sophisticated equipment we have available today.

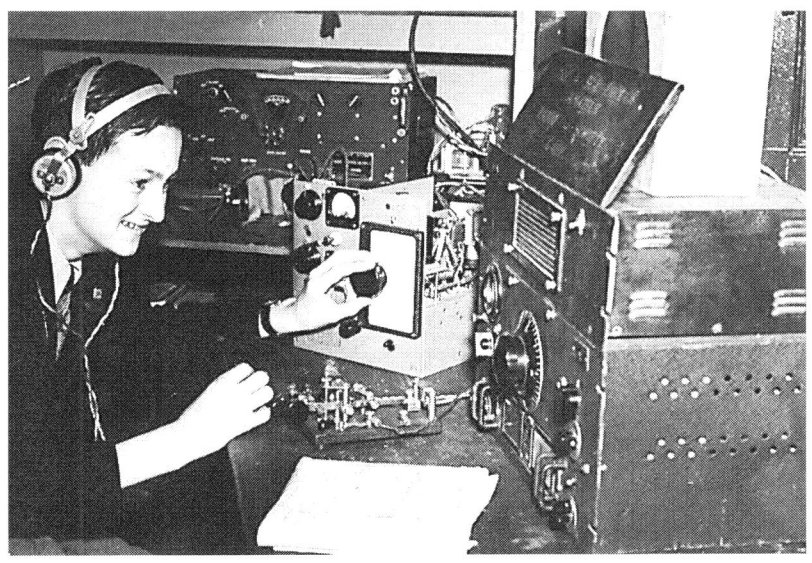

*Above: Here I am 'operating' Scarborough Amateur Radio Society's rig G4BP. Actually it was a mock up photo for the press. I was only licensed as a radio listener so the transmitter had to be switched off.*

I found short wave radio fascinating and met many friends through the medium but school leaving was on the horizon and I needed to find myself a job.

Moving forward to 1955 it was to be my last summer at school and The Yorkshire Lawn Tennis Club had asked for volunteers from the Scarborough grammar schools to assist at the forthcoming tournaments. I was one of those chosen, together with others from the Boys' High School, the Girls' High School and Scarborough Convent.

It was a magical experience – even more evocative almost 60 years later, as I look back.

Journalist Jeannie Swales admirably summed up the atmosphere in a recent article:

*'Each July, all eyes are on Wimbledon Centre Court, but once tennis had another home in Yorkshire.*

*In its heyday, it was considered by many to be the 'Wimbledon of the North'. and whilst the events spread over a week or so, on just one single afternoon, Saturday July 30th, 1955, tennis fans with tickets for Scarborough's centre court in Filey Road could watch some pretty glamorous games: America's Pancho Gonzales v Ecuador's Francisco Segura; the UK's John Pannell v Germany's Ady Laemmken; and Brit Fred Perry and Australian Ken McGregor v Gonzales and Segura.'*

Fans had booked a year in advance for tickets for these matches and I was lucky enough to be there – free – as a ball–boy.

*'Now, [2015] the club that attracted thousands of spectators to watch some of the most laurelled tennis players of the day stands virtually derelict. The old clubhouse is still in use as a sports centre, but the surrounding courts – there were once 18 of them – have*

*either been converted into car parks or are in too poor a state of maintenance to be playable.*

*In its heyday the stands were all painted dark green, with seating right down to ground level, and they'd be packed, perhaps 1,500 people to each set of courts. The players would be brought in through the crowds and people would book their seats a year in advance.*

*The present day visitor can still see a small window, now boarded up, which was where the radio presenters sat to report to the nation. It's at the back of a curvaceous 30s wooden clubhouse, now abandoned and locked up.*

*The clubhouse, however, designed by Scarborough–born architect Sir Edwin Cooper in 1910 and completed in 1912, is considered to be a gem, with both arts and crafts, and Art Deco, influences. It is Grade II listed: English Heritage says it is nationally rare.*

*In 1955, the winner of the singles in the Slazenger Professional Lawn Tennis Tournament at Scarborough took home a grand prize of a trophy, and £150 – not bad at a time when the average house price was less than £2,000, but a trifle compared to the £1.6m which the winners of both the men's and women's singles will pick up at Wimbledon this year.'*

As he had with so many others, Joey (headmaster Henry Marsden) had tried to persuade me to consider teaching. At the time I couldn't think of anything less attractive, possibly remembering how we had all wound up some of our masters. Norman Stoddard, who, as well as being a High School master and Carlyle House housemaster, (I was in Carlyle House), was a neighbour and suggested that as I was electronically adept he could recommend me for a job which was coming up as a trainee in the service department at a local radio and TV shop.

I pondered upon this but felt as a lifetime job I wanted something different. The electronics could stay in the background as a hobby.

In those days university was not a 'right' as it seems to be today for so many youngsters. The sixth form and university were not options for me so I took the view that if I left school at 17 and started earning, financially I would already be a few years ahead of those going on to University or a Teachers Training College. On leaving, they would then have to seek a job. I accept that their qualifications could have led them to higher salaries eventually, but it would still take them a number of years to catch me up and overtake me financially.

So, having made my decision, I left school in the summer of 1955 aged 17 to start work in the big wide world. Eventually I joined Barclays Bank as a junior clerk. However, Barclays was not my first opportunity as I will cover in the next chapter.

To digress, particular school friends Brian Berryman, Graham Burnett, John Found, Bernard Jones, Peter Robson, Geoff Winn and Richard Toft, to name a few, have been like ships in the night over the years. There were years when we hadn't met or been in touch then suddenly, without warning, contact would be re-established.

This happened in the case of Graham Burnett. During our school days we were very close and Graham got his short wave radio bug from me, although he went much further, gained his transmitting licence and is still active in the hobby over 60 years later. We lost touch when we left school but reconnected a few years ago and we exchange e-mails periodically. Whilst we have never met since our school days I feel sure we shall.

This meeting of old friends many years later particularly happened in the case of Bernard Jones. We were at school together in the same class; we joined Barclays Bank within a month or so of each other, we did our national service around the same time, Bernard decided banking wasn't for him so moved on and we then lost touch during our working years, although I often heard snippets from members of his family. We then met up again through the Old Scarborians' Association – the organisation for old boys and masters from the long gone Scarborough High School for Boys. The Association has its own website, holds a Christmas dinner in Scarborough, a lunch in London, and social, golfing and bowling events each year. It also issues a magazine to keep members in touch twice a year.

The High School for Boys had started life as the Municipal School at Westwood overlooking Ramsdale Valley, Scarborough. It opened on January 6th 1902 and was co-educational but in September 1922 the girls moved to a new Girls High School and the High School for Boys came into being, in the previous Municipal School building at Westwood.

They remained there until 24th July 1959 and on 14th September 1959 after the summer break, transferred to a newly built school at Woodlands on the northern side of Scarborough. The new school had cost £236,174.

The 'new' Boys' High School remained at Woodlands until July 1973 when comprehensive education dictated the closure of the vast majority of grammar schools. The High schools – both boys and girls, and the Girls' Convent were three of these victims and the boys' new building at Woodlands was taken over by Graham comprehensive School, the previous Girls' High School building becoming a new 6th Form college.

The Old Scarborians Association was founded in the early 1930's and has helped bring together many old boys years after they left school. In February 2000 it boasted 400 members. Thanks to an energetic committee, and better communication facilities, membership now stands at around 600.

Not bad for a school which closed over 40 years ago!

\*

# CHAPTER 5

# Freddie Trueman bowls a googly
# 1954 – 1957

> **1954: Brief Timeline**
>
> A British Overseas Airways Corporation de Havilland Comet jet airliner crashes in the Mediterranean Sea following fatigue failure, killing all 35 on board; United Kingdom Atomic Energy Authority founded; British Medical Committee report suggests the existence of a link between smoking and lung cancer; Oxford wins the 100th Boat Race;
> Roger Bannister becomes the first person to break the four-minute mile; Fourteen years of rationing during and following World War II comes to an end when meat officially comes off ration; Maiden flight of the English Electric Lightning P-1 supersonic fighter plane; Julian Slade's musical *Salad Days* opens in London; Chris Chataway breaks the world record for the 5000 metres by five seconds; The South Goodwin light vessel is wrecked on the Goodwin Sands with the loss of six of the seven on board; The tanker *World Concord* breaks in two in the Irish Sea; Winston Churchill becomes the first, and as of 2014 the only, British Prime Minister to reach his 80th birthday while still in office; The first UK Wimpy Bar is opened at the Lyons Corner House in Coventry Street, London.

Whilst I was at the High School I had had a few part-time jobs to earn pocket money in order to purchase my Eddystone S640 short wave receiver and to replace my old bicycle with a brand new metallic, forest green, Hercules. I was proud of both.

One job was pushing a sandwich, drinks and sweets

trolley round Scarborough Railway Station platforms so people ready to board a train could get their refreshments. There were no on-station cafés, or on-train trolleys at that time – just a very long branch of WH Smith stationers on Scarborough station and an even longer platform seat which still exists and is reputed to be the longest station platform seat in the world - 456 feet (139 metres) long.

The second weekend job and the one I much preferred was one Percy got me – helping install television aerials for a man called Les Porritt. Les was a real livewire and he installed television aerials for all the television retailers and rental companies in Scarborough – in those days a good number. He charged the shops £5 an aerial installation which doesn't sound a lot these days but it was a good price 60 years ago – especially when the shops supplied and paid for the aerial itself, the coaxial cable, wall ties, aerial sockets and so on. The shops would probably charge £20 – £25 to a customer for a full installation.

Aerials were not then the tiny things which we see on roof tops today. They were massive things initially like a large 'H' on the top of a 12 foot aluminium pole. Each of the verticals of the 'H' was around 6 feet long each but in poor signal areas, instead of having two uprights there could be as many as 5, in decreasing sizes. In some areas, depending on the TV station requirements these monstrosities had to be mounted horizontally. Aerials had to be put together from parts, then wired, and once complete, hauled up to the roof where they would normally be installed on a chimney using special fixing brackets.

There were a number of hotels and boarding houses in Scarborough, particularly in North Marine Road where many were very high buildings overlooking the North Bay. In February or March each year the owners would start to prepare their businesses for the coming season and this was likely to include installing a television set if they didn't already have one.

I was then quite squeamish about heights. But not for long. It could take a four section extending ladder to reach a roof and this then meant hauling a roof ladder up by rope, then hauling up the monster aerial itself. These days, Health and Safety would probably have insisted on full scaffolding but back in the 1950s ladders were the norm.

Woe betide anyone who wired up an aerial wrongly! I recall one installation in North Marine Road – most properties there were 5 storey – which, once installed wouldn't bring a picture to the television screen. A bad contact was diagnosed and the tracing back procedure went from the set, to the aerial cable, to all aerial plugs and sockets, and, if that didn't solve the problem, right up to the aerial itself on the roof. There, we found the wiring was faulty with the metal braid on the cable shorting out the signal which was carried on an inner copper cable part protected by a plastic surround.

Massive though the aerials needed to be in those days, to get a very grainy black and white picture, the screens of the television sets themselves – then cathode ray tubes – were miniscule.

This photo is of a 1952 GEC television which, like many others of that era, had an 8 inch black and white screen. Compare that to the high definition colour sets of today with massive screens.

And imagine, say, a dozen holidaymakers all gathered to watch some event on TV, all straining to be able to see. At the time I was installing aerials the maximum sized screen available was in the region of 14 inches. How technology has improved.

Not only were the aerials huge and the sets miniscule but the definition of the black and white pictures was so poor that invariably all the curtains needed to be closed to have any chance of seeing a reasonable picture.

When I was within a few months of leaving school, I was considering various full time jobs when an advertisement appeared in the Scarborough Evening News seeking a junior reporter. I was very interested.

I suspect the excitement generated in form 3L when we put together that magazine with the encouragement of English master Gerald Hinchliffe, had probably got into my blood and had mixed with what was there already; that of my grandfather Tom Henry Fowler who had been an author and journalist.

No one had invented such things as CV's in the 1950s so I applied to the local paper by letter and was given an interview.

I was ushered into a room to meet the editor, Ray Lazenby, and after no more than 5 minutes general chat he said, 'I have only one question for you. How do you spell rhubarb?'

I spelt it correctly and waited for more difficult questions but he offered me the job there and then. However, the following day I turned down the offer feeling rather dejected as I felt that if it was as easy as that, then did I really want the job?

Over the years I learned more about Ray Lazenby and grew to admire him. At the time of the interview I hadn't realised that, like me, he had attended the High School, but earlier of course, between 1935 and 1940. He had started at the paper as a junior reporter; a similar role to that I had just turned down. He worked his way up and eventually became editor of the then daily Scarborough Evening News – a role he held for an incredible 21 years, overseeing 12,000 editions of the paper before retiring, aged 63 in 1986. He had received attractive offers from much larger, national newspapers but his home was Scarborough and the sea, and he was never tempted to move.

Recently I discussed Ray and his job offer to me with his widow Jean and she said how very keen her late husband had been on the ability to spell correctly. She also said that he was meticulous and would have certainly done his homework before our meeting, probably by approaching the school for a report before he even offered me an interview.

So, having turned down his job offer, I needed to look elsewhere. One interview was for a trainee technician at what we all called 'The Naval Radio Station' on Racecourse just outside Scarborough. This subsequently became GCHQ. I was offered a job but there were two aspects which deterred me. The first was that I was told that GPO engineers were responsible for servicing the extremely high radio masts but that in the case of emergency if they were not available a junior technician would undertake the role and that would have been me. I had coped with television aerial installation on some very high buildings but the height of those masts must have been at least 2 or 3 times the height of the highest building I had climbed by ladder. The second reason was that, whilst I was offered a job, there would be no vacancies for at least 6 months. So I declined, but had I known the following facts, then I would possibly have jumped at the opportunity:

*'The Royal Navy first established a Wireless Telegraphy Station at Scarborough in 1912. Since 1914 it has conducted signals intelligence in support of both the defence of the United Kingdom and of our armed forces. During the Great War the station's role was to monitor the German High Seas Fleet which was making harassing attacks on the East Coast of England. Following the cessation of hostilities in 1918, Scarborough's mission widened to include diplomatic communications, with*

*resources eventually being evenly split between Naval and diplomatic intercepts.*

*At the beginning of August 1939, Y Service, the organisation responsible for intercepting enemy and neutral radio transmissions, was prepared for war.*

*Scarborough intercepted German Naval and Naval Air communications, and controlled a Direction–Finding network.*

*It was during this period that the civilians working in Sigint for the Admiralty became known as the Admiralty Civilian Shore Wireless Service (ACSWS), and the complement soon became a mix of both civilian and service personnel, augmented during the war years by members of the Women's Royal Naval Service.*

*During May 1941, the station at Scarborough played a key role in the location and subsequent destruction of the German battleship Bismarck. The following is an extract from a review of 'Y Work' written by Lt Cmdr WR Rodger, Officer in Charge, Scarborough, 15th November 1945:*

*'The old Y Station in Sandybed Lane (1914–1943) was altered out of recognition to meet increasing demands in equipment and the need for more personnel and space, particularly necessary for aerials and the servicing of [Wireless Telegraphy] apparatus. The buildings on the present site on Scarborough Racecourse were occupied on 1st March 1943 during the course of a forenoon watch, without a stoppage of [Wireless Telegraphy] cover or passing of [Enigma] traffic to Bletchley Park.'*

*The station moved to its present location (some three miles from the town centre on the site of the old Scarborough racecourse) in early 1943. A half–buried bomb–proof bunker covered in hundreds of tons of earth served as the main building at the site.*

*In 1945 the Station's next major task was the collection of Soviet Armed Forces communications during the period of the Cold War, and Scarborough became the main station for the interception of Russian Naval traffic'.*

So, what was I to do? There was no School careers guidance in those days and I really had no idea what I wanted to do, except I had made my mind up I didn't want to teach.

In those days I was quite shy. I kept to my own circle of friends and, looking back, probably a lack of confidence was brought about by that discovery, or, more correctly, non–discovery in Scarborough Library some months earlier.

With hindsight, I realise now that national service was the making of me as it was with so many other teenage boys. But that came later and before then I needed a job. So I joined a bank.

I was offered provisional jobs with the then Martins, Lloyds and Barclays banks. I picked Barclays for the most erudite of reasons; I liked their then dark green embossed letter heads.

The job offer was provisional in that I was expected to get GCE's in 5 particular subjects although I started work before the results came out. Even with those 5 subjects there was a 3 month probationary period, during which the bank, or I, could terminate the employment.

When my results came out and having not achieved the five particular subjects they had nominated I thought I would be looking for a job elsewhere. But Barclays was very fair and merely extended the probationary period. At its expiry they felt I had found my feet and had passed the probationary period satisfactorily. I then spent the next 39 years with the bank, always, I suppose, wanting to give of my best as they had shown confidence in me in those early days.

Before I started work I was handed a form for my father to sign. Effectively it was a guarantee by my parents, that they would 'keep and support' me up to the age of 21. This was because the bank recognised that what they paid me in those early days was peanuts – £12 a month from memory although I cannot recall whether that was before or after tax and National Insurance – and would be insufficient for me to keep myself.

The form was duly signed and, on 15th August 1955 I started work at Barclays Bank's Falsgrave branch in Scarborough.

At my retirement in 1994, Doug Ross, one of the bank's directors, returned the guarantee form to me.

When I joined, the Falsgrave Road branch was a tiny branch with only a clerk–in–charge, a cashier and a junior. The real manager was Stanley Brown, manager of the main St Nicholas Street branch in town and he called in a few times a week to check all was well.

I was the junior and was replacing a man whose name I now forget.

On my first day, I was dressed in my new mid-grey suit, white shirt, black shoes and tie. By the end of the first day my suit sleeve had red ink on it!

The 3 staff were Bill Cooper the clerk–in–charge who also acted as a cashier; Basil Walker, a cashier who also acted as bookkeeper, and a man of about 18 whom I can visualise but whose name has left me. He was junior and bookkeeper and it was his place I was taking as he had obtained a job as a trainee Manager with Marks and Spencer.

He had 2 weeks left at the branch and in that time had to train me in his entire role, which he managed to do, very efficiently. I often wonder how far his career prospered with Marks and Spencer?

Over the following 39 years I was with Barclays the bank kept moving its goalposts.

Sometimes, in the early days, I felt I was not scoring any goals as the goal mouth was either too narrow or the ball too small.

In those early days when goal scoring was limited and I

was making slow progress, I often wondered whether I should have taken up Ray Lazenby's Scarborough Evening News offer. And if I had, where it might have taken me?

Or the job with what was to become GCHQ?

However, over the middle to later years my goal scoring increased rapidly and as I moved forward I was reasonably content.

The goal scoring connotation will become clearer when I give details of my retirement party in 1994.

As I write this chapter the branch at 70 Falsgrave Road, Scarborough has been vacant and on the market for a number of years. It had been one of the many bank closures which all banks claimed were necessary as banking online had become much more prevalent. Falsgrave road branch was similar in layout to most bank branches in the 1950s but would now be thought of as being very old fashioned. If you have watched 'Dad's Army' and seen Mr Mainwaring's office you wouldn't be far off the mark.

From the entrance in Falsgrave Road, the counter faced you – solid mahogany and no security screens in those days. At one end of the 3 man counter was a hatch to give access to the manager's room.

Directly behind the counter was another similar sized desk to give cashiers access to the clerks behind who normally posted the ledgers and statements.

Behind this stood a table – it appeared to be an old dining table – at which Bill Cooper used to work when he was not in his office interviewing customers or undertaking his cashier role.

To the back of the office was a door which led to the ground floor strong room, the only toilet, and stairs which led down to the cellar which housed the central heating boiler and stationary cupboards – as well as a large pile of coke in the corner ready to be shovelled into the boiler.

One of my jobs as junior was to look after the coke boiler which provided hot water and central heating, to the branch and the flat above. Even in those days it was an archaic coke system which produced noxious fumes and often glowed bright red if it was not correctly adjusted. And woe betide anyone down in the cellar when a coke delivery was due as the coal men merely tipped the coke from their sacks through a hatch in the pavement and coke dust landed everywhere – including on my new grey suit.

As one of my duties as Junior Clerk I needed to regularly 'riddle' the burning coke with a special poker to break up the clinker and make sure the burnt coke dropped through to the ash tray beneath. I then emptied the ash tray into a bin in the yard outside.

A good riddling and clean out was especially necessary each evening before going home, as the branch cleaner arrived at 7.00am and she was far from pleased if the boiler had gone out overnight. I can still visualise her waving her mop at me when I arrived one morning and the boiler had gone out and the building was cold.

Two mornings running the boiler went out over-night and Bill Cooper was apoplectic as he had had to have a cold wash and shave. I sometimes got the impression he thought I had let it go out overnight deliberately. After a rant and rave, then another rant and rave as I had pinned certain documents together but not hidden the pin point between the sheets as he had instructed, so he ended up pricking his thumb when he signed the forms, he said it was my responsibility 'to make sure that the boiler was properly serviced each evening'. My claim that the boiler had served its purpose over the years, was on pension and that a new gas fired boiler as most other branches had was the answer, fell on deaf ears.

At around 4.45pm the following evening I went down to the cellar and started an energetic riddling session. I did not intend the boiler to go out that night! I riddled and poked and cleared the clinker, then the ash tray, then filled up the boiler with coke then pulled out the damper in the flue.

Mr Cooper then called me up from the cellar to help lock up the strong room. After doing this I moved my bike from the bank's enclosed back yard into the lane outside. I then had to retrace my steps through the bank so the back door could be bolted and barred from the inside and the front door locked behind us.

All seemed well - until the following morning.

Bill Cooper always came down from the flat after other staff had arrived. That morning his face was as black as thunder as he scowled ferociously and just growled, 'Boiler!'

I looked at him and said, 'Pardon? But it couldn't possibly have gone out last night.'

I thought from his face it had blown up or something. Then the story slowly emerged.

He and his wife had been entertaining customers to dinner in their flat that night. Starters had been consumed and they were all enjoying their main courses. Cold desserts had been prepared and were waiting in a cupboard in the kitchen.

All of a sudden there had been a loud rumbling and shaking noise. Mrs Cooper had dashed into the kitchen to be met by rusty boiling water cascading out of a pipe in the kitchen cupboard – all over the prepared desserts. You've guessed it! The pipe was the boiler overflow and as I hadn't returned to put in the damper, the boiler had been operating at full steam with the boiling water gradually rising up the overflow pipe until the inevitable happened. It's a wonder the whole branch hadn't gone up in flames.

After a bank inspection some months later a new automatic gas boiler was installed.

A few months after my predecessor had left, a new male member of staff arrived as Junior, the son of an existing manager in a larger branch. I was moving up a notch.

The clerk–in charge, (always 'Sir' or 'Mr Cooper' to the staff) said to him one day whilst looking at the branch clock, 'That clock is slow.' The newcomer turned round, looked very slowly towards the clock and said, 'Oh! So it is.' and returned to what he had been doing. Cooper had met his match!

Working in the bank at Scarborough the 4 males were all cricket mad. During the Scarborough Annual International and County Cricket Festival we endeavoured to 'balance the books' and get down to the cricket ground as soon as possible after the bank closed at 3.30pm. We normally got to the ground around 4.00pm but sometimes even earlier if we were lucky. We would catch up on any delayed work the following day.

However, the rest of the staff could never work out how I was able to update them with the latest cricket results during the day. There was no radio in the branch and portable radios were at least the size of a small suitcase so would have been noticed. Transistor radios had not been invented, mobile phones were at least 30 years away and there was no special telephone sports result service.

The reason for my clairvoyance was that I had a friend from my very recent school days who had an aunt who was profoundly deaf – and who was also not short of cash. She was not a customer of our bank but, so abundant appeared to be her bank balance that each time a new hearing aid was put on the market she had to have it.

One day I said to Julian, my friend, 'What does your aunt do with all her old hearing aids? I could really do with one.'

Julian said he'd find out and he later reported that she kept them all in a drawer and he was sure she could spare one for me. A few days later he rang me and said that if we could meet one evening, he had a hearing aid for me and she'd also given him one, both of which he passed over.

Now, whilst her aids were state of the art in the 1950s and far more advanced than the then NHS models, Julian's aunt's aids were not digital or as advanced as present aids which merely consist of a small very high-tech unit which fits over or into the affected ear. The 1950s version consisted of a case about 11 cm high by 6 across by 1 deep – a little larger than a modern I-phone.

To use the 1950s unit it was usual to clip it over the front of a breast pocket so a microphone in the unit could pick up sound, which the circuitry then amplified and fed to an earpiece via a cord from the unit to the affected ear. The case itself contained the microphone, miniature valves, amplifier, a circuit board and a battery. Each of the miniature valves was no more than 3cm long, whereas normal radio valves in those days were a good 15 cm tall.

I was 17 and I mention elsewhere that my Uncle Percy was a keen radio ham. He taught me a lot about circuitry and soldering so I felt confident in removing the microphones from both hearing aids, then soldering leads to the points where they had been connected. These leads then led outside the case to a ferrite rod aerial – a circular piece of ferrite rod, which looked not unlike a short pencil. On to this I had wound the necessary number of 'turns' of copper wire to 'tune in' the 'radio' to the local booster radio station. This aerial rod was taped to the sides of each hearing aid case so that each radio, including the aerial and the existing earpiece, would be no more than 1cm wider than the original hearing aid unit.

I had invented what could well have then been the world's smallest portable radio and after I had tested them both thoroughly Julian was delighted to get his own radio.

During the cricket season I would make an excuse to visit the bank cellar for stationary items where, they, as well as the boiler and the pile of coke to replenish it, were all kept. A few minutes down there gave me the chance to listen to the latest cricket results through the earpiece and then casually reappear in the branch to continue my normal duties, the 'radio' slipped into my suit pocket.

I allowed a few minutes to pass before commenting, 'Freddie Trueman did well getting another 3 wickets this morning', or 'Don Bradman's well on the way to another century.' The cricket mad staff were amazed and never discovered how I kept so up to date with the scores.

The parents of that same school friend ran the Bedford Hotel. This was a commercial hotel and busy each night with commercial travellers. The new Library Theatre in the Round had just opened and in exchange for displaying posters Julian's parents received two free tickets to performances. His parents could never attend because they were busy in the business so Julian and I saw most productions on these freebie tickets. There started my love of live theatre which remains to this day; in particular Theatre in the Round which adds an extra dimension to the traditional proscenium arch productions.

Back to the bank and in those days, there were no security vans trundling round delivering and collecting cash from, and to banks. If we had a surplus, as we usually had, we did 'swops' with other banks if it was coin, or mailed it to the Bank of England if it was paper. Dad's Army without rifles really springs to mind. We had to parcel up the surplus banknotes in brown paper with each parcel holding a maximum of £5,000. This was a considerable amount in the 1950s, and there were usually 2 or 3 parcels to be sent each week. We tied each parcel with stout string, added sealing wax which we melted over the knots with a Bunsen burner, addressed the parcel to a very anonymous address, 'The Bank of England', then stuck bright red and white 'HVP' labels all over the parcel. It didn't take O levels or even the 11 plus to work out that the labels stood for 'High Value Packet'. Then, a taxi or sometimes the Manager's decrepit car, took us to the Aberdeen Walk Post Office where we queued with the rest of the public, to get a receipt for our parcels of money.

Once handed over they were the GPO's responsibility but how did they send this money to the Bank of England? By rail of course – and on August 8th 1963 the Great Train Robbery took place when £2.6 million was stolen.

Bernard Jones, a friend from my schooldays to the present time, also worked for Barclays, but at the time I was at Falsgrave he worked at the much larger St. Nicholas Street, Scarborough, branch. His following anecdotes are worth including:

*As a junior clerk at Barclays, St Nicholas Street I sat at the desk behind the counters and near to the rear staff entrance. I had been told very clearly never to let anyone in outside banking hours, except staff.*

*After closing time (then 3.00 pm) there was a loud knock at the door which I opened slightly to see a man with a strangely familiar face who tried to barge in.*

*'Sorry you are not allowed in here', I said. An angry sounding voice said,*

*'Do you know who I am? I've come to see Mr Brown, the manager'.*

*'Please wait here', I told him politely.*

*By then Mr Brown had come charging over to the door, opened it and said,*

*'Charles, Charles, I'm so sorry. Please do come in', and off they went to the manager's office with Charles red in the face and giving me a look that was intended to kill me on the spot!*

*Later, I was called into the manager's office. 'Do you know who that was?'*

*'No, Mr Brown,' I replied innocently.*

*'That was Charles Laughton the famous film star', he said.*

*'Oh, so I can now let staff AND film stars into the Bank after closing time?' I rather stupidly responded.*

*'GET OUT!!!'*

*In the 1950s I occasionally helped out at the Bank's South Cliff branch to cover for holidays, sickness and other absence. On one occasion an elderly chap had drawn, I think it was £50 in notes and returned very upset because he said that his young grand-daughter had got hold of the bundle of notes and thrown it onto the fire. However he had managed to rescue the bundle only to find that half of it was burned away and this was why he was so upset – £50 in those days was quite a lot of money.*

*'Not to worry,' said the cashier; 'the remaining parts of the notes have a number so we should be able to replace them.' The old man seemed extremely grateful and pleased and went off with his new bundle of £50 with a smile on his face.*

*'Poor old chap,' said the cashier, 'he seemed so upset when he came in and at least I've made someone happy today.'*

*We learned later that he had conducted the same exercise at the Midland Bank with the other half of the original bundle and he was surprised some time later when the police turned up on his doorstep! Little did he realize that both bundles would end up at the Bank of England where they would investigate discrepancies!!*

*One day, a woman came up the front steps cursing and swearing (words I'd never heard before of course!) By chance, all the other cashiers were busy. She made her way towards me pointing at me and still swearing and shouting something I simply could not understand. In these circumstances call the manager! Which I did.*

*'Come this way madam', the manager said politely and in she went still cursing. There was a strange silence. All the staff and customers were spellbound.*

*'Who is she?' one of them asked. No one knew. Suddenly the manager's door opened and the woman crept out, walked down the steps and disappeared to the right. The manager paused for effect then peered round the door*

*with his specs down his nose. Looking over the top of the frame he said, 'Wrong bank!'*

*Everyone simply fell about laughing.*

Back at Barclays' Falsgrave Road branch in the mid-1950s who should walk in but the famous Freddie Trueman. He had a loud voice and a personality to match and all the staff looked up when we heard his 'Good morning'.

Trueman was an English cricketer who married the daughter of a past Mayor of Scarborough. He was generally acknowledged to be one of the greatest fast bowlers in history. Known as Fiery Fred, he played first-class cricket for Yorkshire County Cricket Club from 1949 until he retired in 1968. He represented England in 67 Test matches and was the first bowler to take 300 wickets in a Test career.

He often told of the test match in India in the 1960's when the country was overtaken with the dreaded 'Delhi belly'.

The whole team had suffered on the run up to the first test match, and, come the day of the test, India won the toss and elected to bat. Freddie was opening the bowling and just as he started his run–up he got a violent twinge in his stomach. He carried on with his run–up but instead of releasing the ball he ran past the umpire, down the wicket, past the batsmen, past the wicket keeper, past fine leg, up the pavilion steps, through the members' lounge and straight into the toilet in the visitors' changing rooms.

After about ten minutes of agony, there was a knock on the door and the captain asked, 'Freddie? Are you coming out?'

'No. I'm f…..g not,' replied Freddie. The captain said,

'Well can we have the ball back please? We need to start the game.'

Back to Freddie visiting the branch, Bill Cooper picked up his dip–in pen (he had a habit of pointing the nip, complete with ink, upwards and towards anyone when he spoke, as if he was about to start playing darts), and walking to the counter he welcomed Freddie.

'And what can I do for you today Mr Trueman?' he said.

'I'd like to draw £50,' Freddie replied. This was long before the advent of cash machines.

'Do you have an arrangement?'

'An arrangement? What on earth's that?' Freddie asked.

'Well, you don't bank here and in order to draw money from your account at another branch of the bank, you must make an arrangement with your own branch.'

'Why do I need to do that?'

'Well we don't know who you are. You could be anybody'.

'But you do know who I am. You just called me Mr Trueman.'

'Yes, but the point is we need to have the same rules for everyone or it would get very confusing.'

Of course, Freddie being Freddie said, 'Well it's not confusing to me, only you!'

'Look,' said the sub-manager, 'what I can do is telephone your branch and ask them if it will be acceptable for you to draw £50 at this branch.'

'How much is the call going to cost me?' asked Freddie. Bill Cooper checked and told him. This annoyed Freddie but Cooper wouldn't give in so a 'phone call was made and permission obtained.

We didn't see Freddie Trueman in the branch again!

Together with Bernard Jones, I shot for the Scarborough banks in the Scarborough Small-Bore Rifle League. Matches took place in the range in the cellar of either the then YMCA Club in North Street, or in a couple of converted railway carriages in Gallow's Close – near to where Sainsbury's store is now situated. The breathing exercises and concentration and timing needed for target shooting left us in good stead for national service rifle training, although there we were using .303 bore rather than the much smaller .22. Whilst doing my national service I achieved consistently good scores frequently coming 2nd, and occasionally 1st, but I couldn't beat my bank colleague Bernard Jones who went on to represent his regiment at Bisley.

Until the mid-1980s when Dunblane put a stop to a lot of target shooting I continued to shoot and won a few medals and cups, particularly in the latter years at Driffield when I moved to pistol target shooting which I found much more challenging.

Years later, playwright Alan Ayckbourn (now Sir Alan), referred to my shooting skills on page 33 of the Faber and Faber edition of one of his plays – *Man of the Moment*.

But I am getting ahead of myself as Alan didn't premiere this play until 1988 by which time I was branch manager at Barclays, Malton branch.

Going back to the mid-1950s I used my cycle to travel the two miles to and from work but one weekend I went to buy fish and chips from a shop on Highfield Estate not far from home. The fish and chips were almost forgotten when I saw a notice in the window, 'Scooter for sale £15'.

I asked about the scooter and it turned out to be an ex-paratrooper Corgi motor bike with a 98cc engine and a very low centre of gravity. I haggled and bought it for £10 there and then and had lessons from the fish shop proprietor as part of the deal while he called his wife to deal with the growing, but very interested queue of customers. I pushed EPY 801 home – it was only a few hundred yards – as I didn't then have a driving licence or insurance, although I did arrive home with a cold parcel of fish & chips which came as part of the £10 deal we had struck. The Corgi enabled me to get to work and back each day and most lunch times, and, best of all, it had been cheap to buy and was even cheaper to run.

The badges above the 'L' plate indicated my membership of the Radio Society of Great Britain and the

Radio Amateur Emergency Network. Members of the latter are called out to help with communications in case of national or regional emergencies. Remember, in 1957 there were no mobile phones, home computers, laptops or tablets.

*Bernard Jones' father on my Corgi with me on the pillion with the RSGB and RAEN badges showing above my 'L' plate.*

Pre-decimalisation coin, was much heavier than coinage is now and it was not unusual to struggle 250 yards or so to the nearest Midland (now HSBC) branch with 3 bags of coin in each hand, only to return to Barclays with different denominations – or sometimes notes – in return. No-one questioned the need for security.

Back in the 1950's the few ball point pens there were, were banned from bank use, as were fountain pens. The banks used indelible ink they hoped would not fade over many years, so each Monday morning the junior had to mix special ink from crystals and wash and refill the inkwells in the counter area and in the back office.

Bank inspectors visited branches periodically to check

all was in order. There was no warning and visits were on a surprise basis. All cash in the counter tills and in the safes would be counted and samples of all aspects of the branch work – book-keeping, records, lending, investments – were checked. The inspectors then initialled the records of particular aspects they had checked, as being in order.

One day the Bank inspectors walked into our branch and shortly afterwards I was asked to provide 'orange ink'.

I enquired of the Chief Clerk and was told that I would find various bottles of coloured ink crystals in the strong room on a particular shelf. I was to locate the orange bottle and mix a quantity of crystals with a stipulated amount of water to form 'orange ink'. This was indelible and was used by Inspectors during their visit, to indicate which records they had checked.

There were various bottles of coloured crystals – green, purple, brown and orange spring to mind – and in later years when ball point pens became acceptable, the inspectors moved with the times and used them. But no doubt, some branches of the Bank might still have bottles of ink crystals hidden away in their strong rooms.

Again, going back to the time before computers were brought into general use in banks, and whilst cash was balanced daily, each branch's books had to be balanced on the last day of each half year.

In our bank's case, the financial year end was 31st December so this was the day to which the bank's annual accounts were drawn up. The half yearly balance in June was not as onerous as the annual one, but both had to be carried out after the bank had shut – then at 3.30pm. Whilst the same was the case on 31st December the 'balance' was much more demanding and if you were working in a bank there was rarely the possibility of attending any New Year's Eve revelries.

I well remember that after completing the balance, and

for a few years, I cycled home or used my Corgi for the 2 mile journey, and heard the church clock chime midnight as I passed. In smaller branches, bank records were all handwritten at that time and indelible ink with 'dip–in' pens had to be used for all records to prevent the print fading over the years.

The balance involved first checking all cash in each of the bank's branch premises. This would include cash in each of the tills at the main branch or sub-branches, together with all cash and coin retained in the strong rooms. This work could not start until the branch had closed to the public for the day and each cashier had balanced their own till – to the penny. Balancing each till involved taking the previous night's cash balance, adding to it cash credits taken in by that cashier during the day, and deducting from it all cash given out during that day. In theory the balance of actual cash should agree with the balance arrived at by the above calculations.

In the larger branches and before computers were introduced, staff on comptometers printed the details, but in smaller branches bank statements were handwritten. At the same time, but by a different clerk, the Bank's ledgers were handwritten. Thus, if Mrs Jones paid in £50 in cash to her account, this cash would first be entered into the cashier's till book, then would be entered on to Mrs Jones personal statement sheet. It would then be entered onto the ledger page bearing Mrs Jones' account details.

Individual balances on all customers' Statement sheets then had to be added together, and agreed with the total of all balances on the ledger sheets. If they didn't agree, it was a matter of 'calling' all individual statement amounts to all individual ledger balances to find where the error lay. And that brief description is really a massive simplification of the procedures we had to go through.

For decades the banks insisted upon this rigmarole each year and half year end. The banks said all balancing, had to be done before the 1st day of the New Year or half year, and all summaries, returns and so on had to be posted to head office on 30th June and 31st December. Until computers were introduced!

The bank's senior management – then in 54 Lombard Street London, insisted that the manual system of 'same day balancing' had to be adopted by the computer programmers but the computer whizz kids who set up the systems were adamant that this was not possible as the computers would update a branch's entries overnight and the results would be delivered to branches the following morning.

The computer programmers won and the benefit to the staff was that the lengthy rigmarole of yearly and half yearly balances went out of the window.

Whilst the half yearly balances were in force, it was customary that where Managers lived above the bank – and a flat rent of £1 a week was an attractive inducement to live above the shop – staff would be invited up to the flat for a post–balance drink.

At that branch I recall, sherry was the norm although the Manager's wife always had a 'Gin and It' (Gin and Italian Vermouth).

One year, an initially rather brash new junior clerk was attending his first balance and when in the manager's flat he was asked what he would like to drink. He replied brightly, 'Beer'! There was an immediate hush followed by a few discrete coughs. The manager's facial expression was somewhat disapproving but a bottle of beer appeared and that brash young man subsequently left the bank and went on to become a captain of industry.

In 1956 there was a petrol shortage brought about by the Suez crisis. Petrol rationing followed, which affected Youngman's, the firm dad worked for, as they needed vehicles to make deliveries.

Heinkel and Messerschmidt, the German aircraft makers, were rather canny in bringing out mini cars – popularly called bubble cars. Both are shown below.

They were miserly, using little petrol and having single cylinder 4 stroke engines of between 174cc and 204cc. They were built between 1956 and 1958. Youngman's bought at least two – one of which was often parked on our drive at home.

I yearned after one thinking how much more comfortable they were than my Corgi Scooter.

In 1957 after I had been in the bank 18 months I was called for my national service medical and knew that it wouldn't be long before I had to enlist. The bank knew this as well as they transferred a new clerk to take my place whilst I was away. It was to be a girl who worked in a branch a few miles away and such a transfer, to have female staff working in smaller branches, was virtually unheard of in those days.

Bill Cooper, the clerk–in–charge threw a real wobbly.

'Working with a girl? It is unheard of in a small branch. Everyone will have to curb their language. We shan't be able to take off our jackets when the branch closes, etc., etc. etc. And what of toilet facilities…?'

To answer his last point there was only one toilet – on the ground floor and within easy sight of the main office. Worse still it had a glass – albeit frosted glass – panel in the door.

Initially, he solved the problem by instructing me to obtain large sheets of brown paper, normally used to wrap surplus currency notes, and stick these over the frosted glass with adhesive tape.

The young lady couldn't have cared less when she arrived. Providing she had some privacy for her ablutions she was happy. But the clerk-in-charge was still concerned and discussed matters with his wife. They lived in the flat above the branch and she suggested that Miss Scott use the facilities in the flat and that is what was agreed.

Christine Scott started work at the branch about 2 weeks before I left and in that very short time we became friendly. She was a wonderful girl, very attractive and intelligent with a sharp but gentle sense of humour and before I left for my national service we spent an evening together – the start of a wonderful friendship which continued right through my national service and beyond.

We exchanged letters on an almost daily basis and these meant a lot to me and were very comforting; especially during the hard days of the army's initial training.

As the weeks and months went by our letters got bolder and I remember sending her a copy of a well-thumbed copy of some sex manual of the day, complete with brown paper cover. I had been given it by a fellow squaddie who, by then, felt he had qualified in the subject.

There was no sex education at school in those days – certainly not in our school where we didn't even take biology – and the playground at school, the barrack square, or such books, were the only means of gaining any knowledge.

It was useful knowing what you were supposed to do, although sadly, the contents of the book never got put to practical use at that time.

\*

# CHAPTER 6

# National Service, Elvis Presley, and Shivers up the Spine 1957-59

### 1957: Brief Timeline

Harold Macmillan succeeds Eden as Prime Minister; Cavern Club opens in Liverpool; Manchester United retain the Football League First Division title with a 4-0 win over Sunderland; End of petrol rationing following the Suez Crisis; Britain tests its first hydrogen bomb, at Malden Island in the Pacific; The first Premium Bond winners selected by the computer Ernie; Prime minister Harold Macmillan tells party members 'most of our people have never had it so good'; The cartoon character Andy Capp first appears in northern editions of the *Daily Mirror*; The Wolfenden report recommends 'homosexual behaviour between consenting adults in private should no longer be a criminal offence'; The Consumers' Association begins publishing *Which?* Magazine; David Lean's Academy Award-winning film *The Bridge on the River Kwai* is released; The graphite core of the nuclear reactor at Windscale, Cumbria, catches fire, releasing substantial amounts of radioactive contamination into the surrounding area; Jodrell Bank Observatory becomes operational; The government unveils plans which will allow women to join the House of Lords for the first time; The Royal Christmas Message is broadcast on television with the Queen on camera for the first time.

After working for Barclays Bank for 18 months, I was called up on Thursday, 7th March 1957 for my 2 years national service.

I recall little of the calling up process but do remember that initially we got no papers as such and had to respond to radio and press announcements which instructed those men born between certain dates to register at their local centre.

I then attended a medical at what is now the Lord Rosebery pub in Westborough, Scarborough. Years ago this had been the local Liberal party headquarters – hence the name.

There was a line of doctors, all in white coats and when one had finished with his 'patient', the next man in line shuffled into that place. There were the usual questions, 'cough and drop', handling your 'tackle' with a spatula, eye tests, ear tests, samples in a bottle behind a curtain and so on; but at the end of the day, like most recruits I was passed A1 fit. Some men, of course, tried to fiddle their medical and a favourite trick was to eat soap beforehand. This was said to speed the heart rate so an adverse result might excuse them service.

We then moved on to another room for aptitude tests after which we were asked in which of the services we wished to serve. I opted for the RAF in which my father had served during the war, but was told 'it' was only then taking men who would sign up for at least 3 years. Signing on for 3 years would have meant losing the guarantee from the bank of keeping my job open for me, and, as in those days job security was important for most people, the Army it had to be.

My call-up papers arrived by post a few weeks later instructing me to report to 68th Training Regiment, Royal Artillery, Park Hall Camp, Oswestry on Thursday 7th March 1957. National service men were called up on alternate Thursdays, usually 6000 at a time, and on the other alternate Thursdays around 6,000 were demobbed having completed their service. It really was like a conveyer belt and the logistics must have been horrendous in an era before computers. I remember little of the train journey but do remember eventually arriving at Gobowen – a tiny rural railway station apparently long since closed – and being met by a fleet of Army lorries into which all we recruits scrambled before being transferred to what seemed to be a massive Park Hall Camp.

At the initial induction training at 68th Training Regiment, Royal Artillery, Army numbers ('23375885

Gunner Fowler DG') and kit, ('two of everything' – many items of which did not fit), were thrown across a table which divided 'them' from 'us'. Sizes appeared to be guessed and the throwing came from seasoned soldiers behind piles and piles of uniforms, boots, underwear, socks, shirts, and so on. Later, we had inoculations galore during which some men in a long row of recruits, would faint. We were allocated to billets in groups of long wooden huts called 'Spiders'. A number of huts were connected to each other with a central area between the huts where toilets and ablutions were situated to serve all the huts in that spider.

Each individual hut had a single iron stove in the centre to provide warmth but in winter these were spectacularly unsuccessful.

Early memories are of sheer exhaustion – getting up at some unearthly hour, washing and shaving in cold water ('bum fluff' it was called in those days, but we had to wet shave whether we needed to or not), dashing off to an enormous hall for breakfast, (very high and extremely noisy with lots of condensation), feeling almost nauseous with tiredness, then dashing back to the hut to clean and 'bull' the room and kit before preparing for parade a matter of minutes later.

At the other end of the day I remember 'bulling' boots with a spoon and a lit candle. The spoon was heated in the candle flame then used to flatten the pimples in the leather of the boot. Once a smooth surface had been achieved, lashings of spit and black Kiwi boot polish (it was literally 'spit and polish') were applied with a soft duster by using small circular movements with the index finger, until the boots shone like glass.

We had also to press uniforms with an electric iron and brown paper to put knife edge creases in the trousers and the battledress jacket arms.

Drill, marching, rifle drill, the classroom, more drill, horrible film slides of scabby penises to warn us against the dangers of 'loose women' – and even looser soldiers. – were followed by the free distribution of condoms which, I recall, many of us used as balloons to decorate the huts when it was someone's birthday, or Christmas.

After the initial two week induction training we were split up and some of us moved within Park Hall camp to 17th Training Regiment, Royal Artillery.

It was even more renowned for bull than had been 68th Training Regiment; highly polished buttons – none of the 'Stay–brite' versions then – layer upon layer of No 3 Green Blanco on our belts, gaiters and canvas webbing; boots bulled until the toecaps shone like a mirror; creases in battledress razor sharp, and so on. One ruse was to spread a layer of soap on the inside of the trouser crease, then to iron the crease from the outside using brown paper between the trouser and the iron. This gave a sharp crease which lasted longer than by merely ironing.

One man had what he thought was an even better idea. He got a tube of glue and spread it on the inside crease before ironing his trousers. A very pungent, fishy smell issued forth before the trousers burst into flames. He had some explaining to do!

During this time, memories of home were very strong. Some men became very homesick so we all looked forward to the mail delivery, normally around 11.00am during our 'NAAFI break' when we usually had tea and a bun. Letters and parcels from home from families and girlfriends were particularly welcome. My mother was an excellent cook and knew I liked fruit cake so occasionally she sent me one. These were quickly devoured by those in our billet, who, in turn would share what they had been sent.

On one occasion I had asked mother to send Kiwi boot polish as we found it better for bulling boots than other brands and, for some reason, the NAAFI shop had run out. She carefully packed the Kiwi in the same parcel as a fruit cake, but somehow the tin lid had come loose and the smell of polish had permeated into the cake. We were all ravenous and still devoured the cake in a very short time.

One letter I received around this time had a black mourning border around the envelope. The camp hierarchy went into overdrive, offering me counselling and any help I needed. I should have taken them up on it to gain extra leave. It was from friend Graham Burnett who was writing to tell me that Scarborough Football Club had just been knocked out of the F.A. cup!

One evening some of us had been given the job of cleaning the regimental offices. We were told to dust, clean windows, polish and bump the floor to make it shine; empty the waste paper baskets and so on. The waste paper baskets provided no interesting information, which was disappointing. We kept working hard until one of our number said, 'They really ought to lock the filing cabinets at night!'

We all crowded round and, sure enough, the cabinet drawers were all unlocked. We had a good delve and before long came across the progress reports of our intake. I went through one cabinet and there it was in the 'F's' – '23375885 Gunner Fowler DG – 'Tries hard – but is a bit of an old woman. Needs to loosen up.' It was probably not a bad assessment at the time and it caused quite a laugh.

After we'd been drilled until we felt we could take no more and had regularly fired .303 rifles at targets – remembering to hold the stock tightly against our shoulders, as we had been warned that otherwise the recoil could break our collar bones – our scores were announced and I had scored second highest at rifle shooting. No doubt the fact that I had been in a small bore rifle club at home before enlistment had some bearing.

Drill and rifle drill became second nature and we

concentrated on our trade training – me as a 'Technical Assistant, Royal Artillery'. There was no choice of trade as the RAF seemed to offer and we were all told what our trades would be, probably as a result of more aptitude tests we took.

After 6 weeks of training to become a 'TARA' and learning how to calculate the necessary angles and settings for the distance and height to which the guns needed to be adjusted; then the size of charge needed for the shells to go on their calculated trajectory so they landed somewhere near where they were supposed to land; together with continuing square bashing, guard duty, yet more bull, polishing black lines round the edges of the billet room floor with Kiwi and shoe brushes and, on one occasion, painting piles of coal white for a brigadier's inspection; then travelling in three tonners and towing twenty–five pounder guns into the Welsh mountains, deploying them but then not being allowed to fire them as it was the lambing season and instead we were instructed to pick up a field telephone and shout 'Bang, got you!' ; we were told all our postings would be in regimental orders the next morning.

And so they were. When I pushed through the crush and got to the board I read, '23375885 Gunner Fowler DG – To 1st Regiment, Royal Horse Artillery, Münster, Germany'. Fear gripped me. I'd hardly ever seen a horse, let alone ridden one and my total riding skills took place one weekend when, aged about 7, I had a donkey ride on Scarborough beach. Naïve wasn't the word!

However, when I arrived at the regiment via Woolwich barracks in London, then by train to Harwich, then by the troopship Empire Parkeston to the Hook of Holland and on the 'Blue' train to Münster, Germany – I realised that the guns in those days were sophisticated American M44's, motorised and tracked and not pulled by horses!

In fact the only 'horse' I ever saw in my entire time with the regiment was a pony – the commanding officer's polo pony.

The CO's name was Colonel Teacher and I discovered later that he was related to the whisky firm of that name. That probably explained the cases of Teacher's whisky which arrived periodically.

Münster was a charming old town and on the odd day off I enjoyed visiting, where, for the soldiers stationed nearby there was an excellent Globe Cinema and a NAAFI.

*Me when in Germany. My left shoulder bears the 'mailed fist' badge of the 6th Armoured Brigade.*

On arrival at the regiment we were allocated to modern, centrally heated billets in Waterloo Barracks. This had originally been built as a German Luftwaffe base during WWII. There was ample hot water and central heating and the buildings were very well maintained, compared to those in training at Park Hall camp in Oswestry.

However, until recently I didn't realise what an impact events which occurred at Waterloo Barracks in January 1940 could have had on the outcome of WWII.

The barracks had previously been known as Loddenheide Airfield and in January 1940 an aircraft took off on an unauthorised mission that changed the course of WWII.

The commandant of the airfield offered to fly a visiting staff officer back to Cologne rather than him undertake a long ride by car on icy roads. It is said that the visit had involved extensive alcoholic refreshment. The staff officer was supposed to drive, rather than fly because he was carrying a copy of the current German plan, 'Fall Gelb', which planned the attack on France and the Low Countries.

The aircraft got lost and crashed in Belgium and the plans were captured. As a result Hitler had to change the plan, adopting Van Manstein's 'Sythe Cut' through the Ardennes. This sparked the desperate evacuation from Dunkirk which became known as 'The Miracle of Dunkirk'.

*Developed by German Lieutenant General Erich von Manstein, the plan greatly modified the original 1939 versions by Franz Halder of the invasion plan known as Fall Gelb.*

*Originally, in Aufmarschanweisung N°1, Fall Gelb, the German Army planned to push the Allied forces back through central Belgium to the Somme river, in northern France, like the first phase of the famous Schlieffen Plan of the First World War. On 10th January 1940, the Mechelen Incident occurred, a German aircraft carrying documents containing parts of the operational plans of Fall Gelb crashed in Belgium, thus prompting another review of the invasion plan. While Fall Gelb was revised by Halder, not fundamentally changing it in Aufmarschanweisung N°3, Fall Gelb, Manstein was able to convince Hitler in a meeting on 17 February, that the Wehrmacht strategy should be an attack through the Ardennes, followed by an advance to the coast.*

The morning after we arrived at Waterloo barracks we were all on parade in our bulled up uniforms and boots from our training days. We put the rest of the regiment to shame. 'Step forward TARA's,' shouted the drill sergeant. Around 20 of us who had been trained as Technical Assistants smartly stepped forward. He only wanted 5 and he started at the other end of the line – so it was then a matter of, 'What did you do in civvy street, lad?' When it got to my turn I said I'd worked in a bank for eighteen months. 'Just the thing.' he said, 'We want someone to keep the books in the officers' mess.'

That proved a good move for me. Excused most parades and guards, I could wear shoes, had my own bedroom in the officer's mess – but segregated from their accommodation of course, – and was dangled the possibility of a stripe to lance bombardier after 6 months. But life got better. As a result of my then very rudimentary bookkeeping skills, after a few weeks I discovered the books didn't balance and appeared not to have done so for a few years. I suspected the mess sergeant – effectively a hotel manager in charge of the running of the prestigious 1st RHA officers' mess – was on the fiddle. Crates of beer, spirits, cigarettes and so on were being delivered to his married quarters but the bills had, until then been paid by the officers. There wasn't the normal income there should have been from the sale of beers, spirits and tobacco products. Regular stock orders had apparently just disappeared into thin air. Whether the sergeant had been drinking it all – his speech was often slurred – or selling it on for his own benefit, I never did discover.

I pondered how to deal with it. I was 90% certain it was a fiddle, but in those days I felt my bookkeeping skills were at the lower end of the scale of competence, so I remained a little worried. I decided to have a word off the record with the PMC – the President of the mess committee – a white–haired, whiskery major in his '50s whose name I now forget. 'Leave it with me,' he said. One thing led to another, a board of enquiry was held, statements were taken and the mess sergeant was demoted and shipped back to England. He had been up to his games for at least 5 years and had, until then, got away with it. I hoped the ears of my predecessor Mess bombardier, who had been demobbed, were burning.

Royal Horse Artillery regiments are perceived as élite and for a regular, a posting to an RHA unit is regarded as a significant career advancement. As a senior regiment the 1st RHA did a lot of lavish entertaining and with cigarettes costing under 10s/0d (50p) for 200 and spirits at less than 10s/0d (50p) a litre, it was not hard to see why.

The sergeant's premature departure left a vacancy which I was told would take at least 6 months to fill. A suitably experienced and qualified replacement mess sergeant who would fit into the mess would not be easy to find. A few days later the PMC approached me and said the officers' mess committee had met and its members were very grateful to me for having spotted the 'problem'. They had also agreed that until a replacement could be found I would be expected to run the mess – and still keep the books in order!

I gulped, and so started one of the steepest learning curves I have ever encountered. They kitted me out with uniform 'blues' dripping with gold braid; imagine the Royal Horse Artillery King's Troop ceremonial dress when they fire royal salutes, take away the pill box hat and the horse and that was me. At the tender age of 18 I started work – effectively the job of an hotel manager running a prestigious senior mess for 50 officers and guests, including visits by senior forces officers, judge advocates when a court martial was pending in the area and, occasionally, even royalty.

There was a large German civilian staff and still a bit of post–war feeling, so whilst the civilians were pleasant enough, they were expected to speak in English except amongst themselves. However, they could have stroppy periods when they refused to understand, or speak in English, which meant me having to speak in German. From a halting start, the German teaching from 'Bonn' the German master we all detested at Scarborough High School, rapidly paid dividends and from then on I looked on him as something of a saviour and I frequently mouthed a quiet 'thank–you' to him.

Helga, who undertook seamstress duties and any officer's stitching requirements, had a little room of her own where she worked and told me I was always welcome to drop in for coffee. This became a routine and she soon helped polish my school boy German so I could converse properly with the staff in their own tongue.

After a month or so, Captain Coffey, who commanded RHQ Troop (Regimental Headquarters), told me to look in Regimental Orders the next morning. I did so and was delighted to see my name and promotion to Lance Bombardier with immediate effect. So they had given me my first stripe which I thought was pretty good going. I took the three sets of stripes to Helga who gave me coffee whilst she stitched them on to both arms of my three uniforms.

The second stripe followed after another three months. However, before getting the second I was suddenly told one morning by Captain Coffey that I was to take a squad of long term regulars on a 5 mile march. The regulars ribbed me a bit but it went reasonably well and we all ended up singing as we marched along. I suspected later that it was some sort of test to justify my second stripe. The officers apologised that there was no chance of promotion to sergeant. There was some precedent in the 1st RHA that national service men could get no further than the rank of full bombardier. My predecessor Sergeant had, of course, been a regular.

My duties involved organising and running the mess; making sure the officers and their guests were comfortable; dealing with all catering, accommodation, batmen, military and civilian staffing; buying food in the German shops to supplement Army rations; ordering all drinks – spirits, beers, draught beers, soft drinks and so on; learning about wines, champagne, cocktails, spirits and about how many measures each bottle contained (spirits 26; liqueurs 32) – although Roses bitter, (later taken over by Tetley's) and the occasional sherry had been the extent of my drinking experience until then.

Also stock-taking; arranging functions; dining-in nights and menus; being responsible for the display and security of silver (very large elaborate pieces and normally held in a vault within the camp); being responsible for all mess staff training – military and civilian; and turning a blind eye when officers 'entertained' their girlfriends in their rooms.

*Old-timers almost due for demob – l to r: Brookes, Caton, Pugh and Budd – all officers' mess staff. Brookes, (left) the only one in full uniform, might have been leaving that day.*

One of the batmen - Caton in the photo - was even more naïve than me. One day he approached me dangling a waste paper basket from the room of a tall slim very handsome officer who was known to entertain his girlfriend regularly. The batman held his nose and said, 'what shall I do with these Bom?' In the basket were a few used condoms.

In September 1957 the 3rd Hussars had moved from Iserlohn and taken over York Barracks, Münster from 17th/21st Lancers. This was just up the road from 1st RHA's Waterloo barracks. The Colonel in Chief of the 3rd Hussars was the late Princess Margaret and she visited them on 29th and 30th March 1958.

On 29th, a very large dinner night was held at which she was guest of honour and I was asked to help.

I saw the list provided by Buckingham Palace which 'suggested' that a certain brand of whisky, a carafe of water and a supply of some particular brand of cigarettes, ('Passing Cloud'?) together with an ashtray, be provided by her bedside.

The Harz Mountains were not far away and on many weekends if we were free we would borrow a three ton lorry, load it with hay boxes full of food, take our own drink and skis and head for the mountains. The pure, crisp rarefied air was extremely exhilarating and intoxicating and I look back nostalgically to those weekends so long ago.

I still had to go on all 'schemes' (i.e. training exercises, manoeuvres and 'war games') where we effectively set up the mess under canvas – including the silver – and on one such scheme, possibly at Sennelager or Hohne, one very ambitious regular Army subaltern felt the mess marquee did not look imposing enough for 1st RHA, so he raided the medical supplies and had the batmen and mess staff wind yards and yards of white bandage round the marquee guy ropes.

He was extremely pleased with himself – until the CO arrived! 'Lt M****. Do you not think that's an f*****g stupid thing to do? The men only finished installing the damned scrim and camouflage netting this morning. We're supposed to be bloody hidden from the air and fighting a bloody war and then you go and advertise our presence by wrapping bandage everywhere! You just see. We shall be nuked shortly.'

And just as if the RAF had listened in to his outburst, they came in on cue, spotted us and, to prove the CO's point, bombarded us with toilet rolls. Around 50 must have cascaded down on to our camp. We learned later that it was supposed to be a simulated nuclear attack.

On one 'scheme' in which the Americans were taking part, for some reason the NAAFI was closed and we were told to use the US equivalent – their PX store. There was also a rumour that Elvis Presley was in the vicinity with the US Army.

In the PX store we relaxed, we chatted, we smoked, we ate, we drank and we listened to the juke box.

Then who should walk in with a group of fellow recruits but private first class Elvis Presley, who was doing his national service with the American Army. He was very unassuming, extremely natural and appeared to be just 'one of the boys'.

Everything went quiet and you could have heard a pin drop. Then the whole room erupted and everyone cheered. 'Sing us a song, Elvis', we chorused. He gave a slow, languid smile, nodded his head and in his deep, but very smooth voice he said, 'OK guys. Whadyou wanna hear?'

*Private First Class, Elvis Presley*

The atmosphere in the room was expectant and electric, just like before a heavy thunder storm. Here was the world famous Elvis Presley and he was going to sing – just for us. We could dine out on this for years. The excitement was intense. Simultaneously people shouted out, 'Hound Dog', 'Jailhouse Rock', 'Treat Me Nice' – all were popular at the time.

'OK guys. It'll be 'Treat Me Nice'. He fumbled in his battledress pocket, then removed the jacket and put it on a chair. He moved in front of the juke box, faced us, relaxed, gave that slow languid smile again, spread his legs and gave a few of his famous thrusts of his groin.

Then he turned quickly, slotted a dime on the juke box and the sound of 'Treat Me Nice' echoed round the room. He actually sang and gyrated to the Juke box music. What a showman!

Then afterwards, he apologised, 'Sorry guys – but that was the only way I could 'Treat YOU nice' – mah guitar was back in mah room.'

I actually got the chance to speak with him later and whilst it was a brief conversation it has stayed with me all these years and I have often kicked myself for not asking for his autograph.

By this time the regiment had moved from Waterloo Barracks, Münster to Tofrek Barracks, Hildesheim, near Hannover. Hildesheim is an ancient historical town with many old timber framed buildings which had been badly damaged by bombing during WWII. By the 1950s much restoration had taken place.

That was an unusual move in that the regiment left Münster for their summer camp at Hohne but never returned, moving straight to the new barracks at Hildesheim after manoeuvres. Or at least the regiment didn't return to Münster. I completed half the summer camp, but then returned to Münster as part of the advance party organising the officers' mess move to

Hildesheim and ensuring the 'new' mess in Hildesheim was ready for occupation.

In 1958 the annual 'Admin' inspection took place at Tofrek Barracks. Whilst it didn't directly affect mess staff, for weeks beforehand the rest of the regiment were back to 'bulling' – not their personal kit, although that had to be immaculate for the days of the inspection, but all the vehicles, self-propelled guns and so on.

*Above: Admin parade 1958: From the left are Champs, Centurion tanks, M44 self-propelled guns, Scammell, Saracens and 3 tonners.*

*Below: Admin parade 1958: From left: Centurion tank and M44 self-propelled guns at the drive-past.*

Vehicles were painted, serviced, valeted and polished, until they shone – although in true military conditions all the shine would have been removed to aid camouflage.
On summer camps, schemes, war games and so on, I

always found it most frustrating that we were never told what was happening. At a few minutes' notice we would have to 'up-sticks', strike camp and move to another location – often in the middle of the night without being told where or why.

It was, of course, the principle of 'need to know' and in our lowly positions we were deemed not to 'need to know'. It was understandable, but nevertheless frustrating.

On one 'scheme' for some reason, some of the officers' mess staff were following the main regiment a few hours later. We were in a 3 ton lorry towing a caravan which had been fitted out to contain all the crockery, cutlery, glassware and so on which would enable the officers to live in the manner to which they had become accustomed.

The normal signposting had been removed after our regiment had found its site and we were having a struggle to find them. In 1958 there was no 'sat-nav' of course. Whilst I could read a map over decently marked British roads, finding your way over cart tracks on barren German plains with few identification markers was entirely different and had not been covered in our classroom training sessions. Yet I was given a map and a map reference and told to 'meet up with the regiment'. When we got to the area of the exercises we were on muddy, unmade tracks and at one stage we decided we were going the wrong way. Archie Lowndes, the mess chef who was driving, promptly braked and started to reverse into shrub land in order to turn round. We all forgot about the caravan on the back of the three-tonner until there was a resounding crash when it overturned into a hidden ditch. We got out of the truck and managed to right the caravan and continue on our way with nothing worse than some best china having shattered. After a while I felt we were at the map reference I had been given and we saw a regiment occupying the site. But it wasn't 1st RHA and whilst it transpired that my map reading had eventually taken us to the correct area, in the meantime our regiment had been ordered to move on and this other one had taken their place. We had no radio and no new map co-ordinates so we had to set out to find our regiment by asking each unit we came across. It took around an hour until we were finally back home with 1st RHA.

Luckily we had enough crockery for the officers on the scheme so we got away without embarrassing questions being raised about the breakages.

On one occasion back at Tofrek Barracks, Archie Lowndes, the officers' mess chef, fancied a ride in 2nd Lieutenant Lacey's brand new Riley 1.5 litre car. Lt Lacey was a national service officer, well–liked by everyone, and the car was his 21st birthday present. He would no doubt have given Archie a ride but one evening he had temporarily left the keys in his car.

Empty spirit bottles from the officers' mess were stacked in a particular area before being collected for disposal and Archie, feeling thirsty, decided to mix himself a cocktail from the dregs in the many bottles. Somewhat pie–eyed, he then went for a spin round the camp in the Riley. Needless to say he was not fit to drive and he managed to damage the Riley, dump it, then totter back to the mess. An enquiry followed and I remember having to take him to the nearest Royal Military police unit where statements were taken. I can't remember the outcome but suspect that as Archie's prowess as Officers' Mess Chef was felt to be much more important than the 2nd Lieutenant's Riley (which was professionally repaired and repainted by the REME's transport workshop) he got away with a few days confined to barracks. Needless to say, empty spirit bottles were in future kept in a locked store.

On another occasion the officer in charge of RHQ troop, Captain Coffey – a career officer, very motivated, well spoken, energetic and enthusiastic, called me and said he wanted 2 dozen cases of whisky loading into a champ for 11.00am that morning. The deed was done, he arrived and he said, 'Oh, didn't I say bombardier? I want you to accompany me?' Off we went, him driving and I asked where we were going. 'Oh to the French zone. We've done a deal to swap whisky for vintage champagne!' Off we went, did the exchange and returned to camp much later. How I dealt in the mess books with 12 cases of whisky disappearing from stock and being replaced with vintage champagne, I cannot recall.

It wasn't until 2009 when I was preparing my book 'National Service, Elvis and Me!' and checking photographs from my national service album that a piece of paper dropped out from behind a photograph. It reminded me of an episode I had long since forgotten; the notes gave details of a séance some of us had held, in late summer 1958. One day, talk had got around to the supernatural and a member of the mess staff had suggested we try to see if a Ouija board would come up with any messages for us.

Above the 3 storey accommodation blocks were empty attics, so half a dozen of us went up there one evening with candles, set up a table, sat down and were told by one of the squaddies who seemed to know most about the supernatural, to 'sit down, keep quiet and concentrate'.

He had produced a board and he explained the name 'Ouija' came from the amalgamation of the word 'Yes', in French (Oui) and German (Ja). There was a full alphabet, numbers, and, in each corner 'Yes' and 'No' so answers could be spelt out.

We 'sat down, kept quiet and concentrated' and placed a glass upside down in the middle of the board.

We were then told to each put a finger on the base of the glass and concentrate hard. We then asked the 'board' questions. At first nothing happened, then very slowly the glass started to move and before long it was flying over the board to spell out answers:

'Is anybody there?
*Y–A (Yes)*
What is your name?
*R–U–D–O–L–F  M–E–T–Z–I–G (Rudolf Metzig)*
When did you die?

*1–9–4–4 J–U–N–I (1944 June)*
*Were you an airman?*
*Y–A. L–U–F–T–W–A–F–F–E (Yes. Air Force)*
*What was your rank?*
*O–B–E–R–L–E–U–T–N–A–N–T (Senior Lieutenant)*
*How did you die?*
*K–R–I–E–G (War)'*

By that time even the most blasé amongst us had a shivery creepy feeling down the back of our necks and the room had turned extremely cold even though it was only late summer.

We looked at each other. We spoke to the board. 'We must go now. Will you talk to us if we return another night?'

*Y–A–W–O–H–L. A–U–F W–I–E–D–E–R–S–E–H–E–N (Yes. Goodbye)*

We hurriedly gathered up our paraphernalia and almost fought each other to get down the access ladder from that attic. We never did try to communicate with Rudolf Metzig again. Had it been faked? I don't know, but with us each having a finger on the upturned glass it would surely have been noticed had one man been exerting more pressure than another. And with replies being in German, to English questions it would have needed someone well versed in German and very quick witted, to 'encourage' the glass to move in the correct sequence to give those answers.

As far as I am aware none of us spoke of the event over the following weeks or months. It had been spooky and frightening and the extreme coldness in that attic made us feel that we could have hit on something we were better not pursuing. We gradually forgot the incident.

And there it would have ended until I started putting together my book, *'National Service, Elvis & Me!'* many years later and found the notes together with my photographs of that period. The notes reminded me of the séance and I felt I should maybe look further to try to trace Rudolf Metzig and to try to establish whether he was a figment of our imagination or had existed and might have been one of thousands of airmen who had died in WWII. I didn't hold out much hope but he was surely worth a search on the internet which hadn't, of course, been available in 1958.

I clicked on Google and typed in the name, 'Rudolf Metzig'. The screen responded almost instantaneously with many entries, but not far down the list was an item in German. I opened it to find a long table which looked interesting. It appeared to be a record of military honours awarded by the German Reich during WWII. Google had highlighted my search name – the name of Rudolf Metzig.

His entry read, 'Metzig, Rudolf – Knight's Cross – 9th June 1944*'.

In trepidation I wondered what the asterisk meant and looked at the table on the screen carefully. 'Asterisk denotes Knight's Cross – awarded posthumously', it said.

That coldness, creepy and shivery feeling I recall from 1958 returned.

May Rudolf Metzig rest in peace?

Before my call–up I had been very interested in short wave radio and in anything electronic. As previously mentioned my Uncle Percy was a radio 'ham' and my interest had come from him. Somehow this interest must have become known as the regimental sergeant major got in touch and asked if I would join him in competing in a shortwave listening competition which went on for 48 hours. The RSM? At first I thought I was being wound up. To we squaddies he was more like God than the CO.

He came over to the officers' mess and his idea was that we'd alternate between listening and sleeping as he couldn't have competed himself for the full 48 hours. His short wave equipment was in the spare bedroom of his married quarters, so he fixed my absence for the duration of the competition and his wife kept us supplied with food and drink as we were scanning the airwaves. I recall we won some small prize for our joint effort.

This led me on to think about my pre-service interest in electronics and how it might be of benefit. Portable radios were then the size of a briefcase and many servicemen said they would like a radio to while away the time on schemes and exercises. On these there were many periods of inactivity interspersed with hectic periods of action. I couldn't obtain derelict hearing aids as I had a few years earlier but I thought a crystal set might be the answer. They were simple to make, reliable, could receive local radio stations and didn't need batteries. I got in touch with my sister Phoebe in Scarborough, who got in touch with my uncle, the short wave 'ham'. He provided coils, crystals, tuning capacitors and a coil of connecting wire and sent this lot on to me. From an electric shop in Münster I bought a soldering iron and number of wooden electric light–switch mounting blocks on to each of which I fixed a set of components to make a crystal set. Each set took about 20 minutes to build and test. They required no battery so were ideal for schemes. They would only pick up local stations but I must have sold around four dozen over a very short period of time.

Earphones, which were necessary to hear the radio programmes, were the responsibility of the buyer, although I suspect a number of earphones were 'borrowed' from the signals unit!

Another pocket money earner were battery razors. On schemes, all shaving was 'wet' and all water – unless you were an officer with a batman who would boil it – was cold. Whilst in the '50s electric razors could be purchased, rechargeable battery versions were very expensive, and on schemes of course, there were no power sockets in which to recharge these.

I discovered a German firm, Distler, which had started marketing battery razors in the UK. These looked a little like a torch with the round shaving head being where the lens would be. The standard replaceable batteries were in the barrel of the shaver as in a torch. I bought one and tried it and it was superb. I took it on the next scheme we were on and soon started receiving enquiries from other soldiers and officers. Initially my sister bought a few razors at a time and sent these out to me but as sales increased I approached the manufacturers and they agreed to sell me 3 razors for the price of 2, postage included. I was in business!

I sold them at £3 each which effectively gave me a profit of £1 on each razor and on exercises, in the early morning, the hum of numerous razors sounded like a swarm of angry hornets.

*All was prepared for a formal Dinner night for around 50 1 RHA officers*

By this time my demob date in March 1959 was getting nearer and I was ticking off my last few months on the calendar.

A replacement mess sergeant had still not arrived and did not arrive for well over a year from the departure of the previous one. During this time I was running the mess with the help of Lance bombardier, Jim Lomax.

When the new sergeant did arrive, a short, dour little Scot, he and I got on well after a rather sticky start. He couldn't understand why I was still in bed one morning at 8.00am until I explained that I hadn't got to bed until 5.00am after the previous night's function!

After that episode he was happy for us to share what were then his responsibilities, which until his arrival had been mine anyway. We agreed I would be in charge of the afternoon and late night functions and would sleep in the next morning and he would start early in the mornings, and be on duty at 6.00am for breakfast, leaving in the afternoon. That suited us both – me in particular, as on top of my national service pittance, I continued to receive extra duty pay for work after 5.30pm until whatever time I finished.

There had been a few suggestions that I sign on for an extended period with the offer of a good job and a commission. However, whilst enjoyable and I had learned a great deal, the work had meant long and tiring hours and I was ready to get home to family, friends and Christine.

Shortly before my leaving day arrived the officers threw a demob party for me in the 'Kellerbar' – a small private night club based in the cellar of the officers' mess, and it was a very pleasant change to be a guest for the night rather than me being there to make sure everything ran smoothly.

This night club dated back to Luftwaffe days as Tofrek Barracks had also, like Waterloo Barracks, (1 RHA's previous home at Münster) been a German airfield. The 'Kellerbar' was still decorated with many German Luftwaffe shields and emblems on the walls and what we had thought to be some aircraft-related graffiti on the ceiling.

Research I undertook a few years ago revealed that one piece of 'graffiti' I had seen and wondered about, depicting a WWII biplane with a barrel of Lowenbrau beer on board, had been drawn to commemorate a visit by Hermann Goering, commander–in–chief of the Luftwaffe, whose favourite tipple had been Lowenbrau beer.

By some oversight, no Lowenbrau had been ordered for his visit, so the Reich Marshall–to–be despatched an aircraft to the brewery in Munich to remedy the shortage. This event was later depicted by the painting on the night club ceiling.

I still have the tankard with which the officers presented me before I was demobbed, but, now nearly 60 years later, it is somewhat battered. I don't remember very much of the latter part of the leaving party the officers threw for me as I was presented with a bottle of champagne (not Lowenbrau!) but probably one of those bottles for which we swapped whisky in the French Zone. I was 'ordered' not to go to bed until the bottle was empty. I recall that throughout the evening the officers kept urging me to sign a document which, had I signed it, would have cancelled my demob and enlisted me as a regular. They kept mentioning this possibility during the evening and, as the evening wore on the attractions of promotion and more pay by signing on seemed increasingly attractive. The following morning I awoke with a very thick head, and under the empty magnum of champagne on my bedside table was the re–enlistment form – still completely blank.

The 1st RHA was a wonderful regiment in which to be so closely involved and its officers were gentlemen. It had been a privilege to be part of it.

I held my own demob party at 'Otto's', a local hostelry in a village called Himmelstür about 2 miles from camp shortly before I left the regiment late in February 1959. As we were paying it was a night for beer, not champagne!

*My demob party at 'Otto's' Himmelstür, Hildesheim.
L to R: Lofty Barnes, Scouse Blinkhorn, me, and Paul Derek*

I was demobbed on the 5th March 1959, 2 years exactly after I had been called up and exactly one year to the day before Elvis Presley was demobbed. Co-incidentally, he shared sister Phoebe's birthday on 8th January, but he was 4 years older.

So that was national service.

The upside was that unlike many men I never had time to be bored. I had enjoyed fulfilling experiences and whilst I didn't get further than Germany I enjoyed seeing parts of that country, meeting its people and being a very small part in helping to oil the wheels of a superb regiment. National service gave me confidence, expanded my character, taught me to stand on my own feet, stand my corner and take responsibility. It had been tiring, even exhausting at times but overall it had been a wonderful experience. They said that you would enter national service as a boy and come out as a man and, in my case that was certainly true.

Was there a downside? Well, a few of those in our intake

returned home after national service aged around 20, still virgins. But it wasn't for lack of trying as the following anecdote shows.

*'We got to Amsterdam, in a 3 tonner which we then parked. We eventually found the red light district and ogled the scantily clad girls sitting in their windows. Many were very attractive and some of the dozen of us haggled a price with a particular girl before they entered her premises when the curtains were promptly closed.*

*Later, when we all climbed aboard the truck to return to camp at 11.30pm there was a buzz of excitement but some lads asked why one of the group was so quiet and disconsolate. Eventually he opened up:*

*'It's my birthday today and it was to be my first time. I'd been drinking and I paid her the equivalent of the ten shillings she asked for and she put a condom on me. I was still a bit floppy so she got this motorised thing which buzzed like a hornet and she stroked me with it for a few seconds. In no time at all I'd come!*

*She looked exasperated and asked me, 'Are you queer or something?'*

*'I told her I was most definitely NOT queer but just bloody disappointed as it was my first time, and it was my birthday and I had no more money.'*

*'Birthday? First time?' she asked, 'Why didn't you say? Come back at midnight before I finish and I'll give you a freebie to celebrate your birthday and your first time. I'll make it really good for you too!'*

*'Thanks darling', he had said, 'but the bloody truck leaves at 11.30pm!'*

A personal downside was that before joining up I had intended to study for my Institute of Bankers Examinations whilst doing my bit for my country. I had been assured there would be 'lots of free time' after training, and that studying would save 'boredom creeping in'. Whilst the army even paid for a correspondence course for me, my working hours were so long that my books were hardly opened during my national service period, so study had to be delayed until after demob.

Also back at the bank girls or 'lady clerks' as the bank insisted on calling them in their adverts of those days, had been employed in greater numbers. They had moved ahead in the years I was away so whilst I had been senior to many of them before call–up, on my return they were senior to me and the two years serving my country counted for nothing within the bank.

We also missed our families and loved ones: Christine Hayes (nèe Scott) remembers...

*'We met when I was transferred to his office so that he could teach me the job before he left – I remember thinking how kind he was and very good looking.*

*'He was the first real boyfriend I had – it was all very proper in those days nearly 60 years ago.*

*'We said our farewells on Filey Beach and the evening before he left he gave me a lovely galloping horse brooch which I still have – and then he was gone.*

*'He was in one of the last batches to do national service and left home in 1957. Very soon the letters started to arrive; they were lovely letters to which I replied and for both of us it became an almost daily event. I would meet the postman on my way to catch the bus to work – he would wave the letter and call 'another one today'.*

*'The BFPO stamp seemed very romantic. I think it was BFPO 17.*

*'As time and letters progressed we got a little more daring – I sent him a handkerchief soaked in perfume. It was Apple Blossom by Helena Rubenstein.*

*'His family kept in touch and I sometimes went for tea. I thought they were lovely people and I grew to know them well – perhaps better than I knew him.*

*'He had an aunt who had a shop not far from where I*

*worked. I used to go there and have a sandwich with her at lunch time. She loved to be kept up to date with his letters (I didn't show her them all!)*

*'Because he was abroad, 'leaves' were not very frequent but I remember on one occasion arriving home and being told he was in the sitting room and I felt quite scared to go in. Thinking back I had become comfortable with the letters. We had known each other such a short time before he left that my life with him was nearly all in letters.*

*'I had the impression he enjoyed his time doing national service and I think it was a really beneficial part of a young man's life.*

*'Later, we drifted apart but I like to think I helped him through national service; just as he helped me through those naïve days of the 50s...'*

Phoebe Hawson, my sister, now from Las Vegas USA remembers...

*'Of course we missed you. One minute you were all over the house and the next you were gone.*

*I missed having you around and doing things with my big brother. Of course, we could never understand why a banker had to go into the Artillery and thought that was crazy.*

*There were no overseas phone calls, no computers, no e-mail and no mobile phones so we only had letters to keep in touch. We kept sending you parcels; you would write to us with a list of what you needed and we would go out shopping and mail them off. Mum baked cakes for you and I sent you things you made into radios and sold on to other soldiers. The big one was the crystals and wire for you to make the radio sets. Then there were razor blades; I don't know what you wanted them for! There were far too many to shave with. Also tins galore of shoe polish, but it had to be 'Kiwi'.*

*You sent me a 45 rpm record 'To Know Him is to Love*

*Him', by the Teddy Bears. EP [extended play] was a new format after the old 78 rpms and records were difficult to obtain at that time in England. There was another record you sent which had two songs on it.*

*Two songs on one record was quite rare in the 1950s; I think one was 'Young Love' and the other might have been 'Diana' but I can't remember for sure.*

*You mentioned meeting Elvis Presley but did you tell him he had the same birthday as me? He was 4 years older though...'*

Finally, I had carried a fair amount of responsibility in the regiment, keeping 50 officers and their guests' content, and when I returned to the bank it took me some months to adjust to some of the seemingly petty and archaic practices which still prevailed. However, with hindsight, the confidence, experience and knowledge I had gained during my national service years, stood me in good stead within the bank in the years to come and on looking back I am certain I got further within the bank than I could possibly have done without my two years with the Royal Horse Artillery.

*

# CHAPTER 7

# 'And DO watch the wallpaper...'
# 1959

> **1959: Brief Timeline**
>
> Prime Minister Harold Macmillan held talks with the Soviet leader Nikita Khrushchev on a visit to the USSR; 20,000 demonstrators attended a CND rally in Trafalgar Square; The Chapelcross nuclear power station in Scotland opened; Mermaid Theatre opens in the City of London; First showing on BBC Television of *Juke Box Jury* chaired by David Jacobs; Christopher Cockerell's invention the hovercraft officially launched; Klaus Fuchs released from Wakefield prison having served over nine years for giving British nuclear secrets to the Soviet Union; Cliff Richard and The Drifters release a recording of the song 'Living Doll' written by Lionel Bart; UK postcodes are introduced for the first time, as an experiment, in the city of Norwich; Obscene Publications Act becomes law; Barclays became the first bank to install a computer; The first Mini went on sale; General Election resulted in a record third successive Conservative victory, with the slogan 'Life's better with the Conservatives'; Harold Macmillan increases the Conservative majority to 100 seats; Among the new members of parliament is Margaret Thatcher, who was 34 on 13 October and represented Finchley in North London; The first section of the M1 motorway was opened between Watford and Rugby. It was set to be extended over the next few years, southwards to Edgware and northwards to Leeds.

In March 1959 I was demobbed from national service so it was back to the bank. Barclays gave a guarantee of re–employment when returning after national service, on the understanding that you served the minimum necessary period of service. In my case it had been 2 years.

Whilst on demob leave, I was asked to visit the

bank's local head office in York to speak with the late Bernard Durham, the then local head office manager, to discuss where I was to be placed.

Bernard said there were two vacancies; one in Grimsby and one in Bridlington. Without thinking too much about the implications I opted for Bridlington on the basis that it was only 20 miles from my home in Scarborough so I could travel daily.

It was only when I started my stint at Bridlington two weeks later that I realised the Noel Cooper who was branch manager, was none other than the elder brother of Bill Cooper at Falsgrave Road Scarborough. That branch had only 4 staff when I left it; Bridlington around 20 when I started there, so Noel Cooper was much more senior within the bank than his brother. Not only was he more senior but he was also much more difficult to satisfy.

His daughter Angela attended a private school at Hunmanby some 10 miles away and, after her school summer holidays one year, Cooper called me and fellow clerk Mike Yelland into his room.

'Angela's box for school is all packed and waiting to be brought downstairs. Bring it down from the flat and load it into the boot of my car. And DO watch the new wallpaper.'

What neither of us had realised was that Angela's 'box' was like a sea chest and very heavy. Not only large and heavy, but the staircase to the flat was spiral and quite narrow. We got half way down when it became obvious the box was longer than the width of the stair spiral. We tried to tilt it and it slipped with the result that a dent about the size of an old penny appeared in the wall – and his new wallpaper. For months afterwards he kept reminding me of the dent, yet never mentioned it to Mike. But then of course, Mike lived in Bridlington and was marrying Pat, the daughter of a well-known local family who banked at the branch. That might which just might have had a bearing!

After, in my case, the constant buzz of national service, banking seemed very tame, bland and even boring and it took some time to settle down.

Travelling by train to and from Scarborough didn't fit in with banking hours and I thought a scooter would help and give me more flexibility so I bought a second hand Lambretta to transport me backwards and forwards. (I had sold the Corgi when I started my national service). Ideally, the bank wanted you to live in the town in which you worked, but in summer in Bridlington, no bed & breakfast establishments wanted semi–permanent lodgers as they could make more from the holiday punters. Also, the bank paid nothing towards lodging costs unless you were on 'relief' staff – travelling round different branches relieving for staff members who were sick or absent. With my scooter I had more mobility so occasionally I was sent to other branches on relief. I remember a few days at Pocklington, a market town between York and Hull where, in 1863, my great grandfather had owned the Red Lion Coaching Inn.

From home in Scarborough the journey was the longest I had done on the Lambretta but I arrived early and parked on the paved public forecourt only to have the manager's wife berate me when she appeared with coffee half way through the morning for parking on 'her' flagstones upon which, she claimed, the scooter had dripped oil.

Whilst at Bridlington branch I was still meeting Christine Scott and we had decided to go to ballroom dancing classes in Roscoe Street in Scarborough. These didn't last long!

One winter's day the journey to work in Bridlington on the Lambretta was extremely difficult with frozen snow on the verges and patchy ice on the roads. After about two-thirds of the journey, the Dotterel Inn stands at the highest point for a few miles around. Dropping down a steep incline the road runs under a railway bridge and directly after the bridge is a sharp left bend. I knew the road well but this day the wind had cut across and, unknown to me, the road was a sheet of ice just as it curved after the bridge.

I soon did know as I suddenly parted company with the scooter. I picked myself up, dusted myself down and remounted, riding for the rest of the journey on the grass verge and arriving around 30 minutes late.

Noel Cooper was not happy. He had phoned my father at work to ask where I was and dad had told him I had set off as usual in plenty of time. He was obviously worried. When I got to the branch my ankle was very painful and whilst I should have gone to be checked out at hospital I was conscious that I had arrived late for work and didn't want to lose more time.

For a couple of weeks I needed to use a walking stick to get around and for a long time afterwards my left ankle was very painful. It was only years later when I was having an X–ray for recurrent ankle trouble that they told me my ankle bone was chipped and a piece of bone was floating which was causing the pain. In those days, painkillers were the answer.

Memories remain of Bridlington branch; being told when I started after national service that I would be on the counter – with no cashier training at all – 'that would come later' – and noticing that when one of the bank's largest customers came to pay in – Bridlington Borough Council – the first cashier always ducked under his counter position 'to tidy my empty cloth coin bags'.

The strong room was in the basement of the bank and there was a hand operated lift to get books and cash to and from the ground floor. Books and cash were stacked in trolleys then wheeled into a cage. A sliding gate was then shut, and a handle, attached to a wheel around 3 feet in diameter, had to be turned manually to get the cage to the ground floor. At the end of the day the reverse procedure took place.

In the bank's normal scheme of things, having worked

at Bridlington branch for just over a year I was moved back to Scarborough, to Falsgrave Road where I had started my banking career and to Bill Cooper who was still in charge. In a total of 5 years, 3½ of them in the bank, I had only ever worked for a Cooper.

Christine Scott still worked there and we had continued to meet when we could whilst I worked at Bridlington but she had, by the time I moved back to Scarborough, broken off our relationship. Relationship is probably too strong a word bearing in mind what it implies these days and we should maybe call it a 'close platonic friendship'. I was working at Bridlington branch at the time – but reached home in Scarborough and that night of the parting I cried my eyes out. Yes, we were young but I had thought we might have had a future together.

\*

# CHAPTER 8

# 'That might be fun'
# 1961

**1961: Brief Timeline**
The farthing coin, used since the 13th century, ceases to be legal tender; *The Avengers* television series first screened on ITV; The five members of the Portland Spy Ring go on trial at the Old Bailey accused of passing nuclear secrets to the Soviet Union; Black and white £5 notes cease to be legal tender; The Beatles perform at the legendary Cavern Club in Liverpool for the first time; George Blake is sentenced to 42 years imprisonment for spying, having been found guilty of being a double agent in the pay of the Soviet Union; Prince Edward, Duke of Kent, marries Katharine Worsley at York Minster; Michael Ramsey enthroned as the 100th Archbishop of Canterbury; Barclays open their 'No. 1 Computer Centre' in Drummond Street, London, with an EMI mainframe computer, Britain's first bank with an in-house computing centre; Britain applies for membership in the EEC; Police launch a manhunt for the perpetrator of the A6 murder, who shot dead 36-year-old Michael Gregsten and paralysed his mistress Valerie Storie; Film *A Taste of Honey*, released; Police arrest over 1,300 protesters in Trafalgar Square during a CND rally; Acker Bilk's *Stranger on the Shore* released; The first edition of *Private Eye*, the satirical magazine, is published; Birth control pills become available on the National Health Service.

Whilst I had been working at Bridlington branch, Bill Cooper, back at Falsgrave Road, Scarborough had been promoted from clerk–in–charge to branch manager, and staff numbers had increased to around 10 – an increase from the 3 there had been when I had started working there originally.

Two weeks after I had rejoined the branch I was travelling on my scooter from home to an evening Lambretta Club party on a Saturday, when a van without indicator lights cut across my path and there was an almighty collision. I looped the loop over my handlebars and landed in the gutter. Luckily, I had been servicing the scooter that day and had removed the large windscreen. Had I not done so I could have landed up mangled inside the engine of the van, as did a good part of the Lambretta.

The ambulance crew (there were no paramedics in those days) took around 20 minutes to arrive although I could see the hospital from where I lay in the gutter and when they did arrive they asked if I could stand on the injured leg. Ouch! I couldn't and the nature of the injury was only discovered when my trouser leg was cut off in hospital. I remember asking, 'Won't I be able to get to the party?' The Sister replied, 'No, and you won't be going anywhere for a long time!'

The first question I was asked was, was I wearing my scooter helmet at the time of the accident? I had been and there was relief all round. But both tibia and fibula were protruding from my left leg and it was only then I realised that the injury was serious. The wound was bathed, dressed and a plaster cast added.

With it being a weekend there were no X-ray staff on duty and by the Monday I was in agony. The nurses seemed to think I was causing a fuss over 'a simple broken leg' but after X-rays the diagnosis was that I had comminuted and compound fractures of both tibia and fibula in my left leg. No wonder I had been in pain and there were a few red faces. Recovery was slow and led to an extended hospital in-patient stay. Both bones needed plating so each end of each bone could have time to grow and merge and strengthen with the other end.

Eventually I was released from hospital and got back to work in a full length leg plaster, but not for long. I was having weekly physiotherapy at hospital together with hot wax baths and the head physiotherapist – a customer at Falsgrave branch – said she was concerned and thought the leg was rejecting the metal plates, and inflammation and infection could be setting in. She made a phone call and I was immediately readmitted to Haldane Ward at Scarborough Hospital – then the men's orthopaedic ward – where a decision was made to operate and remove the two titanium plates, each about 6" long.

The subsequent operation to remove them was apparently not without difficulty and I woke up to find a nurse called Rachel Baker – a friend of sister Phoebe's – mopping my brow and saying, 'Thank goodness you're awake. We thought we'd lost you.' There were oxygen cylinders around the bed and there had obviously been some sort of crisis.

I learned later that during the operation my heart had stopped beating and they had to give me an injection to encourage it to restart. I am often reminded of that being my lucky day when I look at my chest and see the tiny red mark which is still there and which resulted from that injection nearly 60 years ago.

Whilst we had split well before the accident Christine did visit me in hospital although her new boyfriend, whom she eventually married, wasn't at all happy and threatened to leave her if she visited me again.

As my left leg had ended up 1½ inches shorter than the right, ballroom dancing was out and whilst I did attempt it occasionally at formal dinners I probably looked, and certainly felt, like a lopsided elephant.

The body can be a magnificent thing and over the years it adjusted to the 1½ inch difference. Yes, initially and over the years I have had back pain but that was bearable with pain killer tablets and it was only very recently that the problems might have resurfaced, although that will be covered in a later chapter.

Barclays had to do without me for almost 9 months –

apart from the brief return in plaster before I was readmitted to hospital to have the plates removed.

After recovering and returning to Barclays at Falsgrave Road I settled down and worked hard. I was grateful for what the hospital and talented orthopaedic surgeon Mr Tupman had done for me as at one stage there was the possibility that I could have lost my left leg and during the second operation I nearly died.

After my recovery I felt I wanted to give something back to the community and was asked, and agreed, to join Scarborough Lions Club. They are a charitable organisation much like Round Table and Rotary and I was then their youngest member. At that time they had over 40 members and met in the prestigious Pavilion Hotel – in the bar of which beer was only sold in half pints – and only in silver tankards.

Since Christine Scott had moved on – she was by then engaged – I had various girlfriends, a couple of them nurses from the hospital I had got to know during my hospitalisation. One, a girl called Jean was a nurse who came from East Ardsley in the West Riding and she told me that was where rhubarb is grown. We went out a few times and she took me home one day to meet her parents and we travelled on the Lambretta. They fed us and I remember Jean taking me into the kitchen and giving me a passionate kiss. After a few months we drifted apart; we'd got to the kissing and cuddling stage but that was usually the limit in those days. Then about eighteen months later I saw her with a man and she was pushing a pram with a baby in it. We both stopped and spoke and exchanged a few words and I wished her well for the future. My passing thought was that he'd had far more luck than I had!

There was Mobelle, who worked in the office of Fairbairn and Laycock, the scooter sales and repair shop I used. She was dark haired, attractive, confident and very vivacious, and drove a Morgan sports car and whilst we went out a few times and to the odd party together we never got beyond the friendship stage.

From the Lambretta Club there was Pauline. I remember her saying very casually one evening, that whilst she felt we both might have wanted to take things further, she thought she ought to tell me that her whole family was emigrating to Australia the following month. And so they did!

Also from the Lambretta Club was Moira. Her parents were bank customers and owned a large men's clothing shop in town. She was very quiet and shy, however, she was adamant that she wanted to go on an all-night scooter rally around the Scarborough area but she didn't then have her own scooter. My pillion seat was free at the time as Pauline had emigrated and Phoebe, who often accompanied me, wasn't free. I remember Moira's mother taking me on one side and explaining that Moira was very quiet and shy and not used to boys and would I please look after her very carefully? Of course I promised I would and I would return her safely home in one piece. And I did. When I next went into the shop her parents gave me a large discount off a sports jacket I was buying, for looking after her. Moira did even better as her parents bought her her own Lambretta.

Elizabet was Dutch; lively, friendly, personable, good looking and affectionate; living with relatives in the town. I met her at what was then the Technical College on Scalby Road where I was studying for the bank exams on an evening. I can't remember what course she was taking or what her job was but she was introduced to me by Judy Nicholson, one of the bank's staff at Falsgrave Road branch. Elizabet and I got on well and went for the odd coffee but apart from seeing her after night school and having a kiss and cuddle in a wooded copse down the road, I can't recall other meetings although she might have joined me as a passenger on odd scooter excursions.

A little later on there was Margaret, whom I got to know as she was the sister of one of my old school friends who was a member of the local Vespa Scooter club. We enjoyed each other's company on and off for a few weeks but then drifted apart.

And that, I think, apart from one, brings my girlfriends up to date until I joined Scarborough Amateur Operatic Society which put on Operettas and later, Musicals, each summer at the Open Air Theatre. But I am getting ahead of myself and details of the Open Air theatre follow shortly.

The girl to whom I refer was called Linda and she was a junior theatre nurse when I had both leg operations in Scarborough Hospital. She was a tall girl, well educated; vivacious and friendly with a ready smile and curvy in all the right places. Linda became a good friend and helped me during what had been and still was a difficult time. In return I said I'd take her out for dinner when I was finally discharged from hospital and in a fit condition.

She made me laugh when she explained happenings during my operations. During the first operation a bee had landed on my toe and the theatre staff had apparently taken bets on how far it would get up my good leg. During the second operation there had been a power failure and she told me later that the surgeon had had to complete the operation by using a manual hand drill. The hospital didn't then seem to have a back–up power supply. This was the operation where my heart had stopped and she explained that this had caused 'quite a kerfuffle!'

Linda later married and many, many years later, she and her husband became bank customers.

When I was seeing her, she had mentioned in passing that her grandfather had been in the RAF during WWII, but it was only years later when I was researching my book, *'God Bless the Prince of Wales'* that I realised how heroic he had been.

*'Dennys Gillam obtained his flying licence in 1934 and joined the RAF the following year. In June 1938, Gillam received the AFC (Air Force Cross) for flying food to Rathlin Island in very hazardous conditions in a Westland Wapiti.*

*During the Battle of Britain he served with No. 616 Squadron very successfully as a Flight Commander. On September 2nd, 1940 Gillam was shot down by a German Bf 110 but he was picked up by an Air Sea Rescue launch off Dunkirk.*

*March 1942 saw him promoted to Group Captain and forming the first Typhoon Wing at Duxford. Subsequently he took command of 20 Sector 2nd TAF in April 1944. In October 1944 he led an attack on the German Staff Conference at Dordrecht which killed many of the senior staff of the German 15th Army.*

*During WWII Gillam was credited with destroying at least 9½ enemy aircraft.*

*He left the RAF late in 1945 but rejoined 616 Squadron in the Royal Auxiliary Air Force. Later he became Director and Chairman of Homfray Carpets in Halifax and Deputy Lord Lieutenant of North Yorkshire. He then returned to his farm with his second wife, the sister of Air Vice–Marshal Bird–Wilson.'*

Dennys Gillam died in September 1991 by which time I was manager of Barclay's Malton branch and lived in the village of Great Barugh. Dennys had lived in a neighbouring village and I attended his funeral which was attended by RAF top brass who provided a fly–past.

Returning to Scarborough and the Lambretta Club was a serious interest of mine in the late 1950's and early 1960's. The club met once a week for a business meeting then usually went for a scooter run as a club each weekend – usually on a Sunday. We were a respectable lot with members aged from 17 up to around 50 and this was well before the time of 'mods and rockers' who used scooters to get around and invade and seriously disrupt seaside resorts; mods normally on scooters and rockers on motor cycles. As well as the Lambretta Club there was a Scarborough Vespa Club but both existed side by side with a degree of friendly rivalry between them. Later on we amalgamated for a few social functions. One weekend there was a scooter rally at Whitley Bay and we all travelled up together to take part.

*The photo above is of a Dinner Dance held in the Palm Court Hotel Scarborough, a joint event with Scarborough Vespa Club.*

Accommodation had been booked in various guest houses and we all had a good weekend. Later we organised our own rally in Scarborough which we called 'Scoot for Loot'. The 'loot' by way of prizes, had been provided by many national manufacturers and participants came from all over the country.

The event went very well and photos and articles appeared in local and national press and the scooter journals of the day.

Another business enterprise, (remember I had sold crystal sets and battery razors whilst doing my national service), was for me to make masts from which scooter owners could fly their club pennants. These masts consisted of a telescopic chrome radio aerial rod to which I added a two way bracket I bought from BSA. This enabled the mast to be fixed in various ways to the luggage carrier most scooters carried behind the rear seat.

Before my accident, a friend, Bob Holmes – another Lambretta scooter club member – and I had decided to join the Scarborough Amateur Operatic Society which put on shows each summer at the then Open Air Theatre. Bob started rehearsals for *Carousel* but I couldn't join him as I was in hospital after the road accident. However, I did take part in the next year's production of *Rose Marie*, and in *Desert Song* the year after. During winter months the society put on a winter show as well as cabarets in various hotels. I became a member of the men's chorus where the talented and well known Leslie Sturdy was chorus master. Leslie was also organist at the Futurist theatre on the Foreshore.

I attended my first rehearsal at Gladstone Road School Hall with Bob – it hadn't changed much since I had attended the school – and a fairly strident girl's voice suddenly called out, 'Oh! It's David! Come and meet the girls.'

It was Judith Lickess, sister of school friend David of school playground wedding, and chewing gum fame, and it became clear that she was in the ballet and the 'girls' of whom she referred were also ballet members. She introduced me to them and in coming months I was invited to parties they held periodically in each other's homes.

There were two girls who took my eye, Christine Tomlinson and Eileen Watson. Christine was very quiet, with blonde hair and a quiet but pleasant personality. Her parents owned a small hotel and some of the parties were held there. Her parents always referred to me as 'the quiet one in the corner' and I suppose I was shy at that time as I was very much a newcomer to the group.

I discovered before too long that Christine had a boyfriend and they eventually married.

Eileen was dark haired, very attractive and vivacious but I discovered she was 6 years older than me, so at first I felt a little inhibited, especially, as at the parties she also seemed to have a regular boyfriend.

However, I felt the breakthrough came when Lilian Hainsworth, the ballet mistress stipulated that the men's chorus all had to be able to dance a proficient polka. Because of the road accident my dancing skills were less than non-existent but Miss Hainsworth told Eileen to 'teach the men how to do it.' So Eileen took us all in hand as a group and taught us to do 'a reasonable polka'. From rehearsals we usually went to the pub. The Northway was favourite as it was relatively near and Eileen and I gradually got to know each other better and gradually became closer. I remember Fred Coulthard, another member, enthusing over her appearance and I said, 'Hands off. She's mine.'

Coming up was Barclays' annual weekend at the Royal Hotel which bank staff, partners and friends from all over Yorkshire attended. I asked Eileen to accompany me to the dinner on the Saturday night but as she then worked at the Royal Hotel as a receptionist she had to seek permission from Esmé Laughton, wife of Tom Laughton who then owned the hotel. The Royal then had a deservedly good reputation and, these days, would have been at least a 4 and possibly 5 star hotel. Eileen was given permission so she attended the dinner with me.

Back to the Open Air Theatre, and after rehearsals in winter and spring, performances were held on Monday and Thursday evenings in the summer. But if either, or both, were rained off before the interval we all had to be available on the following night for a repeat performance. If it did rain, the policy was to try to keep going until the interval. That way we didn't have to give a repeat performance the next night. Also, costumes sometimes got very wet so we were issued with two of everything. It reminded me of national service!

The majority of the 200–300 cast members were amateurs with only the main principals being professionals.

On performance nights Eileen and I used to walk to Northstead Manor Gardens where the Open Air theatre stood, and still stands although it is somewhat different these days. By then the miniature railway had closed for the night so we walked along the track, under the railway bridge and backstage to the dressing rooms. Sometimes we ate out before the performance; sometimes afterwards.

Many years later we were invited to the official opening of the new Stephen Joseph theatre, which had taken the place of the Odeon cinema in Scarborough. During the evening we met actress Julia McKenzie. We mentioned the Open Air Theatre and the 1960 production of Rose Marie, in which she appeared as a principal in the early days of her career. I was in the men's chorus and Eileen was in the ballet – but we were both amateur performers whereas Julia was professional.

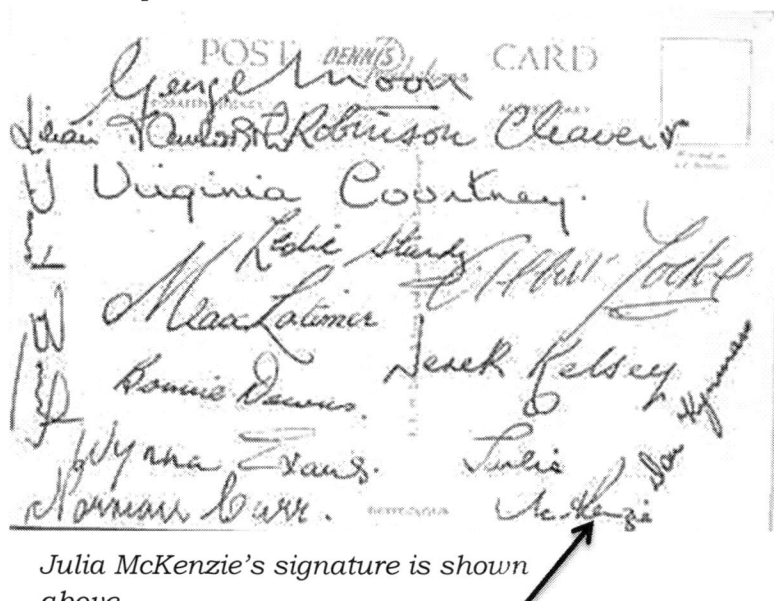

Julia McKenzie's signature is shown above.

Up came actress Maureen Lipman with whom Julia had arrived, to take her away to meet other guests and as they walked away Maureen was heard to say to Julia, 'Who was that couple you were talking with?'

Julia responded, 'Oh, we were all in Rose Marie together at the Open Air Theatre in 1960!' Fame indeed!

By chance, on the internet I came across the postcard on the previous page containing autographs of the principals of that show.

Back to our Rose Marie performances at the Open Air Theatre and I found the Mountie's hat I had been allocated was too large so I had wedged it with tissue paper. At the time we Mounties were at the front of the stage in a long line, all singing the chorus of the Mountie's song:

*On thru' the hail*
*Like a pack of angry wolves on the trail,*
*(We are after you) dead or alive*
*We are out to get you dead or alive*
*(And we'll get you soon.)*

The heavens opened – not with hail but with torrential rain – the paper in my hat dissolved and my hat slowly descended, lower and lower, until it fell over my eyes and ears. I thought no one would notice as there was a lake between the stage and the audience, but the eagle-eyed director Albert Locke, together with his ever present binoculars, was in the front row of the audience and took me to task after the performance.

Eileen and I started meeting more regularly and we became much closer. During this time her father, whom I had never met, died in Shildon, County Durham, and this left her widowed mother, brother Dennis, and sisters Heather, Kathleen and Stephanie, who all lived in or not far from Shildon.

By that time Prudence, the latest Lambretta, which had been completely rebuilt after the road accident, had been replaced by an Austin A30 – by today's standards a tiny car – bought from another member of the Operatic Society, Joe Boag. In turn I sold Prudence to David Robinson, yet another member of the Society.

Late after one Open Air Theatre performance Eileen and I were in the Austin on Marine Drive in Scarborough having a cuddle and I proposed. She surprised me by her response,

'I never intended to marry... but that might be fun.'

I took that for a 'Yes'. Kissing and cuddling was all that went on, as in those days, sex before marriage was taboo although I suppose it did happen and many stretched things so that they participated once they were engaged. But even then, where? Most of us lived at home with parents – in Eileen's case it was in Scarborough with friends of her parents and most parents would not then have allowed shenanigans under their roof. Hotels filtered their guests carefully and certainly, two people with different surnames, or even looking as if they were not married with the girl flashing a Woolworths 'wedding ring' would never have been allowed to share a room.

How times do change! I was surprised to read in a newspaper recently that an official survey had indicated that in 2015 full sex was considered completely normal and usual after an average of only 3 dates!

Apart from advising our families, we kept the engagement to ourselves for a few weeks until we found a suitable ring – and it wasn't from Woolworths! Eileen loves pearls and we found what she wanted when we looked in Lynn's antique shop, then in Ramshill Road in Scarborough. It had been an antique gentleman's thumb ring in gold, consisting of diamonds and pearls. It needed reducing in size for Eileen's much smaller finger and then cost the princely sum of £25. Going through insurance papers I found a valuation of the ring in 1991 at 60 times that figure.

The Saturday we collected the ring we were going by coach with members of Scarborough Amateur Operatic Society to Pickering to see a production of Brigadoon by the Pickering society, so we announced our engagement, and showed the ring to our friends.

We decided to marry some months ahead – on 27th March 1963 – as in those days there was a useful tax benefit by marrying before the end of a tax year. The time sped by and we married at St Luke's Church, where I had been christened, had attended Sunday school so many years before, had rung the church bell to announce the invasion, and eventually, in my teens, had become an altar server. The bank told us not to buy a house as we wouldn't be in Scarborough long, but to rent, so we managed to find a newly converted top floor flat in West Park Terrace, Falsgrave. The flat was ideal with 2 bedrooms, kitchen, lounge and bathroom and Eileen left her parents' friends and moved in before our wedding.

*Our wedding, 27th March 1963*

The flat had no lift so access was by many stairs but the location was convenient for the branch, for the local shops and not further than a brisk walk to the Royal Hotel where Eileen still worked. Our wedding day on 27th March 1963 was wet, but all went well and we had a reception at Scalby Manor Hotel, then run by the well-known local Shipley family. Brian Shipley greeted us when we arrived from the church, thrust a large sherry into each of our hands and said, 'There you are. You'll both need that to relax you.'

The day continued to go well and we were due to leave late afternoon for our honeymoon. We had planned to travel in the Austin A30 to Hull where we had bought tickets for a ballet Eileen wanted to see the following evening. We had then planned to drive on to Mousehole in Cornwall for the rest of the week before returning to Scarborough and back to our respective jobs.

I had had the car serviced by a local garage run by a part disabled retired RAF engineer in Newby.

'Will it be OK?' I asked him when I collected it.

'Aye. It should do you,' he replied, not too confidently, I thought.

Very naïvely, but coming from Scarborough where accommodation was easy to find out of season, we had expected the same to apply elsewhere. Of course it didn't!

We arrived in Hull and we started looking for a room for two nights starting at the 4 star Royal Station Hotel and progressing slowly downwards to small guest houses. Everywhere was full. Hull wasn't a seaside resort with seasons. It was a 52 week a year, commercial and industrial city.

Eventually, the owner of a very small guest house took pity on us and said, 'You can have the bed-settee in the lounge if you like – once the family and other guests have finished watching TV!'

We declined politely and could just imagine the sniggers from other guests so we decided to go for a meal then return to our flat in Scarborough. We would then make proper arrangements for accommodation, set off the following day for Swan Lake, the ballet for which we had booked in Hull, then travel down to Mousehole in Cornwall, the day afterwards.

On the way to Hull the car had been making some disturbing noises but these got even worse and louder on the way home to Scarborough and the car started groaning as if it was in extreme pain. We eventually got to the top of Staxton Hill – an extremely steep 1 in 3 hill about 7 miles from Scarborough when, what only I can describe as an explosion appeared to come from the car's engine bay and the engine stopped. I continued down the hill with only the brakes to slow us down. With hindsight, it was a good job that my knowledge of cars was very limited in those days.

The main A64 Scarborough to York road ran across the bottom of Staxton Hill and we were able to coast over it into the car park of the Hare & Hounds pub.

There were lights on in the pub and the sound of voices but it was after 10.30pm; then the time for village pubs to close.

I knocked loudly on the door and carried out a conversation with a voice inside.

'Please can we use your phone? Our car has broken down.'

'No. Go away. We don't have a phone.'

'But you must have. There are phone wires going through the top of this door. Please open the door so we can talk.'

'No. Sorry.'

And that was that. There were no mobile phones of course in 1963 but I recalled an RAC emergency phone being situated about half a mile away towards Scarborough. So I locked my new wife in the car and I started walking, waving a white hanky as I went.

I hadn't gone 100 yards when a car pulled up. Talk about luck! It was John Morley, a friend from my school days. John was a teacher by then and was associated with the St. John Ambulance Brigade for many years. He was returning from a conference.

I got in, he swung the car round and we rescued Eileen and our luggage and we were on our way.

'Where do you want dropping?' said John.

'Well, we're heading for Falsgrave.' I said.

'So am I,' said John and it transpired that he was dropping off St John's equipment at their offices – only two doors away from our flat. The gods were on our side.

He dropped us at our door, we thanked him profusely and we climbed the stairs. What a racket! There was a party going on in at least one of the flats and the noise could be heard from the street.

We opened our flat door and were greeted by noise, music, merriment and about eighteen intoxicated party goers. Bob Holmes, my best man, came forward.

'Hello David; Hello Eileen; come in and have a drink!'

But the sink was full of dirty glasses and crockery and there was not a clean glass, cup, saucer or anything, so we had to set to and wash our own glasses.

We had a drink but we were both shattered after the journey, excused ourselves and went to bed – to sleep. It was a disappointment but there would always be another day.

The following morning Bob knocked on the bedroom door and poked his head round. He had arrived on his scooter to take Heather, Eileen's sister to the railway station. That morning I got up, dressed and caught a bus to the garage to tell the owner the sorry story.

'Aye. I'll pick it up for you from the Hare & Hounds, Staxton. Mind you, it was on its way out but I really did think it would have lasted you.' Then, looking on the bright side, he said, 'Of course, it was better to go at the bottom of Staxton Hill than the top, or even down in Mousehole!'

I didn't correct him that it had 'gone' at the top of Staxton Hill.

I then went to tell my parents. Mother's expression

when she saw me at the door said it all. I think she'd thought I was coming to tell her the marriage was over already.

We had no telephone so later that day I caught the bus back to the garage to hear the verdict.

'Aye lad. It's a bit worse than I thought. The crankshaft has broken and the force has sent it right through the crankcase. Ye'll need a reconditioned engine. That'll cost ye about £50.'

That was the end of the honeymoon. The meagre funds we had saved, had to go to pay for the car repair.

After our marriage Eileen continued working as a receptionist at the Royal Hotel but she found she was working more late shifts which meant we weren't seeing much of each other as I was at work between roughly 8.45am and 5.30pm whereas she started in the afternoon and worked through until 10.00pm.

A further aggravation was the then head receptionist who, needing to prepare a staffing list for the coming months, asked Eileen to 'guarantee' that she wouldn't become pregnant over the coming months. We felt this was an impertinence Eileen couldn't answer so she started looking for another job.

There was a marriage bureau in Scarborough and she applied and was offered a job there. On her first day she was pointed towards a chair and told that was hers. 'The last 2 girls to use that chair ended up pregnant,' she was told.

Some months later Eileen became the third!

Barclays' Falsgrave branch had been expanding for a few years and now had more staff. The premises had become too small and as the building stood on a corner - on one side was a private house and a butcher's shop was on the other, neither owner wanted to sell so it was decided to expand upwards, into the bank flat. It had been gently hinted to Bill Cooper that he should find a house in which to move and the bank would provide a mortgage. Many months later after deciding there as nothing on the market which suited him he decided to buy a new property which was being built at Cloughton about 6 miles north of Scarborough.

Eventually this new house was ready for occupation so Bill and his wife could move out of the bank flat and rebuilding the branch could then take place. Because the branch improvements involved incorporating what had been the flat into the branch, there was no way we could have continued to work there whilst the work was in progress and for such occasions the bank owned a portable branch; effectively a large wooden hut.

Agreement had been given by the Council for this to be installed on the car park of the Crown Tavern – further up Falsgrave Road on the Scalby Road junction with Stepney Road. The 'hut', which is actually a bit of a misnomer, was single storey and larger in floor area than the actual branch had been, but in winter it was desperately cold.

Bill Cooper tended to be a bit of a miser where expenditure was concerned and one day, in walked the bank's inspectors.

Very quickly they complained of the cold, the staff complained of the cold and the manager was instructed to go out and buy half a dozen electric heaters. He assumed the inspectors' expenses budget would meet the cost but they told him to debit it to the branch profit & loss account which pleased him not one jot.

After a couple of weeks the inspection was nearing completion and for some time it had seemed to me that whilst the manager was keen to recommend female staff for additional salary 'merit rises', only one favourite male had ever got such a payment.

It was customary at the last stage of a branch inspection for the district inspector – in those days Ralph Connell – to interview all the staff individually. When it got to my turn I answered the usual questions then he asked if I wanted to raise anything.

'Yes, sir,' I said, 'please can you tell me what you have to do to merit a merit rise?' This seemed to flummox him but he looked at his papers and said, 'Ah. I think I know what you mean. Where do you see yourself next in the bank?' I told him I wanted securities experience. This was nothing to do with locks and keys but a pre-junior management role whereby legal documents were drawn up to secure a loan or overdraft to a customer, by the customer lodging 'security' – life policies, deeds, stock exchange holdings and so on. At Falsgrave Road the manager did the little securities work that there was so there had been no chance of me getting experience – even had he been prepared to give it.

Ralph Connell appeared to sympathise with me and said that whilst he would do what he could, he was not making promises.

Within 2 weeks of the inspectors leaving the branch, Bill Cooper called me into his room and told me that HE had recommended me for promotion to the securities department at St Nicholas Street branch which, in those days was effectively Barclays' Scarborough head office. There was no mention of me raising it with Ralph Connell but only Ralph could have planted the seed in Bill's mind.

I was to start work at St Nicholas Street in 2 weeks' time and replace Barry Brookes who was moving to York. Les Barker was then in charge of the securities department but shortly afterwards he left to become a head of a department at the new fledgling Barclaycard at Northampton. Roger Griffin transferred from Oxford to join the branch to head the securities department. Eighteen months or so afterwards Roger moved on and I took over as head of the department and Marjorie Rice joined me.

An advantage as head of department was that I was next in line to the branch office manager whose job I deputised for in his absence. Also, on Saturday mornings I would effectively run the branch as he chose to work very few of those. This was more useful experience being gained for the future.

By this time the refurbishment of the Falsgrave Road branch was nearing completion and a new office manager, Frank Kitching, had been appointed to the branch in the hut. Frank was a perfectly reasonable, sensible and friendly man but for some reason – possibly in the past their paths had crossed – he and manager Bill Cooper did not get on.

Whilst the outside of the branch hadn't changed apart from redecoration, the interior was completely new and took in 4 floors including the basement.

Bill Cooper then astonished me by making a special request that I be allowed to move back to the branch temporarily to supervise the move back from the hut to the refurbished premises. He argued that I had assisted in the original move, knew the original branch (even though it was now completely different), and that Frank was new to the branch. Somewhat surprisingly, this was agreed.

Preparations took place during the week, which meant my temporary absence from St Nicholas Street branch and the move itself took place over a weekend.

It would normally have been Frank's job to organise the transfer back to the 'new' branch but Bill Cooper's insistence had carried the day.

The move back went smoothly and the branch opened on the following Monday morning in its original, but refurbished, premises. I returned to St Nicholas Street and contractors moved in to dismantle the wooden hut and store it until it was needed elsewhere.

The move provided useful additional money for the staff involved, as the weekend removal work was all paid at overtime rates.

Around this time, Eileen was sorting the remaining boxes of belongings we had moved with us into the Falsgrave flat and she had come across some mementoes and letters which I had kept from my days with Christine Scott. By then Christine had married and she and Hanson, her husband, would shortly move to the West Riding. When I got home from work Eileen said, 'You won't be wanting these now I suppose?' and I probably confirmed that I wouldn't. Christine and I had been close friends but by then we had both moved on. However, with hindsight, I would have preferred to keep odd items as mementoes of an earlier time, although it was not a big issue and I could see Eileen's point of view.

I had known Eileen had returned the items but not the circumstances as at the time I had been working at St Nicholas Street branch.

Apparently Christine had kept her mementoes of our time together and she later related the story of how she had received back items she had given me.

On the day Eileen had gone into Falsgrave Road branch it was busy and whilst another cashier became free Eileen indicated that she would wait for Christine. Christine recalled that on seeing Eileen waiting she was quite apprehensive wondering what the visit was about, and when her till was free, Eileen stepped forward and pushed the bag of photos and mementoes over the bank counter and said, 'I don't think David will be needing these now so you'd better have them back!'

After Eileen had left the branch, Christine's next customer, who had heard it all, commented, with a smile on his face and a wry grin, 'What a way to get the brush off!'

At St Nicholas Street branch to which I had been transferred, a Mr WC Stainton was branch manager. He was due to retire after I'd been at the branch a few weeks and it was rumoured that a John Baker, who was then in Grimsby, would take his place.

John's reputation preceded him but I find as I see and I saw a larger than life character. He didn't suffer fools gladly and could be bluff and gruff but he treated me well and I learned a lot from him.

A few days after he arrived he asked me to 'go home' with him to meet his wife. I told him I was busy and shouldn't leave the branch but he brushed it aside and said there was always another day for the work to be completed. And anyway, he was the branch manager.

He had bought a flat in Scarborough's South Cliff area which had magnificent views of the North Sea, and when we arrived he offered me a whisky. At that stage I hadn't ever drunk a malt whisky and when he asked if I wanted anything with it and I suggested 'ginger' he remonstrated and said, 'You should never drink malt with anything – except maybe a little water. You need to savour the flavour of the malt.' So, water it was; it was a very valid point he made and on the occasions since then when I have had a glass of my favourite Lagavulin malt, John's face always comes into mind.

John discussed the branch and the staff and his own career and said he was going to introduce tropical fish into the branch and what did I think of it? I can't remember how I replied, but in those days banks were rather sterile places where customers came in, did their business and left.

John however, as usual, was one step ahead and said, 'If a customer comes in to see me, or Ken Forrest the lending manager, or you in securities, and we are busy, he or she sits down and waits. But tropical fish are calming and soporific.

He then asked what I thought of having curtains in the branch. At that time there were large bare arched windows surrounding the banking hall. His thinking was that banks were seen as serious business places a little like a solicitor's office – but to attract the then burgeoning market of guest houses, small hotels and business owners, we needed to make the branch more customer friendly. So curtains appeared.

His third ploy was to provide newspapers and magazines for customers to read while they were waiting. Up to that point the branch had bought the Financial Times, and Yorkshire Post – but for management and staff consumption, to look up share prices and exchange rates and so on. Not for use by customers.

A few weeks later I was working in securities department and John walked in one lunch time. He sat down and started placing obstacles all over the desk.

'Imagine this is a field gun, at sea level, and you want to fire over this hill, 300 feet high. And the hill stretches back for 3 miles to your target. How would you do it?'

He had been an officer in the army towards the end of WWII and was still in the territorials.

For national service I had been trained as a TARA – a Technical Assistant, Royal Artillery to give it its full title, so the answer was easy. Basically the angle the gun barrel was set at, needed to enable the shell to fire over the 300ft hill. And the explosive propelling the shell needed to be adequate to propel it for its 3 mile journey.

John seemed amazed. 'Not bad', he said and I seemed to rise a notch in his estimation.

Bluff and gruff John might have been but as I moved up the ladder through the bank he kept in touch and, when he retired, he occasionally visited me at whichever branch I was then working.

Scarborough Lions Club of which I had been a member since 1961, ran many charitable and fund raising activities, one of which was an annual coal and cash collection. We would leaflet a given area before we visited the next day with a borrowed coal lorry. We shouted, 'Coal, cash or coke!' and householders gave us a bucket of coal or coke, or a cash donation. There were very few houses with central heating in the 1960s.

At one house we were told we could empty a large, but then unused coal bunker to the back of the house. Member David Dennis decided the only way to effectively get the coal out was for him to crawl into the bunker, then from there, to shovel it out. It worked, but when he emerged he looked like one of the then very popular Black & White Minstrels.

It was only much later that I learned that David had been involved in the Dunkirk withdrawal and had been badly injured and left for dead on the beaches. He was very lucky to be alive.

We then had to transfer this coal to sacks and redeliver it to needy households. In odd cases we felt we were being laughed at. At one, a large man with superb biceps and obviously very fit, stood back as we struggled in with a sack of coal. 'Put it there mate,' he said without making an effort to help.

On the lead up to this coal event we had a committee event one evening. Eileen was then pregnant and when I got home she calmly said, 'I think we've had a burglar!'

'Have you called the police?' I asked.

'No', she replied. Luckily she took it all very calmly as it could easily have upset her pregnancy.

We reported it to the police although the only thing I can recall having been taken was a large rubber torch.

It seemed, according to the police, that the burglar had come up the fire escape or over the roof from an adjoining building, then got in to our top floor flat through the bedroom window which was part open for ventilation. There were large muddy footprints all over the lemon counterpane of the bed and it seemed he had been disturbed, then had disappeared the way he had come in. Eileen remembered she had gone to the bathroom nearby and noticed the bedroom door was shut and that's when she discovered someone had entered. He (I assume it was a 'he' from the size of footprints) had obviously heard

Eileen moving and had quickly disappeared the way he had arrived.

The police took a statement and used fingerprint powder but as far as I know nobody was ever caught.

Our daughter Susan Lynne was born on 3rd March 1964. It wasn't an easy birth and Eileen had been confined to bed for some weeks beforehand which meant her missing Open Air Theatre Shows in which she had been involved for many years.

The bank said they felt I could now be in Scarborough longer, having moved to St Nicholas Street branch on promotion so we looked around and after getting back-word on a bungalow we had been keen on at Mere Valley, near Seamer, we found and bought a new 2 bedroom bungalow at Osgodby Crescent, with the bank providing the mortgage.

However, faults in the property became apparent so the developer, Jack Bradley, arranged a site visit and rolled up one morning in his Rolls Royce. He was very amenable, and accepted there were faults and gave us the choice of exchanging the property for any other similar property on that development, or on a new development on which he would shortly be starting work. This was very fair and we therefore moved to Osgodby Grove with the builder paying all removal costs and fees.

We hadn't been in the new house a couple of days when we noticed steam coming out of the fireplace surround and smoke percolating through the floor boards. I phoned the fire brigade for advice and they said, 'OK. We'll send someone out to have a look at it.'

Within 10 minutes we heard a bell (sirens then hadn't been introduced) and a fire engine complete with crew arrived.

They wanted an old pair of woollen socks which they put on the burning fire and before long the smell of burning socks joined the smoke coming up from the floor boards. We were told that there was no immediate danger but that the smoke was caused by a down–draught from the chimney.

The property had early central heating which used a Baxi boiler which fed radiators, but there was an underfloor pipe which was supposed to suck in air from the foundations below the floor, to feed the fire. The pipe which had been installed ended very close to a wooden joist and the firemen felt this caused a possible future fire risk.

Off the firemen went after telling us they were classifying the 'fire' as a 'false alarm with good intent'.

The following day we called the builders in who had to take up a few floor boards to extend the pipe to the required length.

They then investigated the steam which was still percolating into the lounge. This entailed removing the fireplace and they discovered that some workman hadn't tightened the nuts from the water supply to the back boiler. The nuts were tightened, everything was put back in place, and the central heating worked much more as had been intended.

The bungalow itself was far easier to manage with it not having stairs like the flat and we set about decorating and planning a new garden.

All woodwork had been painted and glossed and walls had been emulsioned but we decided we would prefer wall paper. We chose a fairly heavy paper, and bought an intriguing wall papering machine and we were away.

This machine consisted of a wooden base on which was fixed a tray to hold the paste. To one side of the tray there was a wooden roller which held the roll of wallpaper. There was a sponge roller which fitted over the centre of the tray and two stainless steel tensioning rollers each side.

Once it was set up all that was required was to pull the wallpaper through from under the second tensioning roller. It came out ready pasted and by pulling sufficient to provide one vertical length of wallpaper, I climbed up the steps fixing the paper to the top of the wall, adjacent to the previous piece and brushed down the paper to prevent blebbing, then Eileen fitted it at the bottom and trimmed the spare paper.

It was quick and efficient and we soon had the hall decorated.

Until the following morning.

We awoke, opened the bedroom door and saw all the wall paper lying in heaps on the hall floor.

We hadn't realised that the newly emulsioned walls should have been sized before wall paper was added.

When we eventually got the interior decorations to our liking we turned to the garden. Turf had been provided but we needed extra paths so were heaving piles of hardcore, then mixing cement and laying the paths. We then added flowers and plants to provide some colour.

Susan was then about 4 years old and like all little girls, she was interested in ballet. As Eileen had been an amateur classical dancer herself it was natural that Susan would be encouraged.

Susan Richards, who later became a very good friend, had started a ballet school in the then Christ Church Hall in Vernon Road in Scarborough. Susan started lessons but after the first or second she was adamant she wouldn't go back. When Eileen managed to get out of her why not, Susan said, 'Because a boy keeps pinching my bottom!'

Finances just allowed us to have our first family holiday – unless I count the aborted honeymoon in Cornwall – and we booked a caravan on the Norfolk Broads for a week.

It was early in the season and the caravan was on the damp side. This was not surprising as for the entire week it rained. Our first purchase was a pair of wellingtons and a plastic rain coat for Susan, and she sat on the end of a pier happily fishing in the rain.

We had a trip to Skegness, and elsewhere, but Susan caught a cold and after about 5 days we decided to call it a day and drive back home.

Around this time we had acquired a dog, a cross between a spaniel and a labrador. We had been assured he wouldn't grow any bigger but he just grew and grew and got to the stage where he was too strong for Eileen to handle. He was a lovely animal we called Scamp but we reluctantly found a good home for him where he could roam on the cliffs and we often saw the new owner who assured us Scamp was leading a happy life.

Around that time a girl from work was trying to find homes for kittens born on the farm her parents ran. We went to see them and took home a tiny black bundle of fur we called Mischief who was with us for 11 years.

A couple of years went by and a new small development of dormer bungalows was being built at Lebberston, about another mile further out towards Filey. These houses were much more spacious than the Osgodby bungalow, so we moved to Lebberston. This gave us another new garden to prepare.

In 1971 I was told I was being promoted to head Barclays' large Parliament Street, York, securities department.

Before I left Scarborough branch we had a routine inspection and Ralph Connell was again in charge – the same inspector I'd spoken with at Falsgrave Road branch. At that time Eileen and I enjoyed music from theatrical shows and particularly the musical *Robert and Elizabeth* – the story of the Browning family. I hadn't realised, but I must have been humming one of the tunes as I worked, when Ralph said, 'That's from the show Robert and Elizabeth. Did you know that York Amateur Dramatic Society are putting it on? Have you seen it?'

I told him we hadn't but I must have been humming it from the long player we had at home.

It transpired he was treasurer of the York society and we went to see Robert and Elizabeth. Over future years we saw many others at York's Theatre Royal including a memorable production of Lehar's, *Land of Smiles,* all of which we much enjoyed.

My promotion was imminent and it was goodbye Scarborough and hello York...

\*

# CHAPTER 9

# Gliding high
# 1970

### 1970: Brief Timeline

The half-crown coin ceased to be legal tender; The National Provincial Bank and Westminster Bank merged to form the National Westminster Bank; A Boeing 747 landed at Heathrow Airport, the first jumbo jet to land in Britain; Rolling Stone Mick Jagger was fined £200 for possession of cannabis; The Prince of Wales joined the Royal Navy; Paul McCartney announced his departure from The Beatles; Chelsea and Leeds United drew 2–2 in the FA Cup final at Wembley Stadium, forcing a replay; British Leyland announced that the Morris Minor, in production since 1948, would be discontinued; Three civilians were killed and 10 troops injured when British Army soldiers battled with IRA troops in Belfast; Dockers voted to strike and a state of emergency was declared; The last issue of grog in the Royal Navy was distributed; Tony Densham, drove the 'Commuter' dragster, to set a British land speed record at Elvington, Yorkshire, averaging 207.6 mph; BBC Radio 4 first broadcast consumer affairs magazine programme *You and Yours*; British Petroleum discovered a large oil field in the North Sea; The first Page Three girl appeared in *The Sun;* The ten shilling note ceased to be legal tender; Richard Branson started the Virgin Group with discounted mail-order sales of popular records; Nijinsky became the first horse for 35 years to win the English Triple Crown by finishing first in the Epsom Derby, 2,000 Guineas and St Leger.

So we moved to York, buying yet another new house – at King's Acre, Appletree Village – near to Heworth on the northern outskirts of the city. There were a number of Barclays' branches in and around York at that time, as well as the Bank's York local head office, and Appletree Village was favoured by a number of bank staff as a pleasant place to live not far from the city. The house was a 3 bedroom semi-detached with a garage and with oil central heating.

Susan attended Tang Hall School and decided she wanted to take up ballet again so we enrolled her for lessons at a ballet school in York. There were no comments this time about boys pinching her bottom.

At that time the bank's Parliament Street branch was being modernised within its existing historic facade. Like Falsgrave Road branch, work couldn't take place with the builders mingling with staff so the branch operated from temporary premises in Stonebow. This was a comparatively new development which had been built so tenants could develop their own space. As the bank was only there temporarily – possibly up to 2 years – the interior was quite spartan and what I do remember was the colossal noise levels which echoed around the place bouncing off the bare concrete walls. This was a real distraction when our work could be important, complicated and concentrated.

Also, running a department more than twice the size of Scarborough's, and four times as busy, was a challenge and in this respect Pam Varlow, my deputy, was a real help and became a good friend. At Scarborough we had had the time to check and double check everything we did so we knew all the formalities were in order before the bank's inspectors made surprise visits.

At York there was much more pressure and no time to check. Everything had to be right the first time.

There was in excess of 50 staff in the branch – around double that at Scarborough so again this took adjustment. The branch was responsible for sub-branches at villages, Acomb, Haxby, Murton (for the Cattle Market) and Heslington (for York University).

The branch manager was Charles Evans. He had two lending managers Fred Tomlinson and John Lawrence and two office managers, Mike Saul and Mike Yelland. There was also an elderly accountant, Harry Prince, who had worked at the branch for many years and who was nearing retirement.

Decimalisation was soon to arrive on 15th February 1971 and this almost coincided with the branch becoming fully computerised. The bank had a special department geared to instruct and train the staff in the new methods and the local computer manager was Ted Pickering with whom I had worked at Falsgrave Road branch in Scarborough a number of years previously. Ted visited branches giving talks, training and advice, particularly on the changes in routine the computer would make necessary.

At that stage I knew virtually nothing about computers as the securities department had always been operated manually, but Charles Evans, whom I suspect knew even less about them than me, called me into his room one day to say he didn't want the bank's team in the branch as he wanted everything keeping 'in-house', so he wanted me to deal with all the in-branch training. This was an extremely unusual and tall order. I was expected to train the entire staff in something for which I had received no training myself and if we got it wrong the results could be catastrophic.

He was adamant so as a starter I prepared and gave the entire staff a talk – a key part I stressed being that the information put into a computer had to be accurate; that this was paramount and if you keyed garbage in, you would get garbage out.

As the bank's local head office was then in York and I met some staff who worked there most lunchtimes, I quietly remarked to a friend that I was in a predicament. The bank's fully trained team was being side tracked and, without training, I was being expected to step into the breach. I felt that could not be good for staff training or morale, for the general good of the branch, or, for me.

As I had hoped, word got back to the directors and very quickly a special London team was called in to arrange the training for our branch. I gathered that, for face-saving reasons, this had been explained to Charles Evans as 'a change in head office policy'.

One of the perks of working at York was that the local Racecourse was a customer and each time there was a race meeting they needed us to count the cash. There was a lot, as credit cards were in their infancy and debit cards didn't then exist. The racecourse secretary accepted that this was not a 'normal' transaction so we were paid overtime to count the cash after normal banking hours. However, the racecourse allocated a number of tickets for the next race meeting to our staff. Eileen and I had already planned to be away on holiday but my parents normally came to visit and look after the house while we were away and yes, they would be delighted to go in our place. I cleared this with the race secretary and my parents looked forward to the event.

When we returned they were full of excitement at having attended the meeting and we thought they must have had a win.

'No', said mother. 'It was where we were sitting. Right in front of the Queen.' Our cash counting session had certainly made my parents' day.

The then Archbishop of York, Lord Coggan, frequently came into the branch to deal with personal affairs and he was referred to me when management was engaged or when his requirements concerned stock exchange purchases or sales with which my department normally dealt. As well as three management rooms the branch had an additional, very small interview room which I used when necessary and this became known amongst staff as 'The Archbishop's Room'. Lord Coggan was a very friendly and genuine man and left York to become the 101st Archbishop of Canterbury from 1974 to 1980.

Known for his warm welcome, he is commonly credited with remarking that, 'The art of hospitality is to make guests feel at home when you wish they were.'

A 1967 survey revealed that York Minster, and in particular its central tower, was close to collapse. £2,000,000 was raised and spent by 1972 to reinforce and strengthen the building foundations and roof. During the excavations that were carried out, remains of the north corner of the Roman Principia (headquarters of the Roman fort, Eboracum) were found under the south transept. This area, as well as remains of the Norman cathedral, re-opened to the public as part of the new exhibition which explored the history of the building of York Minster.

Some lunch times I used to have a quick sandwich then walk to the Minster to watch the renovation work. The areas the contractors were working on were obviously like building sites and they even had a miniature train running on tracks snaking through the Minster to bring in supplies and take out rubble. It was a colossal engineering undertaking being carried out to underpin the main tower and prevent its possible collapse.

By 1972 I had passed the remaining subjects of the then Institute of Bankers final examinations Part 2. There were two parts to the examinations – each consisting of 5 subjects, and all of which had to be passed. The bank's policy was that you couldn't get to management proper until you had passed all your exams. However, when you did pass them their tune changed to, 'Yes, exams are a requirement but on their own they don't guarantee promotion.' I suppose this was fair as exams alone could create a very unbalanced type of bank manager.

A colleague at the branch had finished his exams at the same time so between us we bought cakes for the staff which were distributed by the branch messenger when he did his afternoon tea round.

I was then a qualified Associate of the Institute of Bankers, the exams then being accepted to be of degree standard so I could legitimately claim I had caught up my old school friends who had gone on to University. Later, in the mid '70's, I was elected to Fellowship – which was an honorary award after I moved back to Scarborough and chaired the local Institute branch.

Whilst work at York branch was enjoyable it could also be stressful. Each June and December, whilst day to day bookkeeping was done by computer, the bank charges and the interest customers had to pay on borrowings, or receive on deposits, all had to be worked out manually. This was done by management and, whilst I was not then officially classed as management, I was included. About half a dozen of us did a normal day's work then stayed on until maybe 10.00pm at night manually assessing and calculating all these bank charges. This could go on for 3 weeks or so and was very tiring on top of a normal day's work.

On one occasion before we started that evening's charges work I was feeling very fragile and was obviously not well. I was locking the strong room door when Charles Evans had obviously had a tip off as he visited the strong room and commented that he felt I was not well and should see my doctor. I did so and the doctor insisted I have 3 weeks off work to recharge my batteries. Had I not done so I suspect a full blown breakdown might have followed.

On occasions in 1972 the branch was without electric power. Candles, and lamps powered by butane had been provided by the bank but these wouldn't power the computers, adding machines and other equipment powered by electricity.

One period of electricity shortages started on 16th February 1972 and a press report of that day announced:

*'Many homes and businesses will be without electricity for up to nine hours a day from today, the Central Electricity Generating Board has announced.*

*Miners now into the sixth week of their strike over pay, have been picketing power stations and all other sources of fuel supply in an attempt to step up pressure on the Government.*

*From today, electricity will be switched off on a rota basis between 0700 and 2400 every day. It means consumers will face longer power cuts, up from six, to nine hours.*

*The shortage of electricity is forcing more and more factories and businesses to close. The Government has already imposed a three day week and a report in today's Times newspaper claims 1.2 million workers have now been laid off.*

*Imperial Chemical Industries, one of the country's leading industries, has given a week's notice to all its 60,000 weekly-paid staff as a precautionary measure.*

*Miners walked out on strike on 9 January in their first national dispute for 50 years. They are demanding a £9 a week pay rise on top of an average wage of £25.*

*The government offered a 7.9% deal – just below its unofficial 8% pay ceiling – but the National Union of Mineworkers refused to put it to the vote. The National Coal Board has since withdrawn the offer.*

*On 9 February a state of emergency was declared. Two days later a committee of inquiry was established under Lord Wilberforce to investigate the miners' demands.*

*All 289 pits in England and Wales are closed and the miners say they are prepared for a long fight.'*

Shortly afterwards, the York branch refurbishment was complete, and we had a weekend to move back into the refurbished premises in Parliament Street. After my 'practice' at Falsgrave Road I was well versed in what was required.

Before the move back, the new branch had been open for customers to have a guided tour and certain staff had been trained and given background information.

A mezzanine floor above the counter area had a castellated effect topping the half height walls, and the girls who acted as 'tour guides' to the visiting customers had been told to say that 'this castellation represents York's city walls and battlements, and the history of the city'.

One girl, unfortunately, when taking a group of customers round referred to the wall being the 'castration representing York's city walls and battlements'. She couldn't understand why titters arose amongst her group.

One day Fred Tomlinson, then the senior lending manager and later to become district inspector, came up to me and said 'I've dropped a piece of carbon paper in your waste paper basket. Destroy it when you've read it.' He winked and moved away. I retrieved the sheet of carbon paper and visited the toilet to investigate. It had been a new sheet of carbon paper which had been used to provide the copy of a recommendation that I be considered for an office manager's job which was arising shortly, in a small branch in Hull. It was a nice touch of Fred's to let me know unofficially and whilst I wasn't offered that particular job, shortly afterwards there was talk that the office manager – by then Mike Saul had moved on and John Angell had taken his place – was due to get an assistant and subsequently I was appointed Accountant of the branch – my first managerial appointment. This helped take some of John's work load off him as the previous accountant had retired some months earlier. Allen Ferguson, who by then was number 2 in securities department took over my previous role as head of the department.

Whilst working and living at York, Eileen and I had taken up gliding at the Wolds Gliding Club near Pocklington. We both enjoyed this, especially as the bank paid the subscription. With hindsight it was a cheek to even ask them but the branch already had a subscription allowance although gliding wasn't on the list so I felt 'if you don't ask you don't get'. The application came back from local head office rubber stamped.

*'RAF Pocklington was an operational flying station of the Royal Air Force during the Second World War, forming part of Bomber Command, and operating primarily Wellington and Halifax bombers. The station, adjacent to the town of Pocklington, opened in 1941, and was closed in 1946. After a return to agricultural use, the station now forms an industrial estate and a restricted use airfield for the Wolds Gliding Club.*

*Work started on RAF Pocklington in August 1940, with the design for grass runways, along with hangars, technical buildings and administration blocks. This was changed during construction to include three concrete runways. Late into the building of the three runways, it was realised that the runway 3 (1,300 yards) posed a threat to the nearby village of Barmby Moor, and so was abandoned in favour of a fourth runway.*

*The first occupants of the site in 1941 were the Royal Canadian Air Force unit of 405 squadron, operating Wellington bombers for 84 raids in eleven months, during which 20 aircraft failed to return.*

*In April 1942, the squadron changed to Halifax bombers, flying a further 20 raids before exchanging bases with the Royal Air Force 102 squadron from RAF Topcliffe, and were the last unit to occupy the station until its closure (although a personnel holding unit was briefly based at the base in 1946).*

*The station transferred to Transport Command the day before the end of the war, operating B–24 Liberator aircraft before their transfer to RAF Bassingbourn.*

*Following the closure of the station, it was mostly returned to agricultural use, with the hangars used as grain stores, but subsequently the technical area became an industrial estate, and a large number of buildings still stand.*

*The original runways are still in use by the Wolds gliding club, who secured the lease to the airfield in 1971, and purchased it outright from the land owner in 1983. Former members of 102 squadron still hold reunion events at the gliding club.'*

We used to go to the club at weekends and although, as members, we were always guaranteed a flight, we also had to take part in other duties such as helping out with launches – holding the wingtips of a glider and running with it until it was airborne to prevent the wing tips clipping the ground, and checking before take–off that no one was trying to land. The signal 'All clear above and behind' had to be passed back to control.

I have never come across anything as peaceful, tranquil and satisfying as gliding itself. After the launch there is just the gentle whisper of air over the wings, with a bird's eye view of the landscape below.

However, before I could go solo the bank moved me to my next branch, the location of which had been a bit of a mystery.

John Angell the office manager at York with whom I worked closely in my new accountant role, took me on one side and told me I was being lined up as office manager of a branch he couldn't name. However, if I got the atlas out and looked for the most inland port in the country I'd have my answer.

There were no home computers or Google in those days but I did get an atlas out and found that:

'*Goole is a town, civil parish and inland port located approximately 45 miles from the sea at the confluence of the rivers Don and Ouse, historically within the West Riding of Yorkshire.'*

So, Goole it appeared to be, and Goole it turned out to be when I was called for interview to local head office in York a couple of weeks later.

*

# CHAPTER 10

# Loitering on the docks
# 1973

### 1973: Brief Timeline

Edward Heath was Prime minister; The United Kingdom, entered the *EEC*; 400 children attacked British Army troops in Derry, Northern Ireland; The Open University awarded its first degrees; Rail workers and civil servants went on strike; Pink Floyd released *The Dark Side of the Moon*; VAT came into effect in the UK; 1.6 million workers went on strike over government pay restraints; The British Library was established; The James Bond film Live and Let Die was released; Football League president Len Shipman called for the government to bring back the birch as a tactic of dealing with the growing problem of football hooliganism; The IRA detonated bombs in Manchester and Victoria, King's Cross and Euston railway stations in London; The film *Don't Look Now*, containing one of the most graphic sex scenes hitherto shown is released; Princess Anne married Captain Mark Phillips; Peter Walker, the Secretary for Trade and Industry, warned that petrol rationing may have to be introduced because of the oil crisis in the Middle East; As a result of coal shortages caused by industrial action the Three-Day Week came into force; Pizza Hut opens its first UK restaurant in Islington; Noel Coward died.

So, Goole it was and the gliding had to take a back seat because of the distance involved and the need for us to sell our York house and buy another one. In the event, the house we bought was another new one at 21, Roseacres, Hook, near Goole. We called it 'Moorings' and it was our first detached house. We also had another new garden to knock into shape.

The builder had a bit of a reputation as a sharp operator, and whilst we had understood the interior of the entire house would be decorated within the agreed price, the wording was not entirely clear. The builder had other ideas and said decoration was extra. Not only that but his prices were steep and funds were limited so we let him emulsion all the ceilings and paint the woodwork and we set about decorating the walls ourselves.

The house was in an ideal position being in the quiet village of Hook with the house itself having river rights and fronting the River Ouse. We had superb views of the river from the upper rooms although views were not as good from the ground floor as at the end of our garden, before our river rights started, was a high embankment, recently increased in size as a flood defence. This embankment had a path on top and was a public right of way.

Large vessels used to plough up and down the river, to and from Selby further upstream. Some of these boats were Russian and when their crews were on deck and we waved we just got surly looks from the crews.

One weekend Allen Ferguson, a friend, and colleague from my York days came to visit and we spent a few happy days exploring the area and reminiscing about our York days in the bank where Allen was still working.

The branch manager at Barclays' Goole branch was Ken Forrest with whom I had worked whilst in Scarborough. There he had been lending manager so we knew each other and there was no ice to break.

Whilst we lived in Hook, about a mile from Goole, the bridge which was to form part of the new M62 motorway to Hull in the east, and Leeds and beyond in the west (this was not the Humber Bridge) was being constructed. What a sight it was to see the massive structure slowly progressing to the stage where it was opened to traffic.

Another bridge, much nearer to where we lived was the railway bridge which went over the River Ouse. One of the vessels which plied up and downstream each day collided with it and engineers decided it was unsafe for rail traffic until substantial repairs had been carried out. This led to alternative routes having to be taken by rail passengers.

I had been a member of York Lions Club and whilst I was still travelling from York to Goole each day, I attended a meeting of Goole Lions with a view to transferring my membership. Goole members were very welcoming and we made lifelong friends with some of them. Two particular friends were John and Margaret Fawbert, both sadly now not alive. As well as being a Lions member John farmed at Hook and he was also a magistrate.

One weekend Eileen and I had been taking a quiet amble round the port of Goole taking in the different ships in the port. We later bought a Goole newspaper and Eileen remarked on the number of people – all seemed to be women – who had been fined for 'loitering on the docks'. Next time we met John and Margaret and knowing he was a magistrate she asked him somewhat naïvely if we would be fined as we had been taking a gentle stroll in the area.

He burst out laughing and said he thought not. He explained that the loiterers were prostitutes seeking custom at the docks from the many seamen who were crews on ships, either recently arrived or soon to sail.

One of the Lions' fund–raising activities was to approach a firm of antique valuers to run our own version of the BBC's Antique Road Show programme.

A national firm of valuers agreed to help and John and I were on the Lions' organising committee so we held a meeting one evening at his farm. During the discussion the valuer said that many valuable pieces had been found in the past in the strangest of places, and cited an attic as one.

John piped up, 'We have an attic full of stuff I haven't looked at for years. I was thinking of clearing it out and burning the lot at the Lions next bonfire night event. There'll be nothing of value up there.'
The valuer was persistent and told John, 'You can never be sure. I don't want to intrude but if you have a pair of steps can I have a quick look? It would be criminal to burn a piece with some value.'

John agreed, somewhat reluctantly, and the three of us trooped upstairs to the attic access. The valuer climbed in and started shuffling around. Luckily there was electric light so he could see what he was doing. Around 10 minutes later he called down to John, 'I see what you mean. A bonfire is probably the best place for most of it. But this picture might earn you a few pounds.'

'Come off it!' said John. 'Stop winding me up. Anything it would fetch would more than be eaten up by your commission and I'd end up owing you!'

The valuer climbed down from the attic. He held up a somewhat battered and very dusty painting of a horse and suggested it go to auction. John was not convinced but the valuer was practised in the art of persuasion and John, somewhat reluctantly, eventually agreed.

Over 40 years later I cannot remember exactly what it fetched at auction but I remember being with John when he opened the envelope from the auctioneer and he took out the cheque.

'Blow me down,' he had exclaimed. I was wondering how I could afford a new roof for the barn. This'll pay for the whole farm to be reroofed – and leave some change!'

Not only did John have a valuable painting in the attic. He also had what he described as a 'Domesday Clock' which was fixed to the farm kitchen wall. It ticked continuously like a Grandfather clock and John said that if it ever stopped ticking it meant nuclear war was imminent and he had to 'get down to the bunker'. He wouldn't say more, or where the bunker was, but he was a JP and could have been one of a limited team of officials who would deal with any nuclear disaster in the wider Goole area from a hidden but secure bunker.

Many years later when discussing this 'clock' with friend Bryan Overall, he did a little delving and came up with a release of details of what could well have been a version of John's 'clock'.

## 'Public Warning in case of Nuclear attack

*In built up areas mains power operated sirens would be operated by signals sent from the Central Control Post. These were often WW2 siren locations and in addition to the receiver they had a control panel to allow local activation. During peace time the fuses to the siren motor were removed to prevent accidental operation.*

### First Generation Receiver

## Second Generation Speaker

*The warning receiver is the part of the system most visible to the general public. The normal telephone line at the premises carried the carrier signal from the telephone exchange to the receiver. In rural areas there were no power operated sirens so receivers were located in premises such as Post Offices, Shops, Pubs, Vicarages or the homes of Police Officers, Council Officials or magistrates, who were deemed "responsible" people trusted to warn the local population by the use of hand sirens, whistles, maroons and gongs. Around 18,000 Warning Points existed nationally.*

*Additionally, a warning receiver was likely to be found on the premises of about 4,000 Warning Recipients who would need to know if it were safe to go outside. These would be Fire Stations, Police Stations, Hospitals, Public Utilities and Feeding stations to name a few.*

*In the earlier carrier receivers, the instructions for the Warning Points were given on a card held in a drawer in the base of the unit. In the later receivers, the instruction card is retained under a clip on the speaker.*

Whilst there are extensive lists of old nuclear bunkers which were situated throughout the country the nearest to Goole appears to be at Wawne, some distance away and equidistant between Hull and Beverley. It seems highly unlikely that this was the bunker to which John would have had to go in the case of nuclear emergency. However, there were probably numerous more 'local' bunkers and it was to one of these that he might have referred.

If any reader can shed more light on John's nuclear clock or the whereabouts of the bunker I would be very pleased to hear from them.

Most social functions in Goole, including those arranged by the Lions, were then held in the Baths Hall. This was actually the town swimming pool but for functions, a wooden floor was placed over the pool itself and we attended some very enjoyable events there, including the annual Lions' Charter night.

The main Barclays branch was in Aire Street but it closed long ago, with the branch now operating from the main Boothferry Road.

As well as Aire Street the bank then had sub-branches in Pasture Road and in the village of Snaith. Howden was across the river but hadn't a branch and in view of new business coming to the area Ken and I discussed the possibility of recommending the opening of an additional sub-branch. This was eventually agreed by local head office and after a build–up period was successful, although I understand it also closed some years ago.

The branch's largest customer by far was the Croda Group. These days it would be nigh on impossible, and even in those days it was most unusual for such a large business account to be domiciled at a small branch, but apparently, the chairman of Croda had started off banking at Goole when his business was an infant and he wished to continue his association with the branch. Also their head office was at nearby Cowick Hall – not far from our Snaith sub-branch run by Goole branch.

At one stage legal documentation needed preparing for Croda's various companies and as Goole didn't have a full-blown securities department I took the blank forms home one weekend together with a manual typewriter and prepared about 20 legal forms and copies.

These needed signing and sealing by the company's board members so Andrew Gibbs – chairman of the York local board of the bank and also a member of the bank's main board of directors in London – arranged to make a visit in a week or so. The forms had already been sent to the company for perusal and had been accepted so it was merely a matter of them being signed and sealed on the day.

Ken Forrest had to attend a meeting at Cowick Hall at around 10.30am then Andrew Gibbs and I were invited at 12.30pm for lunch.

It was agreed that Ken would go by himself, and that Andrew Gibbs would call to the branch to pick me up around noon. He pulled up in, I think an Armstrong Siddeley or possibly a Humber car. Whichever, it was very plush and comfortable inside, and he then drove us out to Cowick Hall and had a general chat which I realised afterwards could have been a sounding out by him to assess when he felt I might next be due for promotion.

We got to Cowick Hall, I arranged for all the papers to be signed, we had lunch and Andrew then returned to York whilst Ken Forrest brought me back to Goole branch.

A few weeks later I got a call from local head office asking me to attend an interview with the possibility of me moving to the much larger Trinity House Lane, Hull branch. I had been at Goole branch fewer than 18 months.

The interview confirmed the job offer which I accepted. This entailed yet another house move but before then we had to cope with a number of days at the Goole branches when electricity supply was restricted.

*'The national power cuts continued until 7th March 1974. The 'Three-Day week' was one of several measures introduced by the Conservative Government (1970–1974) to conserve electricity, the generation of which was severely restricted owing to industrial action by coal miners. The effect was that from 1st January until 7th March 1974 commercial users of electricity were limited to three specified consecutive days' consumption each week and prohibited from working longer hours on those days. Services deemed essential (e.g. hospitals, supermarkets and newspaper print) were exempt. Television companies were required to cease broadcasting at 10.30 pm during the crisis to conserve electricity.'*

On the days when there was no power the bank had to rely on butane gas and candles for lighting. There was no power for electric calculators, comptometers and so on.

Whilst living at Hook, in 1974 we witnessed the Flixborough disaster from the river bank behind our Hook house. We heard explosions and saw clouds of smoke from the tragedy around 30 miles away.

*

# CHAPTER 11

# Our American dream
# 1974

> **1974: Brief Timeline**
>
> New Year's Day was celebrated as a public holiday for the first time; 12 people were killed when a bomb exploded on a coach on the M62 motorway; Architect John Poulson was jailed for five years for corruption; Alf Ramsey, who guided England to World Cup glory in the 1966, was dismissed by the Football Association after 11 years in charge; Inauguration of full electric service on British Rail's West Coast Main Line through to Glasgow; An explosion at a chemical plant in Flixborough, South Humberside, killed 28 people; A bomb exploded at the Houses of Parliament in London, damaging Westminster Hall; Brian Clough was dismissed after less than two months as manager of Leeds United following a disappointing start to the Football League season; The Fast food chain McDonald's opened its first restaurant in Woolwich, London; The Guildford pub bombings at *The Horse and Groom* and *The Seven Stars* killed five people; The second general election of the year resulted in a narrow victory for Harold Wilson; Judith Ward was sentenced to life imprisonment for the M62 coach bombing; Lord Lucan disappeared after the murder of his children's nanny; The Birmingham Six were charged with the Birmingham pub bombings; Former government minister John Stonehouse was found living in Australia having faked his own death.

After being at Goole only 18 months I was promoted to a similar position, but in the much larger branch of the bank in the historic part of Hull, in Trinity House Lane. In those days it was a magnificent, spacious building with much polished mahogany.

My first few days travelling were hairy to put it mildly. I was driving from the small, comparatively peaceful and traffic free town of Goole, to the City of Hull and at the time I was travelling, traffic rush hour hold-ups started around 10 miles from the city.

The branch manager was Eric Poppleton and his lending manager was Neil Aitchison. I joined the management team at number 3 as office manager and there was an accountant – Alan Milner – very much like the setup in Parliament Street, York where I had ended up as the accountant.  At 6' 2" there are not many people taller than me but Alan Milner must have been at least 6' 4"  and it was a strange feeling for me to look up to someone else in the physical sense.

My role consisted of making sure the books all balanced, numerous returns were submitted correctly and on time, cash was correct and balanced, staff training, arranging courses, making staff available for the various departments in the main branch and sub-branches, holidays and holiday cover; all on top of the general day to day nuts and bolts of running a bank branch which had to be taken care of.

When I first arrived Eric Poppleton said he'd give me a few days to settle in then would have a word. From that meeting it transpired that the previous man in my role had been at the branch many years and came from Hull. He appeared to be revered by all the staff and was moving to a small branch in the Hull area as branch manager.

Eric said that he felt there was scope to improve branch systems and he was convinced I was the person to do it but he didn't want things to be done as if an earthquake was hitting the branch. It had to be softly, softly.

This was fine with me and was the method I would have chosen.

I only learned later that an earlier office manager, (not the one I'd replaced), had been an ex-bank inspector. From inspection he had moved to Hull but had apparently upset the staff so much that a staff petition had been circulated and passed to management and then on to the directors. It must have carried much weight as the man in question was removed within a very short time and transferred to the smaller Scarborough branch, whose equivalent office manager had then been promoted to Hull. It had been the ex–Hull man who had been in Scarborough when I was in the branch securities department. I had usually got on with him satisfactorily so whether there was more to the story, I do not know. In any case, whatever had happened had taken place at least 7 years previously, and before Eric Poppleton had joined the branch, so Eric was maybe just passing on to me guidance he had himself been given.

Anyway, the Hull staff seemed to accept me and my methods, which were certainly more progressive and forward looking than those of my immediate predecessor. And the graphs were part of them!

We bought a house, another new one, Pantiles, Saunders Lane, in the village of Walkington near Beverley. This was a village full of character with a good mix of long-standing villagers, and people passing through for a year or so, as were we. There was a duck pond and the village had a vibrant social life.

One annual spectacular event in which we took part in the village was the Hayride where most villagers – and that included newcomers – dressed up in costume and took part. Thousands more lined the route and donated to the charities the Hayride supported. The event was organised by Ernie Teal, a leading light in the village, who recalled:

*'The Hayride traditionally took place each year on the third Sunday in June. It consisted of a colourful procession of splendid heavy horses pulling ancient farm wagons; superb light horses and vintage carriages.*

*'The cavalcade, accompanied by hundreds of collectors*

in beautiful Victorian costumes, left the stack yard and fields of Northlands Farm at 1.00pm.

'Sadly, by 2006, the dwindling size of the procession and the logistics (plus associated costs) of organising Hayride were a serious cause for concern. Rather than allow the event to simply fizzle out the decision was made to go out in style and 2007 saw the 40th and last Hayride procession.

'Since then the village has continued to stage a variety of events on the third weekend of June (barn dances, garden parties, cricket tournaments etc.) and support for local charities continues too.

'The procession made its way through the village of Walkington and onwards to Bishop Burton, one of the most delightful villages in the East Riding of Yorkshire.

'We stayed awhile on the verdant Green at Bishop Burton to rest the horses and sing those beloved songs of yesteryear, concluding of course with Land of Hope and Glory (sung with great gusto and feeling by everyone, spectators included).

'We then left Bishop Burton and proceeded to Beverley's glorious Westwood to be greeted again by very enthusiastic crowds. We sang to them and dwelt awhile before proceeding through the historic North Bar into the beloved town of Beverley – one of the highlights of the occasion. 'We then turned homeward bound for Walkington and arrived back at Northlands Farm generally at about 6.00pm, bouquets verbal and flowery were given out; pies and peas were eaten; the horses fed and watered.

'Yet another Hayride was over.

'Our Victorian Hayride was absolutely unique; nowhere else in the length and breadth of Britain did such an event take place. In more than thirty years of its existence, we have raised over £250,000 for charity, of which we are rightly proud.'

*Above: Ernie Teal, front right, leads the Hayride*

After a few months at the branch it became apparent that Neil Aitchison was under some pressure with the lending side of the business which was growing rapidly, and for which he was responsible. I needed lending experience so I could cover Neil's absences on holiday, courses and so on, but up to then my responsibilities had been to look after the nuts and bolts of the administrative side of the business. So I took on the role of part–time lending manager whilst retaining the main responsibilities of my own job. There was a spare interview room into which I moved and the accountant, Alan Milner, then passed down to department heads the less important parts of his job. This enabled him to support me.

After a year or so at the branch the bank brought in a scheme where holiday could be 'banked'; you could hold a proportion back from one year to another and then take a longer break. Sister Phoebe had lived in America – latterly in Las Vegas – for many years, and wanted us, to visit so we went for 4 weeks in 1976. It was the 200th Anniversary of America and this was reflected all over the country with flags, bunting and events.

Phoebe was working for a large American bank at the time and she arranged for me to call in and see their manager during our visit.

In England, at that time, all interviews were conducted in private in a closed room but in America, this very senior manager had a desk in the banking hall with the American Stars and Stripes flag behind him, and as he met and interviewed customers others passed freely to and fro. It was certainly a different experience.

He and I discussed the differences between banking in the two countries. At that time for instance, all lending in America was by way of loan; overdrafts were unheard of.

We travelled widely, mainly around Nevada and Arizona sightseeing, and at Havasu; the old London Bridge that had been dismantled, exported, imported, and reconstructed, stood proudly; the river Colorado having been diverted to flow under the bridge. Red London buses and telephone kiosks and post boxes, and restaurants with waitresses dressed up as old English serving wenches – but with very American accents – were all the rage.

I had my English banking qualification papers with me and on our travels I decided to call into a few bank branches to see what chances there would be of a job in America. I was amazed. Starting off by doing the equivalent to my then job in Hull, but in the USA, then with promised accelerated promotion, an offer of far better banking perks than in England and of double my then salary, I received at least four offers where I could have started within a month. Housing was much cheaper in America than England, new cars were around a third of the cost of those in the UK, and petrol was much cheaper. And from spending a few days in an American school, daughter Susan appeared to be well ahead of her year group...

All were positives and the three of us were sorely tempted. So why didn't we 'up sticks' and emigrate? Simply because it suddenly hit me hard that when Phoebe and her family had emigrated many years previously my parents had expressed some concern, so I had promised them that I would never leave the UK permanently and would always be around to help them in their old age. And so we were... even if it was the end of our American dream.

When we returned to the UK and Walkington, and me to the branch, Eric Poppleton kept looking at me with a quizzical look. Eventually he said with a smile, 'You're having a job settling back aren't you?'

I admitted I was unsettled and told him of the American dream.

That seemed to settle me; the dream had been just that; a dream. However, from old staff appraisals I was looking at recently I saw the bank had listed me for consideration for any future American vacancies which might have come up.

Until then, direct road access to the south bank of the Humber was via Goole so for a long time the Humber Estuary was a barrier to trade and development between the two river banks. For over 100 years the construction of a bridge or tunnel across the estuary had been talked about. In the meantime a couple of ferry boats transported passengers from one bank of the Humber to the other. One of these was called PS Lincoln Castle, a coal–fired side–wheel paddle steamer, which had ferried passengers across the Humber from the time of the Second World War until 1978. She was the last coal–fired paddle steamer still in regular service in the UK.

Later, she served as a pub at Hessle, and then as a restaurant under permanent dock in Alexandra Dock Grimsby.

The bank held accounts of various involved bodies – The Humber Bridge Board and some of the contractors, so we were kept informed of progress and I recall how sections of the bridge for the Northern part, were built in a yard on land then floated to the bridge site near Hessle.

*'Approval for the construction of a suspension bridge was eventually granted in 1959 with the passing of the Humber Bridge Act and the creation of the Humber Bridge Board, although it was not until 1973 that work finally began.*

*The reasons why a suspension bridge was chosen were twofold. Firstly the Humber has a shifting bed and navigable channels along which a craft can travel are always changing; a suspension bridge with no support piers in mid–stream would not obstruct traffic in the estuary. Secondly, because of the geology and topography of the area, the cost of constructing a tunnel would have been excessive.*

*Work on the construction proceeded for eight years, during which time many thousands of tonnes of steel and concrete were used and upwards of one thousand workers and staff were employed at times of peak activity.*

*When traffic first crossed the bridge on 24th June 1981 many local dreams were fulfilled and similarly many people will have happy memories of the bridge's official opening on 17th July 1981 when H.M. the Queen performed the formal opening ceremony.*

*The bridge 'opened up' both socially and economically, two previously remote and insular areas of England, improving communication enabling the area to realise its potential in commercial, industrial and tourist development.*

*The bridge has saved many millions of vehicle miles and many valuable hours of drivers' and passengers' time – an important factor not only for the drivers and operators of commercial vehicles but also for tourists and holidaymakers who would have had to travel around the estuary to reach destinations in the region.'*

Whilst the bridge was being built – and long before anything appeared above ground, we used to visit Hessle at weekends and gaze at the enormous holes in the river bed, surrounded by reinforced concrete structures to keep the river Humber at bay, and from which many months later the massive northern supports of the bridge would emerge.

Sometime later, after my return from America and Eric's mention of me having difficulty settling down, at a full staff meeting he announced – unknown to me in advance – that I would shortly be leaving and moving to Bridlington as lending manager.

I was then in regular contact with a friend, Richard Benson, who worked at local head office and who was looking for a job similar to the one I had just heard I was apparently leaving. I mentioned the possibility to Richard, and he made enquiries to see whether he was in the frame to move. The proverbial hit the fan!

The directors weren't happy that the moves had become public before they were ready to formally confirm them so Bridlington was out for me and Mike Yelland was given that lending appointment – the same Mike Yelland whom I had helped move Angela Cooper's trunk so many years earlier and with whom I had then worked in York.

A couple of months later Eric called me in to his room and said there was a vacancy coming up at Scarborough's St Nicholas Street branch as lending manager. John Baker was retiring as branch manager. Ken Forrest – who had been lending manager at Scarborough branch when I was last there as head of securities, and who had then become branch manager at Goole when I was his office manager there – was moving back to the larger Scarborough branch as branch manager.

It was most unusual for both top managers within a branch to be moving in at the same time and the thought did cross my mind that, having worked on two occasions before with Ken he might have asked for me to join him. Whether he had or not I never asked or discovered.

Eric looked at me. 'Hold your corn on this one,' he said.

'We don't want this one to come to grief.'

I could well have spluttered as he seemed to have forgotten that it was he who had announced to the entire staff at a staff meeting that I was moving to Bridlington!

But I did 'hold my corn' and shortly afterwards the promotion came through officially from local head office. Not only was I to move back to my hometown of Scarborough, but Richard, my colleague from local head office, was also told he was moving to Hull to take over my position.

Whilst working in Hull, I had transferred to Beverley Lions Club which was the closest to our home in the village of Walkington.

It was a busy, thriving, active club with many activities both social and fundraising. Members made fish and chip deliveries to deserving pensioners each Saturday, ran an annual bonfire and fireworks evening on November $5^{th}$, held music evenings where we learned to enjoy Mahler's music, organised an Antiques Road show type of event, similar to the one we had arranged at Goole and which I would later 'borrow' to put on in Driffield; and each year, collected, then sold, second hand books from an otherwise empty shop unit in the town.

They also organised the annual Beverley Town Carnival and Procession with a different theme being arranged each year. Individuals and members of organisations dressed up and processed through the town where a collection was taken to support local charities.

*

# CHAPTER 12

# A lost bet
# 1976

> **1976: Brief Timeline**
>
> The Prime Minister was Harold Wilson until 5 April; followed by James Callaghan; The first commercial *Concorde* flight takes off; The Queen opens the new National Exhibition Centre in Birmingham; John Curry becomes Britain's first gold medalist in skating at the Winter Olympics; Young Liberals president Peter Hain is cleared of stealing £490 from a branch of Barclays Bank; UK and Iceland end the Cod War; Heat wave reaches its peak. For 15 consecutive days, it reaches 90°F (32.2°C) somewhere in England; This is contributing to the worst drought in the United Kingdom since the 1720s; A fire destroys the pier head at Southend Pier; InterCity 125 trains are introduced on British Rail between London and Bristol; Racing driver James Hunt becomes Formula One world champion; Opening of Selby Coalfield; Denis Healey announces to Parliament that he has successfully negotiated a £2.3bn loan for Britain from the International Monetary Fund on condition that £2.5bn is cut from public expenditure: the NHS, education and social benefit sectors are not affected by these cuts; Inflation stands at 16.5% – lower than last year's level, but still one of the highest since records began in 1750; At one stage inflation exceeded 24%; Opening of Rutland Water, the largest reservoir in England.

It was less than 6 years since I had run the Scarborough branch's securities department, and, here I was, returning to my home town as lending manager of the same branch, after working in York, Goole and Hull. All promotions had necessitated house moves, although I understand that today, most staff are expected to travel each day.

When we knew we were moving back to Scarborough we looked around and were attracted to a new house being built at Field Close Road in Scalby, north of the town. This area included part of what had been the Scarborough to Whitby railway line before Dr Beeching got out his axe. The Council had apparently bought the land and was selling off plots for private housing.

It was a pleasant area, quiet, and away from the main traffic streams yet only a few hundred yards from the old, characterful village of Scalby.

We settled on this house in Field Close Road which was being built to a somewhat unusual design, and we subsequently called it 'Brindlepatch', as it was built of brindle bricks. It bears the same name to this day.

The builder was a very hard working one man band who promised faithfully he would work all hours to ensure we were in before Christmas. And he was doing well until he went to play squash one evening – and badly damaged a hamstring.

We were all geared up to move on 20th December, having sold our Walkington house. And, yes, to be fair we did move in on 20th December, but...

Some of the interior plaster was still damp, there were numerous other minor jobs to be completed, and the driveway – supposed to be raised in height before being tarmacked – was just a mass of mud and hard core with a few planks which enabled us to, just, reach the back door.

Frankly, the house was not really fit to move into but we had my parents, Eileen's mother Sarah Watson, and my uncle Percy and aunt Phyllis, all descending on us for Christmas and our move-in date had been planned in advance for 20th December on which date our Walkington house buyers also wanted to move.

We got in on the 20th – just – when there was a rap at the back door. It was the council's building surveyor who seemed incredulous that we had moved in and said he hadn't passed the house as fit for human habitation. We discussed things with him and said he should be talking to the builder; that we had paid for the house, it was ours legally and we were staying. We suggested he meet the builder and any work which needed completing could be scheduled after Christmas.

He left and we gave a big sigh of relief.

An hour later there was another tap on the door and it was Dudley Ogley, our solicitor. He was a lovely man with a cheerful disposition and very friendly persona and said he had 'merely called round to make sure we were in and everything was in order.'

He realised it wasn't but assured us that all we had to do was contact him if the remaining work dragged or problems arose.

Christmas came and went like a blur and in the New Year the Council building surveyor came back to inspect the house in more detail.

Apart from the drive which still hadn't been started, the plaster work had completely dried out and all he could find fault with was that the open tread staircase to the first floor didn't meet building regulations. Apparently the 'open' part of the tread – that at the back between two steps - was half an inch wider than regulations dictated, and he said 'a baby could get its head caught'. The fact that there was no baby, nor was there likely to be, had no bearing. The builder soon sorted the problem by tacking on a piece of inch wide softwood to the back of each tread to narrow the gap. Then after the inspector had been back and passed the stairs as being in order, the builder came back and removed the pieces of softwood which he had only fixed with panel pins. We then carpeted each tread and the thickness of the underlay and carpet made good any discrepancy.

In the meantime John Baker, mentioned during my earlier spell at Scarborough's main St Nicholas Street branch, had retired and Ken Forrest had been appointed branch manager in his place. The town then had 6 Barclays branches and sub-branches.

Ken was in the process of moving house from Goole; I had moved from Walkington having worked in Hull. The office manager, number three in the hierarchy and already at the branch, was Martin Oxby.

Ken and I had previously worked well together but not without the odd brush. He was an ex–bank inspector so did everything meticulously, looking after a smaller number of customers, but generally the larger ones. However, he must have thought highly of me as looking at my old staff appraisals he regularly gave me 'A's' in all categories. An 'A' stood for 'Performance could not be faulted and targets/objectives were exceeded in most areas.'

I looked after the rest of the lending book and when I had gone to local head office in York for interview about the job, I had been given a brief to 'build up the branch business' although I never did find out whether Ken had been given the same brief.

Whilst we shared secretaries, after a few months Di Fletcher was transferred in as my secretary. She was excellent and we worked well together and subsequently she married Tony Lowery who at that time held an office manager's position in another branch of the bank in town.

My job was mainly lending – but, typical of the bank in those days, they gave you the job and detailed training followed probably 6 months later. The branch had a steady reputation for lending to the tourist industry and this included hotels, guest houses, boarding houses and blocks of holiday flats.

The property market was then buoyant with prices rising continually and the tourist sector then had an average 16 week season although after a few years this started to decline. One reason was that Scarborough, as a seaside resort, was not surrounded by 360 degrees of potential holiday makers – but by only 180 degrees with the other 180 degrees being fish! But the main reason was the advent of affordable package tours which had become popular and through which holiday makers could go abroad for a week or two and obtain guaranteed sunshine.

The branch also had a share of farming customers.

In this, my first full-time lending role, I pondered how to build up business as my masters wanted. Who was involved in selling holiday properties, hotels, guest houses, holiday flats? Yes, you've got it in one. Estate agents, then next to them, solicitors and accountants.

In those days Norman Jackson was a partner in Edward Harland's Estate agents – a very reputable and long established Estate Agent – if then a little traditional.

In the New Year Eileen and I had received an invite to attend a party being thrown by a near neighbour. Norman and his wife Fay were there. I met them for the first time and he turned out to be a country lad, with a bit of a bluff personality but also very hearty and an excellent astute businessman.

We were introduced and when we were alone he said, 'You bloody bankers are all the same. If you were a bit more flexible we could all do business.'

I replied, 'I'm new here Norman. But I'm Scarborough born and bred. I know the town. I know the people. Try me.' And I slipped one of my bank visiting cards into his suit breast pocket.

I thought little more about it and it must have been a couple of weeks later when Norman phoned and asked whether I really felt we could work together. I suggested we should try, but on one firm condition. I said I would welcome introductions from the estate agency to lend for property or business purchases, but the bank had to have the absolute right to make the final decision. We couldn't be using the estate agency as a bank sub–branch with them agreeing to lend.

Norman agreed this was completely fair so he started making appointments for a few potential buyers and, at that time I was able to help possibly 1 in 10. It was fairly obvious why the other 9 couldn't be helped but an estate agency is not versed in bank lending technicalities so at that stage they were actually sending everyone to me who made an enquiry.

I suggested that I prepare a simple tick list for Norman and his staff so they could filter the clients they sent to me and I should, in theory, then be able to help a larger percentage of those they introduced. This would also save their time which they would not then need to spend on hopeless cases. It would also save the bank's time in vetting proposals.

This list contained questions which we would normally have asked the customer direct, had they been in front of us such as:

- What amount was being paid for the property or business?
- What percentage of this price did the client wish to borrow?
- From where was the balance coming?
- Was he/she/they able to pay legal fees and stamp duty or did they wish these to be added to the borrowing?
- Had any property they were selling already sold? If not, was it on the market, at what price and what, if any, borrowing was secured by it?
- Was there any other security in the background (eg another property already owned)?
- What were the ages of the clients?
- Where did they at present live?
- What experience had they in the business they wished to buy, (if any)?
- What were their present occupations and what were their wages/salaries?

- Would one (or both) of a couple continue to work outside the new business?
- Had they any serious health problems?
- Could the bank see 3 years trading accounts for the business to be purchased?
- If they had already been in business could we see 3 years* trading accounts for that business?
- Had the customer approached an accountant to discuss preparation of budgeted income and expenditure accounts for the business they wished to purchase, as the bank would need such budgets together with audited trading accounts to help assess viability?

*3 years accounts was stipulated to see an average flow of how the business was doing. A single year's could have been 'adjusted' to show a particularly strong position in that one year.

It was surprising how many people came to Scarborough on holiday, stayed in a small hotel or guest house and thought the owner had a doddle and that they could do better, without having a clue about all the necessary work there would be in the background.

Norman took this list and passed copies to his staff explaining the reasons behind it. As a result, introductions started coming to us which had been part filtered and where a majority of the questions had received a positive answer. That way, the agency staff's time was not wasted, or the bank's, or the client's, and much business resulted. Word spread that Barclays was the friendly, helpful bank and whilst there had, in earlier days, been an unofficial policy that 'you scratch my back and I'll scratch yours', whereby no local bank manager would poach business from another, the word 'competition' gradually came to the fore.

If we were being given targets by the bank and to achieve them, had to gain new business, it could only come by encouraging good customers of other banks to move to us; or by gaining new business through the likes of estate agents.

Another type of business where we could pass part of the vetting to a professional was in bridging loans – a form of lending which now seems to have died out. A reputable firm of local solicitors often had customers who needed to bridge the purchase of one property until the sale monies of the existing property were received.

They used to send these customers to us and, again there was a high failure rate for one reason or another. So I prepared another tick list for the solicitors, and their managing clerk vetted any clients wanting bridging loans against this list. This often meant that a client, who would lose a property if he didn't move quickly, could then have a good chance of getting it.

As an example, a local accountant, Keith McFarlane, had approached his solicitors. His wife and he had bought a flat but he couldn't settle and the ideal alternative house had come on the market but there was a contract race. The solicitor rang us, gave us the bones of the transaction, I was able to agree a bridging loan very quickly subject to a few formalities and the accountant got his property. I still see him occasionally in town and he says, 'But for you we would never have got the house we've now lived in for nearly 40 years.

John Gledhill was another example. A senior manager for Lucas Aerospace he had the chance of early retirement and he and his wife wanted to buy a sizeable hotel in Scarborough. His accountant introduced him; accounts and budgets were positive, and we were able to help relatively quickly. He and his wife made a great success of the hotel, then moved to an even larger hotel, before subsequently retiring.

I saw John recently and he said, 'We were introduced to you in 1978, you helped us, we did well in business and we've remained friends for over 38 years. I think that's first class.'

So did I, and presumably, so did the bank.

Solicitor, Robert England, was setting up as a sole practitioner in the town, having previously been in partnership after moving to Scarborough from another area. He became my personal solicitor and we have had total confidence in each other for almost 40 years and we still meet for a drink most weeks.

If we had customers wanting a solicitor we would offer to arrange a meeting for the customer or suggest they get in touch direct. Likewise, if the solicitor had a client either not happy with his bank or wishing to move from away to a local bank he would send them to us. There was never any obligation either way but it worked to everyone's benefit.

We frequently hear that bank managers used to do most of their business on the golf course. Possibly, in years gone by that was true when a bank manager was more of a figurehead, but from the 1970's that had all but changed when setting and achieving targets moved into the banking arena.

I did, of course, know some bank managers who were keen golfers but the time most had available was tied to their branches and to visiting customers. Frequently I needed to take work home, as you had to put on new business well before any increase showed in your branch returns. It was not just a matter of the number of accounts, of course, but the makeup of those accounts which counted. This also meant retaining existing business and not letting another bank poach any of the good business you already had. In some cases, of course, you had a customer who was his own worst enemy and you would encourage him to look elsewhere for help.

The bank, in its wisdom, claimed that an increase in business might only be a temporary blip so the increase had to be sustained before there was any hope of you getting extra staff or management to help deal with the additional workload.

In 1976 we had moved back to Scarborough, and in 1978 our beloved cat Mischief, whom we had had since the days we had previously lived in Scarborough died aged 11. He had been a faithful friend and, after some time we replaced him with Tschang, a Blue Burmese, whose name we took from the musical operetta, Land of Smiles, by Lehar.

During 1979–80 I became President of Scarborough Lions Club and I was also President of the Scarborough Centre of the Institute of Bankers, so for about 6 months of the year I held both responsibilities.

*This photo shows the multi seat bike the Lions rode in the Festival parade. I appear second row right, near to the Union Flag and part hidden by a balloon.*

Scarborough Lions always took part in the then Scarborough Festival parade and one year we heard that an auctioneer in Hull had a bicycle which seated, I think, 13 people. We got in touch with him and arranged to borrow it and we rode it in the parade advertising our annual Donkey Derby which was taking place the following evening.

We had one problem with the chain coming off the bike when we cycled up Eastborough – a fairly steep incline from the Foreshore up into town, but it was quickly remedied and as we cycled up town towards Barclays' main branch, Phil Woodcock, then a member of the branch securities department, opened the first floor corner window just before we cycled past and unfurled a large bed sheet on which he had painted in bold lettering;

'From Lion President to Banking King!'

Being President of the Institute was not onerous. We had a members' meeting with a speaker once a month; there were occasional committee meetings and an annual dinner to which members and customer guests were invited. This was held at the then prestigious Royal Hotel in Scarborough and involved the President welcoming those present and making a speech after dinner.

Presidents were normally branch managers and whilst I was of managerial status, my Institute appointment at that stage came about by default.

The job was normally passed in turn between the senior managers of the various banks and David Paddon of Lloyds Bank who was outgoing President, rang me one day to say it was Barclays' turn. Ken Forrest as branch manager had been offered it and for some reason he felt he couldn't accept at that particular time so he declined. David had therefore rung me and suggested I take it and I had willingly agreed, subject to Ken raising no objections.

When Ken had declined he maybe hadn't looked at the ramifications and had merely thought it would be passed on to another bank, with Barclays missing their turn that year.

I told him I had been asked to take on the role and I had agreed, subject to his agreement, but he was a little upset, probably thinking that people might query why he had not taken the job. It might have been suggested that the decision be passed to local head office for a ruling but it didn't come to that as Ken did agree; I was voted in and the year went well. A few years later at Barclays' next turn Ken was approached and at that time he was able to accept. Whilst I had left the town by then I gather he had had a good year as President.

Whilst I was at St Nicholas Street branch, extensive alterations were carried out, partly to make the top floor flat, previously occupied by the Messenger, into part of the branch. This time there was no need to move into a hut on a pub car park whilst improvements were carried out!

Eileen and I had kept up our interest in music and light opera and when we returned to Scarborough we joined SADLOS – the Scarborough and District Light Opera Society. This was not the society which had put on the Open Air Theatre shows in the 1960s and 70's but another, which started off performing Gilbert and Sullivan but then widened its repertoire to include operetta and musical shows. As well as a production in the first half of each year they also put on cabarets during the winter months – often in hotels to provide entertainment for 'turkey and tinsel' bus trips to the town before Christmas.

Irene Beagle was secretary, virtually until her death, and her son John, who was a music lecturer at a college near Middlesbrough, was musical director. Sadly, John died a few years ago.

In a performance of Brigadoon, John livened up the National Anthem which preceded every performance – to have it at the end rather clashed with patrons stampeding for last buses home! – by giving the anthem a Scottish lilt, complete with bagpipes.

Whilst I was not a performer and preferred backstage roles as well as being the society treasurer, John wanted all the clans – in groups of about a dozen – to march from the back of the then Floral Hall theatre down the different aisles and up on to the stage. For this he nominated me to be head of the Cameron clan but the wardrobe department couldn't find a kilt in the right tartan or size to fit me. Tom Martin, a Scot from Edinburgh, who directed the show, said, 'But you can borrow mine, David!'

I had never worn a 'proper' kilt before but Tom's was very heavy, comfortable and warm and had a wonderful swing with it. It was far, far better than the costume kilts the others wore. All the clans marched down different aisles and when ours reached the stage, as clan leader I had to yell the one word 'Camerons'. The recent Prime Minister David Cameron would have approved but, at that time I just thought of the local Cameron's bitter beer! And before you ask? Yes. I was dressed under the kilt!

One year the society put on the musical 'Oliver' and it was decided the cast should tour the town in costume to drum up support and obtain publicity. Eileen had a crinoline for one scene in the show in which long term friend Malcolm Pobgee also appeared in cape, top hat and with a walking stick. I was again helping back stage and looking after finances but Malcolm suggested that, as he couldn't attend and we were much of a size, I borrowed his costume for the procession round town. We walked round the pedestrian precinct handing out leaflets about the show and moved to the car park behind the Lifeboat house for the press to take photographs.

*Eileen and I, front centre, with the cast in costume - but what were these two women discussing?*

TV also turned up and the photo on the previous page appeared in the local and regional press with a short filmed piece appearing on television. We certainly got publicity and this led to good houses. I have always pondered when looking at this photograph what could the couple of women near to the van on the right be discussing?

I was treasurer of the society for a number of years and then became vice-chairman but shortly afterwards we 'modern–day gypsies' – an expression Eileen once used to the bank's directors at a cocktail party – were on the move again.

But before we move on I must mention Sue Richards. Sue was a talented ballet teacher with whom our daughter Susan had originally enrolled when we previously lived in Scarborough. Like all little girls, she had wanted to take up ballet and at that time Susan would have been between 4 and 5 years old but her course of lessons lasted for precisely one session as she said she wasn't returning 'as a boy had pinched her bottom'.

When we had lived at York Susan had got over her fear of bottom pinching and had attended a ballet class there, so when we returned to Scarborough in 1976 and she was 12, she again started classes at Sue Richard's ballet school. Eileen also attended the adult classes having been an amateur classical dancer in Open Air Theatre and SADLOS days. We became friendly with Sue Richards, who used to come to our house on a Friday evening for a meal with us and to listen to music. We had an extensive collection and she picked much of it for future ballet shows she produced.

She really was very talented having qualified in Russian ballet, and she taught from 3 year olds up to around 20 year olds, and included them all in a major production she would put on once a year. On top of all that she ran ladies' classes for the more mature.

One of her productions was Swan Lake in which Eileen appeared as the Queen. Daughter Susan was 'a little swan' where a group of around 6 'swans' started at stage right and danced over to the opposite side.

That was what was supposed to happen! In fact only 5 little swans danced across the stage leaving our Susan, on her own, at the right hand side of the stage, looking completely puzzled and bewildered.

All ended up well as the other five then pranced back again and the rest of the movement continued as planned.

I videoed the performance and always threatened to send a clip to one of the TV shows specialising in filmed and videoed bloops but was always persuaded against doing so.

At one of these dinners Sue Richards came to we were discussing something and we had a bet on some question. Sue said that if I lost I was to appear in one of her ballets. Me! One leg shorter than the other, not a dancer since my road accident in 1960, and with a movement which could only be described as 'lolloping' if I tried to move quickly?

Well, I did lose that bet and thought I'd got away with it until Sue told me a few weeks later that she planned to put on the ballet Sleeping Beauty and that Eileen was to appear as Queen and me as the King.

Luckily, from my point of view it was mainly a 'sitting' role on a throne with Eileen as Queen at my side.

The photo on the next page appeared in the local paper and later in the bank's staff magazine which then had a world–wide circulation. The comments I got! After the last night performance there was to be a party and the Scarborough Evening News had come out with a review in their evening edition. Generally it was very positive and complimentary but, without mentioning the King specifically, there was a comment about 'a rather wooden performance.' I thought I'd got off lightly.

Until, that was, the party was in full swing and the father of one of the dancers came up to me and said, 'You enjoyed the music didn't you?'

I agreed I did.

'I knew it!' he said. 'Your crown had lots of coloured

'jewels' and you were nodding your head to the music. As you nodded, the theatre lights reflected on your jewels and coloured flashes of light streamed right round the interior of the theatre!

*The photo above shows Eileen and I as King and Queen, together with the principals*

A few years later (our) Susan had left school and was working at Barclays', South Cliff, Scarborough branch. Knowing that we were likely to be moved again soon she and three girlfriends decided to rent a house in Spring Bank, Scarborough.

A little later we heard we would be moving to Driffield, some 20 miles away, so we supplied curtains, bedding, furniture and so on, to help get the girls established.

They duly moved to the Spring Bank house and we moved home from Scarborough to yet another new house being built at Beverley Road in Driffield.

*

# CHAPTER 13

# 'There's a rabbit in your room!' 1982

### 1982: Brief Timeline

The lowest ever UK temperature of −27.2°C is recorded at Braemar, in Aberdeenshire; Miners vote against strike action and accept National Coal Board offer; Unemployment in the United Kingdom is recorded at over 3 million for the first time since the 1930s; Laker Airways collapses; The DeLorean Car factory in Belfast is put into receivership; The D'Oyly Carte Opera Company gives its last performance having been in near-continuous existence since 1875; The Queen opens the Barbican Centre; Falklands War begins as Argentina invades the Falkland Islands; The Conservatives have returned to the top of the opinion polls; The nuclear submarine HMS *Conqueror* sinks the Argentine cruiser *General Belgrano*; The Type 42 Destroyer, HMS *Sheffield*, is badly damaged by an Exocet missile and sinks; Official opening of Kielder Water; Falklands War ends 14th June as British forces reach Stanley and arrive to find the Argentine forces flying white flags of surrender; Welsh miners go on strike to support health workers demanding a 12% pay rise; The Provisional IRA detonates two bombs in central London, killing 8 soldiers, wounding 47 people, and leading to the deaths of 7 horses; Margaret Thatcher rejects calls in parliament for a return of the death penalty for terrorist murder; The first child of The Prince and Princess of Wales is christened William Arthur Philip Louis; The *Mary Rose*, flagship of Henry VIII of England that sank in 1545, is raised from the Solent; The Thames Barrier is first publicly demonstrated;

When I started work at Driffield branch, I travelled each day until our new house was ready for us. The first day I got as far as Octon crossroads – about half the distance – and there was a police road block. I wound down the window and the officer said, 'Will you get out of your car please, sir.'

I did so, then was asked to open the boot. After doing so I was allowed to go on my way. Later I discovered the police were hunting for Barry Prudom.

*Prudom was the illegitimate son of Kathleen Edwards, a Leeds dressmaker, and Peter Kurylo, a soldier serving with the British Army. Kurylo played no part in Prudom's upbringing and the two never met. Prudom attended Blenheim Primary school and Meanwood Secondary Schools in Leeds.*

*Although born Barry Edwards, his name was changed to Barry Prudom in 1949 when his Mother married Alex Prudom. After leaving school, Prudom trained as an electrician, then in October 1965 he married Gillian Wilson.*

*As well as being an electrician, Prudom was also a multiple murderer, known as The Phantom in the Forest, and he became the subject of a police manhunt in what was, at the time, the largest armed police operation Great Britain had ever seen, involving 12 police forces.*

*Prudom became a fugitive after killing PC David Haigh on 17th June 1982. Before being captured he killed twice more, shooting civilian George Luckett on 23rd June 1982 and Police Sergeant David Winter on 28th June 1982. Described as an 'avid outdoorsman and firearms enthusiast' Prudom's knowledge of military survival skills, helped him evade capture for 18 days as he hid out in rural areas in the north of England.*

*When eventually found, having been tracked by 'Jungle' Eddie McGee a former SAS instructor, Prudom committed suicide by firing a single shot to his head. It later transpired that Prudom had previously attended survival courses run by McGee, and had made an extensive study of a manual on survival techniques written by the SAS veteran, entitled No Need To Die.*

There was an ironical twist to this story. Prudom was eventually cornered and took his own life, at tennis courts in Malton, the town containing the branch to which I would eventually move after working for 5 years in Driffield.

The house we bought in Driffield, Pantiles, was new and was being built on Beverley Road, just outside the town centre. There were large garden areas back and front and mature trees to the front boundary but the gardens had been a paddock and needed preparing from scratch. We asked gardener friend Ken Gill to come through from Scarborough and sort it all out. When Ken needed to compact the earth for a new lawn he used what we called 'his funny walk'. One foot in front of the other over the width of the garden, then back again adjacent to his previous walk. Backwards and forwards until the whole area had been compacted.

But I'm getting ahead of myself. My offered appointment at Driffield branch had disappointed me when Ken Forrest gave me the news while I was still at Scarborough. Driffield was a higher grade than my Scarborough job but a grade lower than previous interviews and reports had indicated I was next due for. To be fair, I suppose a doubling of my existing grade was not to be sneezed at but it was nevertheless less than I had been told I had earned.

 Another reason for wanting a higher grade was that the next step up was particularly attractive to management as it brought with it the perk of a bank car.

But in those days the bank worked in peculiar ways

and when I went for interview to local head office for this appointment which, frankly, I felt to be beneath what I had been promised, the directors had their ammunition ready.

They sprung on me that I had been picked for Driffield branch as they felt I was largely responsible for having built up the business at St Nicholas Street, Scarborough, so they wanted me to to build up business at Driffield branch as they felt it had the potential to be moved up a grade within a 'reasonably short time'. They went on to say there were few higher graded managerial retirements coming up, that managers who had moved out of the district were due to return and would be expecting the grade of job I had hoped for, and finally, that York district was likely to merge with the much larger Leeds district which had a number of managers already waiting and overdue for higher grade appointments.

They were persuasive and said that by going to Driffield I would be getting my own branch; earning a higher salary than at Scarborough; to a large degree would be my own boss and would be in a position to get the higher grade at Driffield, - but only when I had put the business on to justify that grade.

Persuasive I thought, but Driffield was an agricultural branch and farmers were always reluctant to change their bank. In some country areas the managers of the different banks had informal agreements amongst themselves not to seek to take business from each other.

Finally, the then manager at Driffield had claimed to have built the branch to its absolute optimum – although I was not to hear this until I had started work there.

A decision was needed. I said to the directors that they would be conscious that adding good business was not easy and was time consuming and also caused stress and pressure; yet extra staff members to part mitigate these factors were never made available until the new business had been obtained and branch figures had justified an increase in staffing as being realistic and not a 'flash in the pan'.

Often this assessment was not done until a future branch inspection which could be two or three years away.

I mentioned these points to the directors and asked that consideration be given to increasing staff and management backup on a temporary basis once I had reported and justified that this was needed on the basis of improving business figures.

A discussion ensued; they agreed and I started as Barclays' branch manager at Driffield a few weeks later. The usual press releases were prepared by the bank with the mug shot below accompanying them.

When I arrived at Driffield I felt the branch was quite dated in appearance but it was all on one floor so was convenient for efficient working.

On my first day I met my branch accountant, Chris Larwood. At that time the branch wasn't deemed large enough for an office manager. Chris was a pleasant and friendly man if a little insular, but he had been close to my predecessor and he took some persuading that the brief was to build the branch and, more importantly, that the directors felt this was possible.

After meeting all the staff and establishing basic systems were working well, I called a staff meeting and told them that if we could increase the size of the customer base this could reflect positively on them all. Married girls, for instance, were unlikely to be moved to another branch as, in a country area this could be some miles away from their homes, but if business could be increased in-house, there would be the possibility of them moving up within the branch.

The annual Driffield Show was approaching and the bank hired a marquee to entertain bank customers and serve alcoholic refreshment as well as teas and coffees, sandwiches and snacks.

I suggested to Chris that this would be an opportunity for me to meet customers and make myself known to prospective clients. Chris said, 'Oh you won't have any time for that. Your wife will have to prepare the food and you will run the bar all day long. That's the way it's always been done.'

I told him that now was the time to change the way 'it 'had always been done'. I had a word with the bank cleaner, Margaret Dixon, who was delighted to be asked to look after the food side on the day. She was doubly happy when I said that, of course, she would be paid for her extra work. Girls on the staff who normally worked part time were also delighted to be asked to come in to chat to and look after customers when they wouldn't normally have been at work and these changes allowed Eileen and I to be free to talk to and get known by customers and potential customers.

Back at the branch, which still had to open on Show Day, Chris was left in charge with a depleted staff. It was normally very quiet at the branch as everyone in town was down the road at the Show.

For some time Chris still appeared a little negative and was convinced that there was no chance of increasing business. He spluttered a bit and said that there 'wasn't a cat in hell's chance' of building up the branch; that my predecessor had got all the business possible and that was why he had been promoted and had moved.

I replied, 'Give me 6 months Chris. We shall see.'

Gradually Chis saw the light. I had set up graphs similar to those I started in York and whilst these flat lined at first, they slowly started to move upwards and he became a convert – suddenly realising that if the branch put business on and justified more staff, he could gain promotion himself from accountant to office manager.

From then on he was entirely positive, a great help and I certainly give him credit for helping increase, not only the size, but the profitability of the branch.

Then happened a traumatic event in our personal lives. daughter Susan had decided that she wished to move into theatre on the technical side so she had applied for a place at Mountview Academy of Theatrical Art in London. There were very few places available and many hundreds of applicants, but, possibly because she had a good CV; possibly because she had a good job in the bank which she was prepared to give up, or, most likely, just because she was very good and would have come across well at interview, she was offered one of the few places available. She was due to start at Mountview in September that year.

She and her girlfriends had decided to go to the south of France on holiday before they separated and moved on in their various careers. One day, on holiday there, they had hired bikes and were cycling on a main road when a vehicle drove straight in from a slip road, scooping up Susan and a couple of friends. They were cycling in line, with her at the end so she got the brunt of the impact.

She was taken to the French equivalent of hospital intensive care. We knew absolutely nothing about this, and Susan, when she started to come round, couldn't understand why we were not with her or in touch.

This was simply because we weren't aware. Eventually one of the other girls' parents contacted us and asked why we hadn't been in touch. Their daughters had not been badly hurt so had got in touch with their parents. Susan, of course, was not in a position to do so. These parents gave us the name of the local travel agent whom we contacted and this branch of a national firm did not cover themselves in glory; their sole response being 'she is over 18 so we don't have to tell you anything'. And they didn't.

I then made enquiries through Barclays who confirmed that Susan had taken out holiday insurance with the bank. They put me in touch with their insurance department who traced the cover and were extremely helpful, making contact with the French hospital, dealing with any language difficulties and eventually flying Susan back to Heathrow, then on to Leeds, then by private ambulance from Leeds to our new home in Driffield.

We had only been in the house a few weeks and the day Susan was due to return home was Driffield Show Day, always a very hectic day. The ambulance bringing Susan home from Leeds/Bradford airport arrived at our house in the evening just after all the show entertaining had come to an end. After embracing, very gently because of her injuries, she said the highlight of her day had been the private ambulance paramedics who, feeling peckish, had suggested stopping in York for food. Sue voted strongly in favour and they all sat in the back of the ambulance eating fish and chips before continuing the final leg of the journey.

They eventually arrived in Driffield in the evening and after our doctor had visited her and examined her the following day, he said there was no possible chance of her taking up her Mountview place in September.

Susan, however, can be very determined and she insisted she would be fit enough to be there for the start of term. As she said, she had fought hard to get the place and had already given in her notice to the bank so 'there is no way I am going to miss going to Mountview'.

She progressed well and had intensive physiotherapy and whilst she was not 100% fit by September she was fit enough to enrol at Mountview and we drove her down to

London. Her fast recovery did lead to problems much later when the suggestion was made that she had actually recovered too quickly as healing scars had covered up road gravel still deep inside her head and this and other aspects of the injuries caused her problems in years to come.

Sadly, Tschang our Burmese cat died just after we had moved house and we were without cats until, later that year we bought two brown Burmese brothers which we called Ayckbourn and Todd. The origin of their names follows later.

At that time it had been the norm for the branch manager at Driffield to be responsible for all borrowings; business and personal, large and small. Chris, as accountant, had his own responsibilities but if he could pass down some of these to a senior girl to undertake under his guidance, that would enable him to take on some of the smaller advances and leave me more time to concentrate on building the branch.

Chris accepted this willingly as it would increase his responsibilities and experience and stand him in better stead for future promotion. Likewise, the staff who took on some of his duties would be gaining more experience which would stand them in good stead.

The graphs which I had originated at York, then used at Goole, Hull and Scarborough, enabled staff to see how we were doing with internal targets – those we had set ourselves – and later, with targets the bank started setting for each branch, but which first had to be agreed each year in advance by the manager with local head office. This helped involve all staff in the progress of the branch and regular staff meetings reinforced this.

Before I delegated any borrowings to Chris I suggested we carry out a simple in-branch survey. Many private customers got their salaries on a regular day each month and some were in the habit of overdrawing a few days before this was received as weekends could intervene. There was minimal risk to the bank as the incoming salary would repay any temporary borrowing within a few days.

Probably unheard of in the early 1980's, Chris and I went through all the personal accounts and marked overdraft limits to a usual maximum of one month's income although in most cases, and depending on circumstances, these internal limits were much smaller. The customers were not made aware of these arrangements – but this prevented numerous, very small unauthorised borrowings arising before the monthly pay days and prevented 'chasing' letters having to be sent when an unauthorised overdraft occurred. Such borrowings had previously appeared on the branch daily 'refer list' which had to be scrutinised in detail, with action being taken on all accounts out of order. So, by reducing the number of entries which appeared on the list, and the number of phone calls or letters we otherwise needed to make, at least a couple of hours work a day could be saved.

Many years later the bank introduced this system as standard throughout the bank – but I like to feel we were there first with it at Driffield branch.

By passing some of my work down to Chris and by him passing some of his further down the staff, Chris gained time which enabled him to deal with personal customer interviews whilst I could concentrate on business customers.

I then worked on a similar internal limit system for business customers where we knew their cash flow was positive but where there might be a slight hiccough when month end payments–out caused a blip before payments–in arrived. To increase the business portfolio I reckoned that many new introductions could be gained by existing customers recommending Driffield branch to their friends and colleagues as 'the bank to be with', but to do this I needed to get to know all our business customers, to make sure they were happy with the branch service and to encourage them to recommend us to others.

The branch held a lot of agricultural accounts whereas Scarborough, although a larger branch had a smaller number. To get to know business customers I preferred to meet them on their own patch so would often go out to their business or farm to carry out regular borrowing reviews. This was time consuming, especially in a country area but it did pay dividends and to see a customer 'on their own patch' often gave a completely different and more positive impression, than meeting them at the bank.

One such well-established and successful farmer I visited was a Miss Latham. She had asked me to visit and had shown me round all the farm buildings and then set off at a fair trot across a field.

I followed. In one far corner was what looked to me like a cow. We got nearer and I realised it had a ring in its nose and it was taking an interest in us with some aggressive foot stamping. Gulp!! I assessed my position and thought, 'If SHE can walk the field without being upset by a bull, then I certainly can,' and I followed her as quickly as I could.

We got to a gate at the far side and let ourselves out and she turned round and smiled. 'OK Mr Fowler. I was just testing you out. You've passed!'

She had planned it all along.

We got along fine after that and she had obviously mentioned me positively to friends and colleagues as new agricultural business approaches started to appear.

Progress was plotted on the graphs and the different coloured ink lines moved slowly upwards.

Margaret Dixon was the cleaner who worked in the branch each evening and when Eileen had back problems we asked Margaret if she would give us a morning each week to help out with the house cleaning at home, for which, of course we would pay her ourselves. She willingly agreed and was happy to have the extra work.

One day Margaret was in the dining room at home when Eileen heard a bit of a commotion. She came downstairs and Margaret appeared petrified and, hand in mouth, pointed to the corner of the room. 'Mrs Fowler, Look! Look! Your cat has brought in a rabbit!'

Eileen looked into the corner and sure enough there was Ayckbourn guarding a rabbit almost his own size. How he had managed to catch the rabbit, then drag it to the back door and get both himself and the rabbit through the cat flap without the rabbit escaping was a mystery. Ayckbourn was patted, the rabbit was returned to the field and peace reigned once more.

In the early 1980's I was a member of the St Catherine's Hospice fund raising committee in Driffield which helped provide money which eventually provided a hospice in Scarborough. Driffield would be within the hospice's catchment area which extended to around a 25 mile radius of Scarborough.

I was invited to the official opening of the Hospice in Scarborough which was held on April 29th 1985. Princess Margaret, Countess of Snowden was to open the Hospice.

As I parked my car, I met local entrepreneur and philanthropist Don Robinson – for whom many years later I researched and put together his biography - and walked over the road to the hospice with him. He told me his wife, Jean, had actually been invited to the opening as a guest but couldn't attend so Don told me he had gone in her place. But even in those days security was extremely tight and there was quite a hiatus as Don handed over Jean's invitation and explained she couldn't attend.

He was questioned and a number of phone calls took place to prove he was who he said he was. My identifying him counted for nothing! I went in and joined the welcoming party and eventually the door opened and we all expected to see Princess Margaret appear. But in stepped Don, who made his entrance somewhat sheepishly a couple of minutes before the Princess arrived to officially open the Hospice.

In 1982 we felt it was time to be more adventurous on holiday so we decided to spend a week in Russia with the second week in the then Yugoslavia. We flew from Manchester Airport to Dubrovnik, then changed planes for a flight to Kiev arriving at the very modern and impressive Kiev airport at 10.45pm, Russian time.

At Kiev we had to go through immigration and whilst the staff members were polite and efficient one asked why we were travelling on our Queen's [official] birthday!

Our hotel in Kiev was the Hotel Dnipro, Khreshchatyk Str.1/2, Kiev, and, according to Google, it still appears to be trading.

We were allocated room 609 on the 6th floor which turned out to be a 4 roomed suite with a large hall, dining room–cum–lounge with fridge, drinks cabinet, TV, radiogram, 3 piece suite, large bedroom, and bath and shower room.

By this time it was 1.30am Kiev time so we slept well.

At 10.00am the group set of by coach for a tour of the city which had colourful and well–kept gardens, parks and tree lined streets. We visited St Sophia Cathedral, the Unknown Soldier's grave and memorial, and the statue of the Motherland.

St Sophia Cathedral in the snow

A rather strange thing happened throughout the week when, if the coach which took us on our sightseeing tours, was late back for a meal, the meal still appeared on the table, course by course, as if we had been there. So, if we returned at, say 1.30pm, it was likely that the full meal would have been served in our absence and be there, on the table, waiting for us, comprising cold versions of whatever should have been hot!

That afternoon we visited the Church of the Cross, Monastery and caves, where mummified bodies of dead monks had been buried; and then The Museum of Ukrainian Art before returning to the hotel.

Dinner was at 6.00pm and, that day consisted of a starter of smoked salmon and cucumber, a main course of chicken Kiev (somewhat appropriate!), chips, peas and carrots and a choice of dessert.

At 7.00pm that evening we left the hotel for Kiev Airport to take the flight to Leningrad, arriving at 11.15pm - when the sun was still shining.

We stayed at the Leningrad Hotel in room 713, and again the room was excellent with a good view over the River Neva. It was very much like Venice but on a much larger but less intimate scale. Before bed we visited the bar which had only water, grapefruit juice or Coca Cola for sale.

The next day, Monday 14th June we had a tour of the city including the Winter Palace, Revolution Square, Peter and Paul Fortress, and the Piskarevskoye memorial to the ½ million who died in the siege of Leningrad between 1941 and '43.

We returned to the hotel for lunch, then, in the afternoon were taken to Pavlovsk and Pushkin, both names still applying to one of St. Petersburg's most famous imperial villages. The summer home of the Romanov tsars for centuries, Tsarskoye Selo, or the Royal Village, was renamed Pushkin following the communist revolution in honour of one of its other well-known residents, the poet Alexander Pushkin.

A day later we visited the Hermitage Museum which had been the Tsar's Winter Palace. This is a remarkable museum of fantastic treasures and we could easily have spent a whole day or more, wandering round rather than the hour or so we were allocated.

After the visit had lunch in the Sadko restaurant for lunch – caviar, cured fish, salad, beef with vegetables and potatoes, followed by ice cream (with one plum!) and coffee. Wine was included and available throughout the meal.

In the afternoon we went to Nevsky Prospekt to shop; then on to a Beriozka shop which was their equivalent of duty free and had lots of goods at what appeared to us to be ridiculously cheap prices.

To book ballet, opera and theatre tickets was quite a performance in itself. You missed breakfast and queued to book and pay for what you wanted. There were only a few seats reserved for tourists and much demand so you then returned to the hotel at 4.00pm to see if you had been lucky. If so, you were given tickets for that night's performance; if not, you got your money back and missed breakfast the following day if you wanted to try again.

We got back to the hotel and found we had been lucky in obtaining tickets for the ballet Swan Lake, by the Kirov Company at the Lensovjeta Theatre. (People's Palace of Culture). We took a taxi to the theatre where Swan Lake was an excellent production throughout; costumes, lighting, sets, orchestra, and, of course, the ballet itself.

When we left after the performance it was raining hard. We couldn't get a taxi so went to the underground. We asked a guard but he seemed to indicate there were 3 Metro changes, and with all station names and signs being in the Cyrillic alphabet, that might confuse us. He stopped a fellow traveller – a Jewish looking gentleman with beard and black coat and homburg hat and appeared to explain our plight. This gentleman took us back up the escalator, tried unsuccessfully to get us a taxi, stopped us getting on a 49 bus (which we had been told earlier was the one we wanted), as it was going in the wrong direction, then put us on a trolley bus and faded away into the night before we could even thank him.

We hadn't a clue how to get a ticket but two girls explained in sign language that you had to put the correct amount into one machine, get the ticket, then cancel it on another machine. They helped us by taking the right amount of cash from a handful of coins and they then told us which stop we should get off. The hotel was just over the road.

The following day we were due to fly on to Moscow but first, in the morning, we visited the historic Aurora ship and museum at its anchorage, then went on to Peter the Great's cottage.

Late in the evening we arrived in Moscow at the Hotel Cosmos which had been built for the 1980 Olympic Games.

One of us missed breakfast on Thursday June 17th and tried to get seats for a ballet or the opera Madame Butterfly. Again, the system was the same, and we were told to return at 4.00pm when we found we had been unlucky.

The tour that morning was of Moscow and covered Red Square, the University, and the Olympic Games site. In the afternoon we missed the tour to the Soviet Achievement Park and at 4.00pm managed to get seats from a cancellation for the ballet Coppelia that evening. It was a first class performance and had a very large orchestra. Tickets - if you could get them - were a real bargain with seats costing the equivalent of £4 each.

We were accompanied on the daily tours by Ana Marjanovic, our Yugoslavian guide, but she was not allowed to 'guide' us in Russia so the authorities nominated their own guides at each of the three cities we visited.

By the time we got to bed it was already 12.30am on 18th June – both our birthdays and coincidentally Ana's as well. We also discovered that Nadia, the Russian guide, Liz or Pam – I cannot remember which – and Hazel and John, who were all in our group, had birthdays in the same week so we decided to throw a party in our room for the birthday people after the planned events on the 18th.

After breakfast on the 18th we tried to get tickets for the Bolshoi but the theatre was fully booked – reportedly for a conference.

The morning tour was to the Kremlin and we saw Stalin's tomb and in the afternoon we were taken for a trip on the Moscow underground.

We were then taken to a GUM department store on one side of Red Square. We were not impressed. It was unlike our large department stores and more like a covered market.

We then moved on to a Beriozka shop in a large hotel near to the Kremlin and there I bought a real fur hat – which from memory cost me around £5. We also bought 4 bottles of Russian champagne for the party we were to hold later.

Then back to the hotel for our evening meal, and Nadia, the Russian guide had arranged 4 birthday cakes – one for each of the tables occupied by our group.

After dinner we all left for a visit to The Moscow State Circus on Ice, at the New Circus Theatre. This event had been planned for the whole group and was included as part of the tour so there had been no breakfast queuing.

There were some very clever acts and effects, polar bears, pigeons and an eagle or vulture although I cannot remember the details.

We returned to our hotel and the party in our room for the birthday people started around 10.15pm. The Russian champagne proved excellent and very potent and the party broke up around 1.00am.

On Saturday 19th we were to fly back to Dubrovnik. With the time difference it would mean a 27 hour day but the following week in Yugoslavia was intended as relaxation and we made sure that life moved at a much slower pace.

In 1983 we decided to travel to Hua Hin in Thailand. We flew from Heathrow on 11th June landing in Bangkok where we were greeted by our courier who was to take us the 200 plus mile journey south, by taxi, to Hua Hin. As we drove past the shanty towns and barren landscape I wondered what ever had we let ourselves in for. It seemed extremely primitive when compared with home. Eventually we arrived at the hotel, but what a difference; it was a real oasis of peace and calm, greenery, fountains and even a sign to greet us: 'Welcome Mr & Mrs David Fowler to the Sofitel Hotel, Hua Hin.'

The hotel was spread over acres of green grass interspersed with swimming pools. There were tropical birds, and a baby elephant had free rein over the hotel grounds. It was peaceful, very relaxing... and very hot!

Towards the end of our stay I started to feel decidedly groggy and a touch of sunstroke was diagnosed. Eileen took herself off into the town, booking a bicycle rickshaw to find a pharmacist where she could buy pills for me. She found it fascinating shopping with the locals where the norm was to buy a pill at a time from vast arrays. She eventual found what she had been told to get and returned to the hotel. The pills worked, I recovered and was fit enough to travel home. But, this time, instead of a long car journey to Bangkok, we were flown in a tiny plane from a small airstrip at Hua Hin, to Bangkok where we caught our plane back to Heathrow.

Back to the Driffield branch of the bank and I then found that customers whom I had looked after at Scarborough were making appointments to see me at Driffield and asking to transfer their accounts. This was potentially embarrassing. It was not usual to seek business from branches of your own bank – the other banks were the targets. But I was not seeking this business; it was coming of its own accord. I did refuse many accounts but when a customer said, 'If you won't let me transfer I'll move to another bank', I would look into it more seriously and a number of accounts did transfer to me at Driffield.

Ken Forrest, still branch manager at Scarborough, was said to be not happy – quite naturally in the circumstances – although he never approached me directly. However, in a conversation with a colleague from local head office it was hinted that Ken had 'made a few ripples' about the transfers.

I explained that I felt it was fair game in the cases where the customer was threatening to move to another bank. Any rumblings eased and those few accounts which had transferred – and a number, by that time were personal friends – helped the graphs to move ever upwards.

The Great Yorkshire Show was an annual event branch management attended but the stand was run by local head office directors and staff although we attended and visited the bank's pavilion at given times so we could meet any customers who were asking for us.

Whilst at Driffield, I was still rifle shooting but transferred to pistol which, whilst much more challenging and demanding, gave me more satisfaction. I won a number of small cups and medals and shooting (at targets I hasten to add) was a vent for built up frustration caused on occasion by the odd customer who would not stick to their side of a bargain, or a disagreement with head office.

Daughter Susan by this time had passed out from her course at Mountview Academy of Theatrical Art and had obtained work in the theatre in the West End of London.

Whilst she had had to train in all aspects of theatre – including coming home with green hair on more than one occasion – she had specialised in the technical side; sound, lighting, effects and so on.

At one time she was one of only two female chief electricians in West End theatre. For equity purposes she coined her first names to Sulyn (from Susan Lynne) and that's how most people know her to this day so from this point onwards in this book Susan becomes Sulyn.

One influential customer at Driffield branch was Marcus Whickam Boynton, owner of Burton Agnes Hall and Estate. He invited me to the Hall a few times and, in turn, I took him to the Bank's local head office at York for lunch. Whilst he was elderly and very slightly eccentric we got on well together and I remember him enthusing about his Japanese car – a Hyundai, I think it was, which must have been one of the first Japanese cars in or around Driffield at that time when all other farmers seemed to drive Volvo cars.

*Burton Agnes Hall*

'Burton Agnes Hall is an Elizabethan manor house in the village of Burton Agnes, near Driffield in the East Riding of Yorkshire. The Hall contains a number of fine 17th–century plaster ceilings and chimneypieces. The ceiling of the Long Gallery was restored in two stages by local architect Francis Johnson between 1951 and 1974.

The plan, attributed to John Smythson presents a square block with bay windows and a small internal courtyard. All of the display has been concentrated on the entrance facade, which includes many windows and many shaped projecting bays, two square flanking the central entrance, two semi–circular at the ends of the projecting wings, and two five–sided around the corners. Variety in the skyline is created by gables alternating with level parapets.

The main facade is built a story higher than the rest of the house to contain a long gallery running the full length of the second floor, with the result that the minor side facades are asymmetric.

The estate has been in the hands of the same family since Roger de Stuteville first built a manor house on the site in 1173. In 1457 Sir Walter Griffith came to live there.

The Griffiths were a Welsh family who had emigrated to Staffordshire in the thirteenth century and inherited the Burton Agnes estate.

The present Elizabethan house was built nearby in 1601–10 by Sir Henry Griffith, 1st Baronet, after he was appointed to the Council of the North. His daughter Frances Griffith, heiress of the estate, married Sir Matthew Boynton, Governor of Scarborough Castle and the first Boynton baronet. On her death in 1634 the estate was bequeathed to their son Francis, later the second Baronet Boynton. According to legend, the skull of Sir Henry's youngest daughter Anne is bricked up in the Great Hall. It is reputed to be a screaming skull, and to return to the house whenever it is removed.

The widow of the 6th Baronet married John Parkhurst of Catesby Abbey, Northamptonshire, known as 'Handsome Jack', who squandered much of the family fortune and neglected the estate.

On the death of the eleventh Baronet in 1899 the house passed to his daughter, who had married Thomas

*Lamplugh Wickham, and who had adopted the additional surname of Boynton. On her death it passed in turn to their son Marcus Wickham Boynton, who operated a successful stud farm on the estate for many years and was High Sheriff of Yorkshire for 1953–54. He died in 1989 and left the property to a distant Cousin, Simon Cunliffe–Lister, then aged twelve, grandson of Viscount Whitelaw and son of the 3rd Earl of Swinton. Today, the estate is owned by the Burton Agnes Preservation Trust and is managed by Cunliffe–Lister and his Mother, the Hon Susan Whitelaw.'*

Sadly, Marcus died in 1989, 2 years after I had moved from Driffield but he left us a 'bequest' about which we would not become aware until I had been at Malton branch for almost 3 years.

\*

In 1984 we holidayed in Rome and Sorrento in Italy, and then in 1985 we travelled to Verneuil near Paris with Driffield Lions club members who were twinned with Verneuil Lions. We stayed for around 4 days and they really made the trip memorable. They took us to Paris where we were booked for dinner and the show which followed at the Lido. The show was magnificent and we hadn't realised as we dined that our hosts had booked tables next to the stage which emerged from the floor and gave us an excellent view of the show and all the dancing girls in, and in some case almost out of, their magnificent costumes. The girls were so close that as they danced, pieces of their black fluffy feather boas floated across to us and landed on our table.

One event the French Lions arranged for us was a Sunday lunch which started around 11.00am and went on well into the afternoon. Suddenly, one of the French Lions looked at his watch and gabbled away far too quickly for us to understand. We were all bundled into cars and off we went, soon to arrive at the medieval town of Chartres where the main stop was the Cathédrale Notre–Dame de Chartres

'Not only is Chartres Cathédrale one of the greatest achievements in the history of architecture, it is almost perfectly preserved in its original design and details. Chartres' extensive cycle of portal sculpture remains fully intact and its glowing stained–glass windows are all originals. Chartres is thus the only cathedral that conveys an almost perfect image of how it looked when it was built.

In addition to its architectural splendour, Chartres Cathédrale has been a major pilgrimage destination since the early Middle Ages. Its venerable history, exquisitely preserved architecture, and centuries of fervent devotion make for an atmosphere of awe and holiness that impresses even the most non–religious of visitors'.

The Cathédrale had a deep and poignant significance to many of the French Lions who in effect, were making their own pilgrimage. They had served, or had relatives who had served in the Resistance during World War II and Chartres was apparently an important Resistance centre. Each year, at the same time, they visited the Cathédrale to remember those far off days.

St.Basil's Cathedral

In June that same year, 1985, we returned to Russia, arriving at the Cosmos Hotel in Moscow. This tour had been advertised as The White Nights Festival and was split between Moscow and Leningrad. In Leningrad it never appeared to get dark at night at that time of the year.

Various tours were included – some of which we had done on our earlier trip but many new; The Kremlin again, and St Basil's Cathedral, with its colourful, onion shaped domes, the central tower of which we climbed.
 We saw a stunning performance of Paggliachi at the Stanislavski Theatre, then the following night we obtained tickets for a ballet called 'The Little Humpbacked Horse', at the same theatre.
 Again, the lighting, effects, orchestra and dancing were all excellent.

We noticed the front two rows contained elderly ladies dressed in black and we made enquiries. They were the wives of the orchestra's all male members who apparently were given free tickets. With it also being a music festival, orchestras from all over Russia played in Moscow in June so, for the wives it would be a holiday while their husbands worked.
 On June 19th we visited Gorky Park by underground. We went on our own and having just read the book *Gorky Park,* the 1981 crime novel written by Martin Cruz Smith, we were fascinated to see in reality what was so vividly portrayed in the book; the park, the big wheel and the outside cafe; they all seemed to come to life. The following day we were due to fly to Leningrad, as it was then called. However, we had time in the morning for a short walk and came across a small church from which came the most beautiful singing. We opened the door and entered, quietly standing by the closed door and just listening. From the outside the church looked almost derelict, but the inside was magnificent and full of gold leaf and wonderful paintings. Numerous candles cast shadows and a service was obviously in progress, possibly Russian Orthodox, but

we hadn't time to stay and find out as our flight was soon due.

We arrived in Leningrad and were taken to the Pulkovskaya hotel on the outskirts of the city. It now appears to be called the Park Hotel and is one of the Radisson group.

This being our second visit to Leningrad we gave up the thought of missing breakfast and queuing for theatre tickets we were unlikely to obtain, and decided to do it the Russian way. We discovered a kiosk down in the Metro with a poster advertising theatre tickets. We didn't speak Russian and the proprietor didn't speak English but we got by on schoolboy and schoolgirl French.

She got us tickets for a Symphony Concert by the Leningrad Symphony Orchestra for that night. It was an excellent performance in a beautiful hall with eight huge chandeliers.

*The Kirov Theatre, (now called the Mariinsky Theatre)*

The following morning we missed the planned tour and made our way to the Kirov Theatre. It was magnificent and we discovered that each night a number of seats had to be kept free for 'heroes of the state'. If these heroes hadn't claimed their free tickets by 4.00pm they were put on general sale. At 4pm we returned and obtained tickets for that evening's performance of Prince Igor. It was unbelievable to be actually sitting in the Kirov watching such a wonderful performance. As well as the principals and a full chorus there were also around 70 members of the Kirov ballet taking part. The whole experience was breath–taking.

The next day we went on a tour of the rivers and canals of Leningrad and the day after our group visited Pavlovsk to see the Tsar's restored summer palace.

In the afternoon we visited our friendly ticket booth lady and obtained seats for Lohengrin at the Kirov for that evening. It was another excellent performance.

This time, when we returned to the hotel after yet another performance there was a little murmuring and apparent jealousy from other members of the party who could just not understand how we managed to obtain tickets. For most it was their first visit. As our second, we felt like old hands. They had queued and missed their breakfast, only to be turned away at 4.00pm, so were spending their evenings in the hotel bar. We gently explained that hotels weren't the only place to try to obtain tickets.

Wednesday, June 26th, found us all heading for Petrodevorets in a hydrofoil.

It was a magnificent palace after recent restoration and the extensive gardens and parkland are full of fountains, covered in gold leaf.

The next day saw us at the Hermitage and we were able to see much of what we had had to miss on our first shorter visit to Leningrad – including wonderful paintings by El Greco, Leonardo, Rembrandt, Rubens, Titian and much more.

We also managed to get precious tickets for Eugene Onegin at the Kirov. The soloists and the orchestra were excellent and the whole production first class. I particularly take notice of the sets, lighting, scenery and sound and I certainly wasn't let down in the 3rd Act – the ballroom scene – which was faultless.

*Petrodevorets*

The following day it was raining so we had a leisurely morning before going to the ticket kiosk to see what Ana could offer. Our communication in French had improved over the days and she offered two seats for the ballet Sleeping Beauty at the Kirov that evening. She apologised and said there was a snag. These seats were in the 'Gods'. However, the design of the 'Gods' at the Kirov just proved what talented theatrical architects and designers could achieve. We were in the middle of the very back row and could have touched the ceiling of the Kirov but we had a full, unobstructed central view of the entire stage. The whole production was first class.

I have never, ever, before or since, heard such prolonged applause after any production. It lasted for well over 20 minutes with countless curtain calls and numerous bouquets of flowers being thrown on to the stage for the principals.

The following day we came down to earth with a bump. We flew home and it was back to work at Driffield branch on the Monday morning.

Customers who were memorable as excellent farmers and who became good friends were Robin and Basil Aconley and their sister Annie. They were arable farmers who invited me to visit and walk their farm before harvest each year. Eileen was invited and chatted with Annie until we returned when the five of us had supper together.

When I moved to Malton branch in 1987 we lost touch with them but in 2014 we were in a Scarborough restaurant and I was sure the three of them were sitting at a table together with another lady. The next time we were there they also appeared so I approached them.

'Excuse me. Are you by any chance Robin Aconley?'

The youngest one looked at me blankly and said no, he wasn't, and he gave his name.

'Sorry,' I said. 'Mistaken identity. It must have been nearly 30 years since I last saw him.'

This drew even more incredulous gasps and laughter until I realised that the man I had spoken with was only then around 40, so couldn't possibly have been the Robin I knew who would have been around that age, 30 years earlier.

Business built up rapidly at Driffield, so much so that the branch was upgraded and I got my first bank car – a BMW 316 automatic. Increasing business led to Chris Larwood being promoted from accountant to office manager and branch newcomer Mike Sankey was transferred in as accountant. Mike was a sensible man who, although quiet was a thinker and a real asset to the branch. He was able to take over a lot of Chris's routine office management work and this left Chris the time to take over more of the personal lending book.

Increased business led to the premises becoming too

small for our needs as we had gained extra staff and we needed additional interview rooms.

By that time the elderly bank spinster who lived in a flat above the branch had died so plans were prepared to enlarge the branch by redesigning it, putting in a larger counter, providing additional interview rooms, moving some departments and the staff room into what had been the flat upstairs, and adding a cash machine. It was also to be refurbished and carpeted throughout.

There were many stages to go through but work eventually started and it seemed from the very early stages that there was a difference of opinion between me, as branch manager, and the builder's foreman. I was responsible for the entire branch and its security but the foreman had somehow got the impression that they had taken over the entire branch and it was our job to fit round them.

Things came to a head when the builders propped open the back door and started knocking down a wall when we were trying to get cash from the tills to the strongroom.

I stressed to the foreman that in other branches in which I had worked whilst building work was taking place, the branch was partitioned with builders having a specific area or areas in which to work and the bank likewise having an area in which they could work without disruption and which would be security protected at all times.

The foreman would not agree and claimed that it was our responsibility to work within their requirements. I was going to phone head office but before I created a fuss I phoned colleague Colin Porter who was branch manager at Bridlington branch at the time, and who had previously been on the bank's inspection team so knew all the requirements about security during branch renovations. I explained the position and he got in his car and came through to Driffield immediately.

Colin was aghast at what he saw so I rang head office,

he backed me, and it was confirmed to us that the bank's property department was responsible for day to day branch security whilst improvements were taking place, so they would be instructed by head office to confer with the builders and tell them what they could, and could not do. The bank had to be in charge.

Katie Colley was then local head office premises officer and when she realised what the builders were up to she was very supportive – as she has been in any of the branches in which I have worked which were having premises work carried out.

I cannot now recall but I think the foreman was replaced. Problems settled down and after nearly a year's work conversions were completed. The finished branch was excellent and a considerable improvement. The redesign had retained the character of the old building but had brought in modern touches such as woven light green wallpaper and electrical halogen uplighting. Even air conditioning had been installed.

On moving to Driffield I had transferred from Scarborough, to Driffield Lions Club. Many of their members were farmers or connected with the agricultural sector and they worked hard but made sure they had a good social life.

At one meeting I was asked to chair a committee to arrange some event for the Christmas and New Year period. For Scarborough Lions we had organised occasional fancy dress parties which had been very popular and successful and with tongue a little bit in cheek I proposed we do the same at Driffield using the large first floor private Maple room of the town's historic but recently upgraded Bell Hotel.

After I made the suggestion there was an embarrassing silence. Remember this was an agricultural area where all events were very conservative – with a little 'c'.

Then a voice took pity on me and piped up and said

what a good idea it was. It was time the club moved into the present century and no-one need feel embarrassed at dressing up as it would be a private function in a private room at the Bell Hotel. All members and wives and guests would have to do would be to arrive in costume, enjoy themselves, then leave in costume or even change at the hotel. And a large raincoat to arrive or leave in, would soon cover up any costume, if any member or guest was really embarrassed...

The evening went ahead and was a great success but one farmer, with a reputation for having a rather dry sense of humour and being a little staid, turned up in his Sunday best suit with shining polished shoes and a smart dark Crombie style overcoat.

'What have you come as Keith?' I asked with a twinkle in my eye as he arrived.

'Ah've cum as a bloody bank manager!' was his reply. One up to Keith Beal!

In 1986 Sulyn graduated from Mountview and was due to start work in London West End theatre so we spent a few days in London with her, but in August that year we flew to Italy spend a week in Verona, then spent the rest of the time in Lido di Jessolo which was an easy water bus ride into Venice.

Verona is the wonderful town of Romeo and Juliet fame, and the supposed site of the lovers' balcony is a real draw for photographers. The massive amphitheatre hosts opera performances each summer and we were fortunate to see three of our favourite operas.

As tickets were collected at the entrance to the arena every patron was given a small brown envelope. On getting to our seats – actually massive marble slabs warmed by the summer sun during the day – we opened the envelope to find a few birthday cake candles. With the sky darkening, the orchestra striking up with the overture and the arena lights going down, everyone lit their candles and held them up. The atmosphere and sensation caused by thousands of candles flickering in the darkness was worth the ticket money alone. The arena at one time held 30,000 patrons, but 'health and safety' has now interfered and capacity has been reduced to 15,000. Traffic in the town is banned during performances, the acoustics and productions are excellent and the experience is really memorable.

The years went by and I realised I would soon have been at Driffield branch 5 years. It was the longest I had been anywhere in the bank although this was normal in management and some managers stayed at the branch where they had first been appointed until retirement. The staff collectively had achieved excellent results; I was proud of them but I felt I was due further promotion and I had sufficient energy to take another branch forward.

I had a friend in local head office, Geoff Aitken, who would phone and pass me cryptic and very brief titbits of what was, or wasn't going on. One such titbit was that 'Sam Telfer retires from Malton branch in November'.

Now, that was a branch to which I aspired. Agriculturally based, as was Driffield, it was a much larger branch; mainly because it held a lot of the larger businesses in and around the towns of Malton and Norton and it had a much wider customer catchment area of around 20 miles radius, compared to Driffield's 10 miles.

I let my colleague know I would be very interested, but in those days the directors made appointments from their own assessments and you couldn't apply for a job which was coming up.

A couple of weeks later he rang again, 'They've asked for a few staff files including yours.'

After a few more days the message came back, 'There's a guy from the south who is due to return to the district and they need a similarly graded branch for him.'

Then another, 'It's between him and you.'

In early October I was asked to attend regional office – by then in Leeds – where I was delighted to be offered Malton branch with a takeover date of Thursday 5th November 1987. Bonfire night!

Shortly after that meeting my successor came to Driffield to take over what had been my branch and after a week or so I moved to Malton to take over from Sam Telfer.

It was goodbye to Barclays Driffield as Barclays Malton beckoned...

*

# CHAPTER 14

# 'Please drop the latch when you leave Castle Howard'
# 1987

### 1987: Brief Timeline

Golliwogs are banned from Enid Blyton books and replaced by politically correct gnomes; Cynthia Payne is acquitted of controlling prostitutes in her London home; It is alleged that six Nazi war criminals are living in Britain; National Health Service prescription charges rise from £2.20 to £2.40; Winston Silcott, a 28-year-old black man, is sentenced to life imprisonment for the murder of PC Keith Blakelock; Christie's auction house in London sells one of Vincent van Gogh's iconic *Sunflowers* paintings for £24,750,000; MP's vote against the restoration of the death penalty by 342–230; The jewellery of the late Duchess of Windsor is sold at auction for £31 million, six times the expected value; The 1987 General Election sees Margaret Thatcher secure her third term in office; £60 million is stolen during the Knightsbridge Security Deposit robbery; Novelist and former Conservative MP Jeffrey Archer wins a libel case against *Daily Star* over allegations that he was involved in a vice ring; The Channel Tunnel is given the go-ahead; Moors Murderer Ian Brady claims that he committed a further five murders; Construction work begins on the extension to the M40 motorway between Oxford and Birmingham; Swedish retailer IKEA opens its first British store; Retired English jockey Lester Piggott is jailed for 3 years after being convicted of tax evasion.

On Monday 26th October 1987, I travelled to Barclays Malton branch to start the takeover period from long serving and much respected predecessor, Sam Telfer who was retiring.

It had been rumoured that Sam had wanted one of his previous office managers to be offered the job; it would have made sense as he would have known the branch and known the customers from his days there. However, if this was true Sam didn't mention it to me and he was friendly, helpful, supportive and professional from the word go.

I feel fully justified in saying that Sam was Mr Malton. He had worked at the branch many years before, then returned some years later as branch manager; he had run the branch successfully for many years; was known to everyone; was a member of the Middleton Hunt; and was widely respected throughout the whole Ryedale area and beyond. He would have been the most senior bank manager of all banks in the area.

What an act to follow!

On top of that, and again presumably unknown to Sam, the brief given to me was to build up business – as had been the case at Driffield where the branch team had worked hard to achieve a substantial increase in business and profitability. Following Sam, I was far more diffident about being able to pull the proverbial rabbit out of the hat than I had been when I moved to Driffield.

Initially I travelled from Driffield to Malton each morning, and after checking necessary paperwork and reports, Sam took me round to meet customers.

What a variety! Many farmers and agriculturally based businesses of course; many racehorse trainers (which was a completely new category for me); an abattoir, solicitors, accountancy firms, shops, hotels and pubs, a large bowling centre, a very large sheet steel manufacturing company, and, on the private side, a few titled customers.

I did wonder, when Sam took me round the abattoir, whether he was doing a repeat of the lady farmer at Driffield who took me across a field containing a bull.

The firm running the abattoir was situated some miles from Malton. I had never seen an abattoir in action before and can only liken it to a production line with the animals going in one end and coming out as carcases at the other. It was quite gory and one man's duties seemed to consist of waving a hose pipe in full flood around to swill all the blood and guts down the drain.

Future negotiations with the firm's directors were conducted either at the branch or in their offices!

As well as these visits, Sam had two retirement parties where I met yet more customers.

A short time after Sam had retired, one of the girls knocked on my door and came into my room. Rather diffidently she told me the staff members were holding an autumn barbecue at her house in the country on the following Saturday and my wife and myself were welcome to join them if we wished. I thought it could be an icebreaker so we agreed to attend. It was a wonderful sunny November day and not cold. Seating was in folding deckchairs and after Eileen had been given one, the only remaining free one was on a hilly bank. I sat on the chair and shortly afterwards someone cracked a joke and I laughed out loud and leaned right back. Being on a slope the deck chair collapsed and I flew through the air landing a few yards away spread–eagled on the grass. There was a very polite, deathly hush which was only broken when I burst out laughing.

Everyone else laughed, the ice was broken and the following 7 years went on to be some my happiest and most productive in the bank and staff members were some of the friendliest and most supportive I had ever known.

Malton branch was in an old building – just like Driffield's branch had been. Both had been modernised internally within the last couple of years but, to my mind, Driffield was far more attractive, work friendly and better laid out. The modern had been blended with the old and with the character of the building. For example, we had uplighters in the management rooms whereas Malton had standard fluorescent tubes for lighting. I don't know what say the branch staff had in the interior design at Malton but at Driffield we were given a choice of alternatives at every stage.

Malton's interior decorations were more muted and traditional and access to some of the internal office space was a little cumbersome, although structurally, it would have been difficult to change this. It was also a leased building as opposed to the freehold the bank owned at Driffield.

However, branch decorations do not reflect the spirit of any branch. The staff at Malton appeared happy and worked extremely well together, as had Driffield staff when I left, and to me this was much more important.

I had taken over as branch manager at Malton on November 5th and a few weeks later I got a phone call from the new regional inspector. My place at Driffield had been taken by an ex-inspector from London and we were obviously different in our approach to business. My outlook was that you couldn't make progress and get new business without accepting some element of risk arising in the future; I was also fully aware that when this happened, accounts at risk were more time consuming to administer than normal accounts which would usually almost run themselves.

As an ex-inspector himself, my Driffield successor would be used to commenting during inspections about accounts he felt might be at risk. But possibly, he didn't have the experience to nurse such accounts himself with the aim of bringing them back to health.

The district inspector said that my successor had mentioned to regional office that he was under pressure as he felt a few of the Driffield lendings were risky and he was having to spend time looking after them. The regional inspector asked for my views. I explained I had been appointed to Driffield – and later Malton – to increase business, and increasing the number of new accounts always increased the risk of a few bad debts which manifest themselves at a later stage. On previous inspections of the Driffield lending the inspectors had been relaxed about the percentage of risky accounts, which fell within the branch's agreed target percentage.

The new regional inspector thanked me for being frank and finished the phone call by saying he would send a report to regional office but I would probably hear no more about it.

I didn't.

In those days bank cars for management were exchanged by the leasing company, a bank subsidiary, every 3 years and with the latest branch upgrading at Driffield I had been able to exchange my BMW 316 automatic for a Mercedes 190E automatic.

At Malton branch, the lending manager was Allen Ferguson and we had been friends since we first worked together in York. John Douglas was office manager so at that time the management team consisted of three of us.

With a happy, cohesive and supportive staff to start with at Malton we could start on the difficult process of expansion much more easily.

The graphs similar to those I had introduced at York, Goole, Hull, Scarborough and Driffield were set up to chart progress so all staff could see exactly where we were, or weren't making progress, although John Douglas was in charge of these from the start. I think that by that time they were probably becoming standard across the Leeds region of the bank – by this time York Local Head Office had been absorbed into Leeds Regional Office.

We held management meetings each week so we could discuss progress and any problem areas or bank policy changes. The internal overdraft limits for most private customers which I had brought in at Driffield were introduced, as were similar limits for business customers. These were internal limits, and were not advised to customers. But, properly controlled, they were sensible and saved many hours work a week and I was interested to see a few years after I had retired, that the bank adopted this system throughout the country – although I gather the computer was then in charge of assessing the limit which was marked. Customers both private and business could, of course, negotiate higher overdraft limits where circumstances justified it.

The majority of buildings in Malton are owned by one of two Fitzwilliam trusts – those in the centre of town and including the bank premises were owned the Fitzwililam Malton Estate:

*'The Fitzwilliam family has been investing in Malton for over 300 years. Fitzwilliam Malton Estate (FME) is the trading name for its interests in central Malton. Sir Philip Naylor–Leyland, grandson of the last Earl Fitzwilliam and his heir Tom Naylor–Leyland look after the interests of this company.*

*Sir Philip says, 'For over 300 years, my family has been closely linked with the fortunes of Malton. I am committed to managing our property portfolio for the continued commercial well-being of the town.'*

*Tom Naylor–Leyland, eldest son of Sir Philip Naylor–Leyland, and his wife Alice have a family home in the centre of Malton and work with the promotion of the town...'*

Just over a month after I started at the branch I had 4 days holiday due in which we planned to move house. We had sold Pantiles, Beverley Road at Driffield and on Thursday, December 10th we moved to Old Church House, Great Barugh near Malton. In the meantime I had travelled each day, often calling in to Great Barugh after work, to check on progress with the house which was being converted from the old village church.

The move itself was somewhat traumatic.

My sister Phoebe had arrived on a visit from Las Vegas where she has lived for many years and had been staying with us in Driffield from early December. The move from Driffield was planned for Thursday 10th but at that time Eileen had badly damaged her back, was having intensive physiotherapy and was on crutches. Phoebe was a great help and the three of us managed to get all the necessary packing done before removal day. We then drove to Great Barugh to be there before the removal van and Phoebe helped with the unpacking before returning home to America on Sunday 13th.

Before the house move, the cats went to Mrs Wastling's cattery near Driffield, the only cattery I have ever seen where the inmates had carpeted pens. I collected them a week later after the new house was about ready to accept them. At that time we had Ayckbourn and Thomas. Ayckbourn was a pedigree brown Burmese, bought a few years earlier together with his brother, Todd. A short time later Todd was unfortunately killed by a car on Beverley Road, the main road running through Driffield.

After Todd's death, Ayckbourn was bereft and had pined for his missing brother and after a few weeks he arrived home accompanied by a straggly looking, disreputable stray. Gradually the stray gained confidence and Thomas, which we named him, who was certainly not a pedigree, became Ayckbourn's surrogate brother, the two of them becoming inseparable.

The names of Ayckbourn and Todd came from Alan Ayckbourn (now Sir Alan) and Paul Todd. Both were friends of ours and were respectively artistic director and musical director of Scarborough's Theatre in the Round. Alan in particular, thought it was a hoot having a cat named after him but he was a Burmese cat lover himself, having a champagne coloured cat – appropriately called Bollinger, or 'Bolly' for short, which had been given him by Andrew (now Lord Andrew) Lloyd Webber.

The property, which we called Old Church House, was

newly converted from what had originally been the village church dating from 1853; it was later used as a Church of England Mission Hall and had become known as The Old Mission Hall. In more recent years it had been unused until being sold by the church to a developer and then converted into a house.

The builder had started converting it for his own use but his circumstances changed and he placed it on the market part converted. Agreement was reached that he would complete the conversion – the stained glass windows had already been moved to another church – but to our requirements as, whilst we wanted to retain the character of the building, we also wanted fixtures and fittings to be modern and practical.

In 1987 the asking price of £95,000 seemed steep and we got little more for it when we sold in 1994. But a couple of years ago we were told that it had been valued at almost £400,000. Old Church House, when the new garden had matured, became a wonderful property and both Eileen and I say it was our favourite of the 10 houses we had then lived in since we married.

It was not only a property with much character but was situated in a wonderful hamlet, as Great Barugh could not claim to be a village. It had a pub – the Golden Lion which in those days was the hub of activities; there were no shops, but it did have a post box and a telephone box, and around 20 houses. There were long standing villagers who had lived in the area most of their lives, some newer incumbents, then around ten couples similar to ourselves who wanted to make the most of living there while they could, as we all knew that eventually we would have to move on. We used to enjoy parties in the pub; in each other's homes; and we would go out for trips to different restaurants, Trenchers Fish Restaurant at Whitby being a favourite at that time.

Old Church House still had the original bell tower. This was a bit of a misnomer, but it can be seen in the following photograph to the immediate right of the front entrance just sticking above the roof line. The bell had been refurbished and rehung but there had been some concern in the village that the buyers might have children who would ring the bell incessantly. When we moved in we told our neighbours that the only time the bell would be rung was on Christmas morning at noon.

*Above: Old Church House, Great Barugh. There was also a double garage, workshop above, stable and small paddock.*

*And below: The rear of the property... in winter*

And so started a tradition, as we came out of the front door, rang the bell and raised our glasses to all our neighbours, and they came out and raised theirs in return.

I had just moved into the branch when I was told about the annual Dickens Festival which was being held little more than a week later. Eileen was enthusiastic so we hired costumes from the festival's supplier, and joined in the celebrations. The branch staff asked if they could dress up to bring the Festival into the branch, and I said we'd all dress up; I took the view that we all worked as a team.

*Staff in costume: From left: Mark Wray Mitchell; Judith Abbiss and Robert Pollock – all from Securities Department*

*Right: More staff members in costume in the branch during the Dickens Festival*

*Above: An illuminated Yorkersgate, Malton, for 'A Dickens of a Christmas', 1987. Barclays Bank is the entire building with the 5 windows lit up on the right.*

Details of the annual Festival are given below in an extract from the Dickens Festival website:

*'Malton and Norton have strong and solid connections with Charles Dickens, insomuch that Charles Smithson born in York House, Malton was a close friend of Dickens. The two met while Charles Smithson was training at Smithson and Dunn an associate family law firm in London. It was through the famous author's friend, Thomas Mitton, that Dickens first became acquainted with Smithson. Mitton had borrowed £1050 to buy a third share in the firm of Smithson and Dunn, in order to practice as a Solicitor. Charles Dickens acted as surety for the sum and it was during these business transactions that Dickens and Smithson first met. Charles Smithson was forced to return*

*home to Malton and take over the running of the firm following the death of his brother Henry in 1840.*

*Dickens travelled extensively in the United Kingdom, Europe and North America during the course of his writing, using the experiences gained as material for his books. During his English travels he would often visit his friend in Malton where he would stay with him at Easthorpe Hall.*

*The Yorkshire Gazette recorded on July 8 1843: 'We understand that Charles Dickens Esq, the admired and talented author of 'Pickwick', etc is now on a visit with his lady at Easthorpe, the hospitable abode of Charles Smithson Esq. Solicitor, Malton, and that he has visited Old Malton Abbey and other remarkable places in the vicinity.'*

*It is known that Dickens did a number of story–telling performances at venues in Malton, one place being a now–demolished hall in Saville Street.*

*Dickens wrote or developed the ideas for a number of books in Malton with 'Barnaby Rudge', 'A Christmas Carol', and 'David Copperfield' reputed to have referenced to characters he met in Malton. The Smithson family were informed by Dickens that their office in Chancery Lane was the model for Scrooge's Office.*

*In recent times a Dickens Festival has been held in Malton just before Christmas to commemorate the connection that the famous author had with the town. It was during this period that it was decided to re–enact an event that had taken place in December 1841 when Dickens received a huge pie sent to him by local Malton and Norton butchers: he shared it with the poor and needy. He later related in a letter to his Malton friends, 'There never was such a pie. We sit and stare at it and grow dizzy in contemplation of its enormous magnitude'.*

*The Dickens connection is as alive today as it has ever been with a Dickens Museum and a Dickensian Christmas Festival as a celebration of all that is good in Malton.'*

I had been only been at the branch a few weeks when I

received an invitation to attend an inaugural meeting of the Macmillan Cancer Relief committee which was to be held at Castle Howard. The invite came from Annette Howard, then chatelaine of Castle Howard. I found Annette to be a very friendly, personable and positive woman in whose dictionary the word 'cannot' did not feature. Meeting her and serving on the committee was the start of a friendship which was to last until we moved to Scarborough following my retirement and, shortly afterwards Annette moved away after she and the Hon. Simon Howard divorced.

I first met Annette at this meeting and it transpired that she had been approached to either revitalise an existing local area committee, or to form a new one.

In any case she had been asked to chair the committee and she asked me to take on the treasurer's role which I was happy to accept. That was the start of my association with Castle Howard, an extremely warm, friendly and happy place when I got to know it in those days. At a future meeting at Castle Howard we were all discussing some matter and taking our time when Simon popped his head round the door to remind Annette that they were shortly due to leave for another engagement. Five minutes later he called in again with another somewhat firmer prompt, so Annette said, 'I'm sorry everyone. I'll have to go. You carry on the meeting David. Just let me know what transpires, and oh, please drop the latch when you leave!' The meeting finished around 15 minutes later and I duly 'dropped the latch' ... of Castle Howard.

Later, most meetings were held at the bank as Malton itself was more convenient for most other committee members although some future events organised by the committee took place at Castle Howard.

Farming was going through a difficult period at that time and fairly early on I visited one customer who had diversified by rearing young livestock, sheep, rabbits, and so on which he kept in special enclosures. He then offered visits to schools from towns and cities and made a small charge per head. It made a day out for the children and most of them had never seen, let alone actually visited a farm.

He let the children wander amongst the young livestock, and explained, in a space he used as a classroom, how the farm operated; how animals were born and reared and crops were sown and grown, and how these provided the food we eat.

At the end of one such trip and after answering the children's questions the teacher sidled up to my farmer customer.

'Can you show the children please, where you mix the powder and bottle the milk?'

'Eh? Pardon?' said the farmer, scratching his head.

'You know. Where you mix the powder into milk.'

I thought this was a joke the farmer had picked up from somewhere but he was deadly serious and told me, 'If that teacher didn't know that milk comes from cows heaven help her pupils in future years. No wonder education is in the state it appears to be in.'

Wilf Ward was a very astute but friendly and unassuming customer, even though he and his brother had built the large Ward Group from very tiny beginnings. They had expanded very successfully into farm and factory prefabricated buildings at Sherburn, between Malton and Scarborough and subsequently the company grew to produce many large industrial prefabricated buildings. At this stage they had been advised to go public. This they did and the sale of some family shares gave both brothers capital with which they intended using to benefit others. Ward's was the branch's largest customer.

*In 1988 the branch had a BarclayBank machine installed. Now you see them everywhere but in those days they were allocated much more sparsely. In the photo to the left, Wilf Ward from Wards of Sherburn is drawing the first cash from the machine, the cash being donated by the bank to Wilf's own charity.*

Whilst Wilf remained on the Ward's board as chairman – his brother Frank became ill and later died – he and his wife Phyllis used their share of the sale money to benefit others and they started the Wilf Ward Family Trust, a charity they set up in 1976. It was founded on the principles of providing support, accommodation and respite care to those with learning difficulties; disabled people, and their families. A purpose built home, Isabella Court, was built at Pickering, since when a number of other homes have opened throughout the region. In 1984 Mr Ward was honoured with an OBE. Sadly Wilf died in 2005 aged 88 by which time the number of his trust's care homes had grown to seventy.

In March 1988, Eileen and I flew to the Maldives for our 25th wedding anniversary which fell on 27th March that year. The flight was long and tiring but I shall always remember the first sight of the islands, each surrounded by sand which was lapped by shallow turquoise sea, as we circled before landing on the small airstrip at the capital, Male.

It was a relaxing, peaceful holiday on Bandos, the island on which we stayed. Male, the capital of the Maldives was about an hour away by motorboat and there was an uninhabited island near to Bandos on which we held desert island barbecues.

The gentle lapping sea around each island was crystal clear and warm and by wading out only a few yards you were surrounded by numerous shoals of brightly coloured fish which knew no fear.

On our 25th Wedding anniversary, the 27th March, we went for our evening meal and word had got around as a cake with candles was produced together with a bottle of wine.

From the restaurant it was about 300 yards to walk back to our bungalow across the sand and I suggested we walk round the island before turning in. To walk right round the island only took around 40 minutes and we usually did that each morning after breakfast.

We started the walk on the soft sand dotted with palm trees and I thought what better way to celebrate our anniversary than by making love under the many Palm trees in the dark evening sky, lit only by the moon and numerous stars.

I should point out here that Eileen had been brought up as a Primitive Methodist and from what she had told me about them, and knowing how reserved she could be in intimate matters – although a glass of red wine could often help! – I didn't hold out much hope. Anyway, I broached the possibility and got a much more positive reply than I had expected. Eileen said, 'Maybe, but I'm not promising.'

We walked on, me full of hope, and when we got nearer to our bungalow she stopped and pointed,

'Look someone's in our bungalow. The light's on. We've got a burglar!'

Bang went my hopes of a romantic open–air interlude under the stars! We turned towards our room and on entering were met by the two single beds having been made into a double, then brightly coloured flower petals – real petals not paper – having been spread all over the bed.

The room boys had also got the message about it being our anniversary and had merely forgotten to turn out the light when they left the room after they had rearranged it.

That was the end of the romantic night time walk round our desert island.

Later that year for my 50th birthday we decided to have a party at home. It was a fine evening so the garden was in use as well as all the house and most of our village friends were there, together with a few bank staff, a sprinkling of customers and many friends.

A customer who ran a pub rigged up a bar for us from which beer and wine could be dispensed on a self-service basis in the utility room, and the village pub – the Golden Lion – had prepared the food. The evening went very well.

The following day one neighbour, and very good friend Rosemary Davies, who lived over the road from us, asked, 'Who was that intriguing, well-spoken man I was chatting to who said he spent a lot of time in London and answered my questions in riddles, and wouldn't tell me what he did?'

I laughed and told her it was Alan (later Sir Alan) Ayckbourn who had come with his wife Heather on condition that during the evening he remained incognito. That made Rosemary's day and she was on cloud nine.

The following year, 1989, we had booked to fly to Kenya and as part of the preparations we took our cats – then Ayckbourn and Thomas, to Mrs Wastling's cattery near Driffield for the three weeks we would be away.

At the cattery we wandered around and saw a large, long haired cat who looked very woe begone and unhappy. Cattery owner Mrs Wastling – the cats even had carpets in their pens – explained that his owner had had to go into a convalescent home and the cat, then called 'Torki', would have to be put down if a home could not be found for him.

We flew into Mombasa, Kenya, on 2rd April and stayed at the Nyali Beach Hotel which had extensive grounds and, as its name implied, ran straight on to a large sandy beach.

*The Nyali Beach Hotel, Mombasa, Kenya*

Two memorable events spring to mind from this holiday. After settling into Nyali Beach and investigating what trips were available we decided to go to Amboseli game reserve to stay for a few nights and, hopefully to see some wild life.

We booked for this trip and had to be up early the morning we flew, as the flight left around 7.30am from Nairobi airport. We were collected from the hotel by car then taken to the airport where the formalities seemed to be far less onerous than back home. Someone glanced at our passports, someone else was nominated to take us to the plane and we were merely told 'to follow'.

Follow, we did, and we were soon on board a tiny

Cessna propeller driven plane with 7 seats including that of the pilot. At first we thought we were the only passengers but we flew up the coast to Bamburi where 4 Swedish visitors joined us. We took off again, this time heading for Amboseli and we flew quite close to the snow-capped Mount Kilimanjaro. That was a magical experience.

*Above: Elephant with Mount Killimanjaro, Tazmania, in the background.*

Somewhat more concerning was when the pilot, who hopefully had put the plane on to auto-pilot, got out his newspaper, spread it out, put his feet up against the front windscreen and started to read the day's news!

We stayed for a few days in Amboseli and on the second day an early morning game drive had been arranged. There were only the two of us and the four Swedish people in a minibus and as we set off into the bush the driver explained that he was looking for clues showing where and which animals had passed by during the night or early morning so we could get closer. He seemed to be having little success until one of the Swedish guests called out in somewhat nervous, fragmented English, 'Excuse me. Are there supposed to be elephants behind us?'

Very quickly he swerved the minibus off the track on which we were travelling and through some forestry. He then turned back towards the track and told us to keep quiet and still. Shortly afterwards the mother elephant and her baby, which had been following us, passed by safely on the track. He explained he had got off the track quickly as mothers are very protective and had she thought her baby could have been harmed she might have charged us.

The second memorable event was a visit we made – again for a few nights – to Shimba Lodge. This was effectively a hotel built into the trees, with a rectangular shaped wooden walkway jutting out at the back through the trees, about 3 yards wide but probably 20 yards long on each of the three extended sides. From this structure you could look down into a lake and see wild life coming to drink, normally at dusk.

You may remember journalist Alan Whicker on television presenting 'Whicker's World.' One of his programmes covered Shimba Lodge and he also produced a Barclaycard advert on the lodge's walkway when he had a (tame?) tiger accompanying him.

At Nyali Beach and as a souvenir of Kenya we bought a large soapstone hippopotamus which was far too heavy to get home as hand, or even hold, luggage. The hotel shop said, 'no problem', and agreed to send it on to us. We got it eventually, and still have it, but it took around 6 months to arrive – and that was only after the Nairobi branch of Barclays Bank had intervened for me and persuaded the seller to speed despatch.

We returned home on 25th April 1989 and collected the

cats as we had arranged. 'Torki' was still in the cattery and Mrs Wastling said there had been no interest from anyone wanting to rehome him. We had room at Old Church House for a third cat and there were plenty of fields behind the house in which they could roam but Mrs Wastling was obviously concerned that Torki could be a little vicious as she always wore heavy gardening gloves when handling him. We told her we were interested and a bargain was struck where she agreed to take him back if we felt unable to cope. So 'Torki' came back to Old Church House. His long haired coat was matted and Eileen gently groomed him over many days. He actually began to look like a lion so we renamed him 'Shimba' after Shimba Lodge in Kenya. That seemed to give him pride and he gradually gained confidence and was readily accepted by Ayckbourn and Thomas. So Shimba became part of the family living with us for a good few years.

Another later addition to the cats at Great Barugh was Chloe. This had been Sulyn's cat in London but she felt unable to look after her properly because of her theatre working hours so Chloe came up by British Rail Red Star and Eileen went to Malton station to collect her.

The cats had their beds in the large utility room at Old Church House, in the outer door of which was a cat flap through which the four of them used to come and go, usually together in procession. The garden fence into the field behind, had a hollowed 'burrow' beneath one corner which was their access to and from the field. We nicknamed this their 'snooky hole'. After harvest you could seem them walking round the perimeter of the field of stubble but as the crops grew they were almost invisible with only Chloe's ginger tail tip pointing vertically above the crops to indicate where they were.

At Malton branch an important sector of business was race horse training. We had a number of trainers on our books – some very well-known and others less so. Visiting the stables was usually a real pleasure as the horses were always kept in tip top condition and many were horses I'd heard of, or seen during races on television.

Malton has had a history with horses stretching back to Roman times, as the town then had a cavalry fort and for the past 200 years thoroughbred racehorses have galloped in training across the gentle turf of Langton Wold. At least 20 trainers were then based in or near Malton, including famous names like Easterby and Tinkler.

One of the earliest trainers I went to meet was Nigel Tinkler at his stables at Langton, Malton. His yard was immaculate and the horses and their turnout were a real credit to Nigel and his staff. He now has a 2 furlong round all-weather track, an all-weather arena and an undercover horse-walker as well as gallops. At any one time he has an average of 40 horses in training.

Nigel has been in racing all his life, originally riding winners on the flat, hurdles and steeple chases. By the time he was 16, he had already ridden 250 winners. He then began his accomplished horse training career which has continued over many years.

Nigel has trained over 1000 winners including two Cheltenham festival winners with *The Ellier* in the Kim Muir with Gee Armitage, and *Sacre d'Or* in the Mild May of Fleet with Graham McCourt as jockey.

Some of the racehorse owners have been with Nigel since he first started training. He welcomes individual owners and syndicates, the latter of which have included *Full Circle* (which had 52 winners in one year), *Elite Racing* and many other partnerships.

Another trainer I particularly remember for different reasons was in a much smaller way of business. I will not name him for reasons which will become obvious, but he was an Irish trainer who decided to build a large therapeutic swimming pool for horses near Malton. He already had his own yard but asked the bank for limited financial help towards the heavy cost of this new pool. This seemed to be a sound proposition, as there were no similar facilities in the area so it was probable that if the enterprise was run professionally other local trainers would take advantage of the pool. In fact it did do very well for some time but then repayments to his bank loan started to dry up. I tried to contact him but the phone seemed dead so I went out to his stables to find him. There he was, very apologetic, saying he'd hit a bad patch and the phone bill hadn't been paid so had been disconnected. The upshot was that he said he was moving, but was adamant I couldn't know where. I told him that as he owned money to the bank we must know where to contact him. He kept wringing his hands together and he was obviously in great distress and kept looking around as if he felt a gunman would walk round the corner.

That sounds very melodramatic but was not far off the truth as eventually the story came out. The comparatively small amount the bank had lent towards the total cost of the pool was 'merely to make the transaction appear normal'. The vast majority of the building costs had been lent by the IRA which was most unhappy that their repayments had fallen well behind schedule. In fact, threats had been made against our customer and he was actually in fear of his life.

From memory, the bank had to write off a small part of the amount we had lent, but this trainer must have overcome his difficulties as I see from a recent internet search that he is still training, but from a different address.

A short time after having first met Annette Howard I had a call from Castle Howard. Ian Martin, the promotions manager to ask if I could go to lunch on a given day to meet him? I could and I did. Ian had an office and a private dining room on the ground floor of the castle and the staff provided excellent food and wine. Not only was he promotions manager of Castle Howard but he was also the Northern Chancellor of the prestigious Association de la Jurade de Saint-Emilion. We shall learn more about that organisation later.

When Allen Ferguson, the lending manager at Malton branch, was also invited we had to take it in turns to drive home as the entertaining was so lavish. Ian became a good friend and asked later if Eileen and I would be prepared to attend evening functions, some at short notice. Thinking back, Annette might have had a hand in this but we were more than happy to agree and it appeared that if a function was not fully subscribed, or there were late cancellations, the policy was to build up numbers, a bit like a theatre giving a few free tickets to give the impression of a full house.

Some evenings I would get home from the bank and the phone would ring about 6.00pm, 'Can you get to Castle Howard for 7.00pm in dinner jacket?' and Ian would give us details of which event we were attending. Invariably we could, and we attended some wonderful functions.

Some events were hosted by the Hon. Simon and Annette Howard themselves and occasionally we and other people were invited and asked to host one of the tables so the Howards would know all their guests were being looked after.

Ian Martin, a one-time police officer, was also an accomplished and very humorous after dinner speaker and even though we heard some of his jokes numerous times he always added a new twist and always picked someone from those present whom he could wind up. I was often that somebody and I remember him claiming that after a bank holiday we had opened the strong room at the bank and Shergar strolled out. On other occasions he claimed it was Lord Lucan coming out of the strong room when we opened the door.

*(Shergar was the prize winning race horse kidnapped by the IRA 33 years ago which was never found.*
*Lord Lucan, 7th Earl of Lucan, disappeared after his children's' nanny, Sandra Rivett was murdered on 7th November 1974. Hundreds of reports of sightings of him have been made in various countries around the world, although none has been substantiated. Despite a police investigation and huge press interest, Lucan has not been found and is presumed dead).*

Not all the events were dinners. At one time the estate had been busy dredging and cleaning the lake and waterfalls and repairing and renovating various fountains, some of which had stopped working over the years. On completion of the work the Howard's held a lunch in a large marquee overlooking the lake to celebrate completion of this mammoth task. We were invited and were seated next to a pleasant but obviously well-to-do couple. I asked them where they were from and they replied 'Bolton Abbey Estate'. Look up Bolton Abbey and you will see it is owned by the Duke and Duchess of Devonshire.

Castle Howard also put on many indoor musical events. I remember Julian Lloyd Webber, the celebrated cello player, Sarah Beth Briggs an international pianist, and many other performers – most events being held in the first floor, Long Gallery. These were wonderful evenings we were privileged to attend, but to me, what really brought home that we were actually being entertained in Castle Howard was the fact that the painting of Henry VIII, by 'the workshop of Holbein the younger', stood on an easel just inside the entrance door to the Long Gallery during events.

Castle Howard announced in 2014 that it, and other treasures were to be auctioned by Sotheby's. A figure of £965,000 was reportedly achieved for this single painting.

There the painting stood, nearly 500 years old, and to

me, that picture symbolised Castle Howard itself; the actual castle being a mere stripling at only 400 years old compared to the Henry VIII painting. It is interesting to compare that Willyam Fewlar, the first of my ancestors in the Fowler family tree, was born in 1541, one year before 'Henry' was painted.

Castle Howard was a wonderful place and I felt privileged to have been involved - albeit in a miniscule way.

*King Henry VIII, 1542. (One year after the start of our Fowler family tree) Workshop of Hans Holbein the Younger and recently sold by Sotheby's for a reputed £965,000*

When he rang me recently Allen Ferguson, friend and ex-colleague, reminded me to include the fact that we often paid for our attendance at these concerts 'in kind'. There was the time a grand piano had been hired and had to be taken downstairs from the Long Gallery after a concert. There was no lift and although a gang of Irish removers was being employed to do it they felt they needed additional help so Ian Martin collared 3 or 4 of us and said, 'Right you lot. Can you help get the piano downstairs safely?' We did.

On another occasion a harpist was playing and after the concert she and her partner were struggling to get the harp downstairs and into their vehicle. Again we helped and we were just leaving, having loaded it into the vehicle when we heard the sound of breaking glass. The harp was safely inside the vehicle so the partner had slammed down the rear tailgate. However, the vehicle's rear window sloped rather sharply so had shattered and they made their way home with a broken window and part of the harp sticking out into the night air.

Around late 1989 my bank car, the Mercedes 190E was 3 years old and due for replacement. By then the bank had changed its policy and instead of letting managers pick any car they chose, subject of course to cost; they had decided that cars could only come from Nissan or Ford, as both firms gave the bank much better discounts. I ended up with a metallic dark blue Ford Granada Scorpio automatic. Whilst not the BMW or the later Mercedes with which the bank had provided me, it was very closely matched and turned out to be an excellent car with many extra features included. It also grew to know its own way the five miles or so, back home from Castle Howard after the numerous functions we attended there.

One morning in June 1990 Eileen rang me at the bank in a state of high excitement.
'We've had a letter from Buckingham Palace,' she said.
'A letter? Crikey!! So what's it say?' I replied thinking she was winding me up.
'I don't know! I haven't opened it.'
'Well, open it then you can tell me.'
She did and I heard a long drawn out breath. She then said, 'Good heavens! We're invited to a Garden Party at Buckingham Palace on 24th July at 4.00pm. Are we free? Can we go?'
She was bubbling over with excitement.
'Yes, if it's not a hoax, of course we can go', I said.
'We'll sort it out when I get home.'

The invite was obviously not a hoax but I was intrigued how we had come to receive it and who had recommended us. It was not the sort of thing you just booked yourself. I was involved in various charities at the time and thought it could have been one of these or possibly one of our titled clients had made the approach.

*The Lord Chamberlain is
commanded by Her Majesty to invite*

*Mr and Mrs D. G. Fowler*

*to a Garden Party at Buckingham Palace
on Tuesday, 24th July, 1990 from 4 to 6 p.m.*

*Morning Dress, Uniform or Lounge Suit*

It was some time later that we discovered it had been Marcus Whickham Boynton from Burton Agnes Hall, near Driffield who had put our names forward whilst I worked in Driffield. Sadly, he had died in 1989, the year before, so I could not thank him. It was his bequest to me.

We arrived in London by train the day before the event, and the day of the garden party dawned bright and sunny. The hotel booked us a taxi to take us to the palace and the driver said the Mall would be very crowded and all taxi drivers had been instructed to take clients into the Palace grounds through the back entrance. The guidelines we had received did give that as an alternative but also said the main front entrance could be used so I told him that if at all possible we would prefer to use the front entrance as it was very much a 'one–off' for us.

The driver made his way up the Mall and everyone must have taken the official advice and gone in the back way as the journey was easy and we swept through the gates of Buckingham Palace like royalty. He dropped us only a few yards from where a new prime minister's car would stop, we gave him a generous tip and he drove away smiling.

After our invitation had been glanced at we were then told in very subservient tones to go through one of the front doors, then through the interior of the Palace and various state rooms, before we left the building through French windows at the rear.

What was surprising was that we were not accompanied although were probably being watched electronically.

*With Eileen after the Garden Party, outside Buckingham Palace, 24th July 1990.*

Our route led right through the Palace before arriving at steps down into the gardens at the back where the garden party was being held. It was a wonderful day and an experience not to be missed. Our access through the actual palace building was a real bonus as this was in the days long before official tours of the palace had been introduced. Guests arriving through the back entrance arrived direct into the garden and missed the entire 'Palace experience.'

We said a silent 'thank you' to Marcus.

In April 1990 members of Malton Lions Club visited Paris for a long weekend. This trip wasn't linked to a French Lions Club as had been the visit from Driffield to Verneuil Lions, but Malton members had thought it would make a pleasant break to spend a long weekend there. And so it was. Wives were invited and we visited all the tourist sites, stayed in the same hotel together and we had time for any visits couples wished to make on their own.

One amusing episode was when we were all returning to the airport under our own steam, to catch our flight back to Leeds/Bradford airport.

Eileen and I had left plenty of time and we decided to have a meal in a Paris restaurant. We found a suitable looking place and went in, only to find member Mike Elvy there with his wife Anne. We joined them at their table and ordered, the Elvy's already having done so. I ordered a very well done steak and when it arrived it was dripping blood. I mentioned this to the waitress and it went back to the kitchen only to return a little later still very rare.

I attempted in my poor French to explain, but in all, this damned steak made three journeys back to the kitchen before I admitted defeat and cringed as I thought of eating it.

Mike and Anne's meals then appeared. His steak was wonderfully charred and I looked at him in envy, but he turned up his nose and said he'd ordered a rare steak. It was his with which I had been served! We swapped and laughed and both of us were happy, especially when Le Patron came out from the kitchen and apologised that as the steak hadn't been to our liking there would be no charge. However, we did leave a much larger tip than would have been normal as we realised we had contributed to the problem.

Each year there was Malton Agricultural Show, together with shows at Ryedale, Driffield, Thornton Dale, the Great Yorkshire Show and the Royal Agricultural Show, all to attend.

*This photograph was probably taken at the Great Yorkshire Show, where I was presenting cups which the bank had donated. In this case they had been won by customers of the bank. I appear far right in the photograph.*

Following our Buckingham Palace visit we spent two week's holiday in Italy; in Rome and Sorrento in 1990. In Sorrento we stayed at the Tramontano Hotel in a room overlooking the harbour and sea.

Our 1991 holiday was spent in Madeira – the first of two visits. We stayed at Reid's on this first visit as we had obtained a very good deal as the hotel was celebrating its centenary. When we compared prices the following year they had doubled. Even so, apart from an excellent breakfast served in our room overlooking the sea we only ate in the hotel once for a centenary dinner they arranged, as prices were so high.

That same year we had to have the front foundations of Old Church House underpinned. Because of a few dry summers the clay on which the village had been built had dried out and a few cracks had started to appear in the front brick and stone work. Luckily we had a very good bank surveyor customer who arranged everything through our insurance company, and the entire house frontage was underpinned. It was done in stages by excavating the land lying around the foundations for a metre span, then replacing that with new foundations formed from blocks of reinforced concrete cast on site. Each block was around a metre cubed in size and individual blocks were then linked with the adjoining block by protruding steel bars. The original foundations were found to consist of two layers of thin limestone blocks – apparently the norm at the time the building was built as a church. When the work was complete there was no evidence of all that had been done. The surveyor and builder had done an excellent job.

For our birthdays in 1991 (both are on 18th June) we had the chance to hold a barbecue at the boathouse at Castle Howard.
This was a wonderful outdoor venue with a large veranda and capacity within the boathouse itself to take everyone if the weather turned against us. Luckily the elements were kind although this was an evening during a drought and the Castle Howard boat; a refurbished Edwardian, now battery driven passenger vessel, was not able to get out of its own boathouse to give us rides round the lake. Ian Martin acted as MC and an excellent evening was had by all.

*The venue of our joint birthday party was a barbecue at Castle Howard. I am at the back raising my glass, with Eileen in front with Ian Martin who acted as MC.*

*Another photo from the same party with Eileen dancing with Canon John Manchester, then Vicar of Old Malton. Front left, facing the camera are Margaret and John Fawbert, both now sadly not alive, who feature in the Goole chapter of this book, ('Loitering on the docks')*

I would hate to give the impression that it was all play and no work at Malton branch. Far from it. Every member of management and staff worked very hard, and the graphs showed consistent upward rises in all important areas. When we met or exceeded targets we would periodically have a 'profits party' – not to spend the additional income – but to thank the staff for their efforts.

Each year we also arranged a Christmas lunch for all the staff although, as it was at lunchtime and the bank was open, we obviously couldn't all be together so we had two or three sessions so everyone was included.

Just as had been the case at Driffield branch, Malton, together with the adjoining town of Norton, had their own joint agricultural show at which the bank was represented. I was asked and happy to become a Vice-president of the Malton and Norton Agricultural Society.

*Malton Show, June 1988, with the Portakabin we then used for customer entertaining. Front left is Doug Ross, Regional Director, I am next to him in the light suit and staff complete the picture. Not all staff could be there as we had to keep the branch open in town.*

For the show, we used similar arrangements to those I had introduced at Driffield, which enabled Eileen and I to be free to entertain and talk with customers and potential customers.

Allen Ferguson, who had been a friendly, efficient and very effective lending manager, well-liked by both customers and staff, gained well deserved promotion to Beverley branch, and in his place Paul Newlove moved to the branch. John Douglas was office manager but a later bonus because of the new and increasing business we were obtaining was that John was promoted from his role of office manager to lending manager to look after the majority of the branch's personal business. With John's promotion, Russ Grimshaw moved to the branch as office manager.

Allen's pending leaving, and John's internal promotion left Paul and I able to concentrate on growing the business portfolio; part of my own existing portfolio which I was then able to pass on to Paul.

Incidentally, even after that shuffle I was still left with around 1200 business customers of my own to look after and I was still personally responsible for all borrowings made by the other lending managers at the branch. This, to me, seemed entirely illogical. They had all been on courses and were all trained and proficient to lend. Had they any doubts about a proposition they would see me and we would talk it through before making a decision. Yet I took the can if any of their lending went wrong.

Around 1993 the bank started to carry out a countrywide survey on managerial workloads. We heard on the grapevine that there was a possible feeling amongst the bank hierarchy that many managers were underworked. Some managers might have been, but this was certainly not the case at many branches, including Malton, and I felt the powers-that-be would get a shock from the survey results.

These results appeared shortly after I retired in

September 1994 but I heard that, had I still been at the branch, and as well as the overall managerial responsibilities for which I had always been responsible, I would have been responsible for no more than twenty business customers compared to the 1200 for which I had actually been responsible. No wonder I had felt overworked at times and had had to take work home many evenings and at weekends. The rules also changed whereby subordinate managers all became individually responsible for the safety of their own lending.

With hindsight I do suspect that the survey was the start of the bank's decision to introduce computerisation into the lending sector. The computer would then make most lending recommendations and from there would come the modern phrase, 'the computer says No!' I also feel sure that the same survey also led to many branches being downgraded, closed or merged into larger branches, to enable management numbers being cut.

Allen Ferguson's promotion date drew near and he arranged a retirement party at the hostelry of one of our customers. The girls on the staff were giggling a bit and I wondered what they had arranged. Then in walked a 'policewoman' to 'arrest' Allen. She jangled her handcuffs, he spoke with her and I heard him say, 'Oh heck. It's you. I know you. We'd better go through with it for the benefit of the girls.' So they did and he was duly arrested.

Just after Allen left the branch we had a farmer customer – one of mine – who had hit hard times and whose farm we had been on the point of repossessing. We felt we had given him enough rope and various opportunities to turn his farm round; but this had not happened and things were going from bad to worse.

Some weeks before, and known to the customer, the bank had taken all the necessary legal steps to repossess the farm with which he had appeared to agree, albeit reluctantly.

However, he had been very confident he had found a private buyer, so our final concession had been to give him three weeks to get contracts exchanged for a private sale. Failing him achieving this, the bank would take control and would sell the farm.

That extension was due to run out on the day he phoned me; the same day his sale contract exchange was planned to go ahead.

Had that private sale gone ahead, the bank would have lost financially but we had agreed that the customer could be left with sufficient funds to enable him to move away from the area. In such difficult circumstances everyone would have lost but from the bank's point of view that would have been a better option than to allow interest to pile up unpaid on a dormant borrowing.

On the morning the sale was due to be completed the farmer phoned me and started arguing about the agreement saying he wanted the bank to meet all legal fees and various other expenses and to guarantee he could have a much larger proportion of the sale proceeds. I refused point blank, telling him he either agreed to let the sale proceed that day for which we had his earlier written agreement, or he would be worse off if we took possession then sold to a buyer at a lower price. We finished the call in a somewhat heated manner and, feeling somewhat exasperated I put the phone down.

Allen's successor, Paul Newlove, came into my room and I started telling him about how this customer had tried to put pressure on us at the 11th hour and how he thought he could take me for an idiot. I ranted on for a while about the customer and his lack of morals.

Then the phone rang. It was the same customer! The telephone line hadn't disconnected properly and he had heard every word I'd said. He promptly called off the sale calling me every name under the sun.

I immediately phoned regional office who in turn, phoned the bank's agent who had acted in the original repossession proceedings which were temporarily on ice.

These arrangements were still legally valid; they had merely been delayed. The agents knew the customer's intended buyer, approached him and did a quick deal, selling the farm for the same amount but obtaining a higher sum for the bank than the customer had arranged. How? It transpired that the customer's own deal with the buyer had included one price for the bank and another, which included a good few thousand pounds, for himself.

The branch car park was situated behind the bank so involved a walk of around 50 yards to the front door. One day another farm customer, Alec Taylor, came in, saw me in the banking hall and said, 'Giv us yer car keys lad. Ah'll bring 'em back.' And he did, about 10 minutes later. When I got to the car later and looked in the boot there was a large cardboard box containing a butchered lamb. Thank you Alec!

Other popular gifts from farmers were game; grouse, partridges, and pheasants. These were dead of course, but normally complete with plumage so a quick lesson was needed in hanging, defeathering and gutting them and preparing them for the pot. All went well until one day I got a mouthful of lead shot which dislodged a couple of fillings in my teeth. I have not happily eaten game since.

One special event was held at Castle Howard and involved my intronisation as a Vigneron d'honneur de La Jurade de Saint-Émilion – (Les Brown, French master at the High School for Boys would have been proud of me).

The Jurade is a body based in Bordeaux in France which was originally chartered on the 8th July 1199 (yes, 1199) and whose members are tasked with ensuring that wines bearing the Saint-Émilion label are of the highest quality.

I was 'intronised' (in other words, inducted) into the Jurade as an honorary member with a few others in 1993. Ian Martin, the promotions manager at Castle Howard, was then the Northern Chancellor of the Jurade and he was there together with members of the 'Jurat', the officials of the association, who were mostly French. Whilst it was usual for intronisées to have first attended at least two events, often the 'Bans des Vendages' (the declaration of the new grape harvest in Saint–Émilion, in September), they dispensed with this for me as the association's UK banker. Subsequently we did visit Saint–Émilion a number of times in early September and had some superb experiences; including pageantry and not only visiting very prestigious vineyards and chateaux in the area, but sampling their excellent wine as well. Members are presented with a red wax sealed parchment scroll, written in mediaeval French and, for formal Jurade occasions, a scarlet and ermine épitoge, worn over the left shoulder is the badge of office.

As well as Jurade events being held at Castle Howard one memorable visit by the French Jurats included an evening service at York Minister, and others were held at the excellent White Swan Inn in Pickering where proprietor Deirdre Buchanan put on superb food and accommodation.

*Me, being intronised as a Vigneron d'honneur de la Association de Saint Emilion*

Another wonderful evening was a small dinner party Ian Martin put on at his home on the Castle Howard Estate. We knew his son James was a well-respected chef in a restaurant in the south of the country and had trained at The Yorkshire Coast College in Scarborough. Ian had arranged for James to cook for us and Ian's daughter Charlotte would be 'front of house' and serve and look after us. It was a magnificent meal and evening made even more enjoyable by Saint-Émilion wines.

Not much later James appeared on television, then appeared in a weekly Sunday colour supplement series reviewing exotic cars he had test driven, since when his career has taken off at similar speed to some of the cars he tested. He is now a well-known celebrity.

A few years ago James became executive chef adviser to the Talbot Hotel in Malton and built up the standards of the recently refurbished hotel. This building had previously operated as a hotel for a number of years although latterly it had become tired. The Fitzwilliam Estate which owned the freehold, renovated the building and launched the restaurant and its reputation is now very high. An online review follows:

*'In the heart of the thriving market town of Malton, The Talbot Hotel provides 5-star accommodation. The 17th Century property has its own bar and restaurant, and meadow gardens that stretch down to the River Derwent. Roaring open fires and traditional cream teas in period style lounge rooms make for a classic country retreat. Guests can relax with a book in the elegant drawing room, sample some whisky by the wood-panelled bar and grab light bites in the atrium. Executive TV Chef James Martin oversees the Talbot's restaurant menu, and meals are served in the grand dining room with floor-to-ceiling windows overlooking the grounds. Rooms are bright and airy and decorated in light pastel colours. Each has an en-suite bathroom with luxury Penhaligon's toiletries, and*

*views look out over the town or gardens. The hotel has free Wi–Fi internet throughout. The Talbot Hotel is just 10 miles from the North York Moors National Park and 18 miles from York.'*

One day a customer called in to discuss his business and mentioned in conversation that he was part owner of a Cessna light aircraft. It was based at a small airfield near Hull and he had use of it a couple of times each week. Would I like a flight sometime?

I jumped at the opportunity so we arranged a date and I met him at the airfield on the agreed afternoon.

Eileen and I lived in Great Barugh about 7 miles north of Malton, so a round trip from the airfield near Hull, to Barugh, where we would circle our house, then back again to the airfield was arranged.

Before we set off he had marked his route on a map which he had presumably lodged with air traffic control, then showed me it, and off we went. We seemed to be more or less following the route, but occasionally he would ask if I saw anything I recognised and whether it showed on the map. I recognised Driffield then Old Malton Church as we went on our way and we eventually arrived at Great Barugh. There was only one problem. We were very high and whilst he had asked for permission to fly lower it appeared that the RAF had a low flying exercise that day so we had to keep to a minimum of 5000 ft. We spotted Eileen in the garden waving but afterwards she said the plane looked like a pin prick although she thought she saw it waggle its wings.

After a few circuits we turned and headed back to the airfield where the same procedure took place.

'What do you recognise?' 'Are we on route?' and so on.

We arrived safely back at the grass airfield, even though on the approach I thought we were going to hit power cables and then the landing seemed to be a little bumpy. I thanked him for the experience then said, 'Can I ask you one thing? Why did you keep asking me whether we were sticking to the route and where we were?'

He smiled and coloured up a little. 'Ahh' he said. 'My sight is poor without my spectacles. ...And I'd left them at home!'

In 1993 when I was 55 the bank circulated an offer that voluntary managerial redundancies might be available upon request. This was a reasonably attractive offer but contained a reduction in pension in view of the earlier than normal retirement date. 5 years in my case would have been deducted as the bank would have been paying my pension for 5 years longer. The bank was hoping to lose a layer of management and a number of us were initially interested.

Shortly afterwards I discussed this with Doug Ross, the director from regional office in Leeds who was my point of contact with the hierarchy, when he was visiting Malton branch. His off the record advice was to 'hold on if you can' as his own view was that within a year a more attractive offer would have to be made, to secure the number of retirements for which the bank was looking.

And so it turned out to be. The later scheme proposed no reduction in pension for leaving early, so that anyone in management who was accepted for the scheme could retire at a date in the future to suit the bank, with a pension of two thirds of final salary at the date of actual retirement.

It was an extremely fair – even generous offer. Eileen is 6 years older than me; the bank was changing into a sales and very target orientated organisation, branches were being amalgamated and some were being closed with online banking being encouraged. I could see my round peg trying to fit into a square hole if I stayed much longer.

Also, up until then, managers had made lending and management decisions based on a critical analysis of the facts available to them. These were, of course subject to head office guidelines. Whilst branches used computers for bookkeeping purposes, managers had not been issued with them – but later, when they were, the computers analysed lending proposals and made the decisions.

I passed on Doug's comments to one or two other manager friends who had been thinking of retiring under the earlier scheme then on offer. All were grateful and decided to stay, and see if the later scheme was announced.

It was, so I, together with a number of other managers applied to leave under the terms of the new scheme. My application was approved and my paid service was to end on 30th September 1994, although I actually left just over 3 weeks sooner because of accrued holiday I had to come.

At the time I took early retirement as branch manager, Malton branch had 2 other lending managers and an office manager. I was responsible for a branch lending book with borrowing limits totalling over £50m – at 1994 values – and net profit had increased substantially to around £1.6m a year, which, for a comparatively small country branch was substantial. Malton branch was earning the highest profit per head of staff of any branch in the entire Leeds region.

Computers were being given more prominence and whilst, up to then, as well as for bookkeeping, they had been used for preparation and analysis of customer's trading accounts and balance sheets, this was to change. These days, it seems the computer decides who can borrow, and how much, and unfortunately a lot of the personal contact has gone.

By this time, we had lost two of our cats, Ayckbourn and Shimba. Chloe was to follow a short time later. There would only be Thomas for us to take with us into retirement and he was almost blind having had to have one of his eyes removing.

My retirement date grew nearer and an invitation

arrived for me to join the directors for lunch at Leeds where I was presented with a heavy cut glass bowl about 15 inches in diameter. Later, I was talking with a colleague who was leaving, and he was a little miffed as his bowl was only 6 inches in diameter. Somebody must have been trying to tell me something.

Following the lunch, I received a letter from David Lovell, the senior regional director, and he wrote:

*'We wish to place on record the Bank's sincere appreciation of your excellent service over your career.*

*We are appreciative of your stewardship of Malton [branch] which has gone from strength to strength, and I know how pleasing it is to you that you should head the league in cost income ratio terms and per capita profit.'*

In non-bank parlance the latter referred to the fact that Malton branch had risen to become the most profitable branch per head of staff, in the entire Leeds Region, which then comprised 109 branches of various sizes. Larger branches, for instance in Leeds itself, made more total retained profit than Malton, but, of course had greater staff numbers so their 'per capita profit' was lower.

This was not just a pat on my back. It reflected well on every single member of the branch team and in the seven years I was at Malton I can recall very few members of staff who, I felt, didn't fully pull their weight. Staff came and went, of course, and not all were there for the full 7 years I was branch manager. But whilst each of them was at the branch, they rolled up their sleeves, knuckled down, and did their utmost to help to gain the superb results we achieved over 7 years.

Head office supported the Premier Football league and had there been a cup for the Premier branch it would have gone to Malton branch.

It would be invidious to pick out particular members of staff for praise as everyone contributed to the progress of the branch through their own departments. However, without a strong, cohesive management team, all hopes of raising performance, meeting targets and raising branch profit levels would have gone out of the window.

Allen Ferguson, Paul Newlove, John Douglas and Russ Grimshaw were all totally supportive and without their efforts we would not have been able to make the progress we did. Two other departments which worked closely with me personally, were securities and the secretarial departments. Securities department, (absolutely nothing to do with locking doors and windows as some people might think!) was responsible for making sure any security we took to support advances, was legal and watertight. This was effectively a legal role and they all performed admirably. The other was the secretarial department, which was front line, in that they dealt with incoming phone calls, making appointments, preparing files for coming interviews, all typing, mailing and secretarial duties and keeping management informed of snippets the secretaries might have heard about customers from elsewhere.

Occasionally, a farming customer might arrive, or phone at 3.00pm (one even phoned me at 6.00am!) and say they wished to bid in an auction for a farm the following morning. They had done their homework but didn't appreciate that we needed to do ours. Invariably, the amount they required was of the size where head office was involved and this meant preparing a detailed application for funds, getting it all typed and mailed to head office, in the hope that we could get agreement before the auction the following day. It was all paper and Royal Mail in those days. You couldn't just e-mail an application to head office. If typing suddenly arose at going home time there was never dissention and I particularly thank my own secretary, Anne Guest, together with the whole secretarial team over the 7 years of Janice Bendell, Trish Hartley, Gill Hunt, Jill Sturgeon and Ann Morton. Thank you ladies.

*Some of the Malton branch staff – those available on June 23rd 1994. Shown from the left are: Front: Russ Grimshaw, Paul Newlove, John Douglas; Back: Kath Coulson Linda Welsby, Ann Morton, Helen Kirk, Angela Jewitt, Louise Hall, Debbie Towse, Jane Goforth (at the back), Margaret Wilson, Anne Guest, Mike Wrathall, and Steve Toal.*

To conclude this chapter before moving on to my actual retirement we had a well-known local titled customer, Lady W. who, at one time had been lady-in-waiting to the late Princess Margaret.

Lady W was a wonderful woman, elderly, very friendly and easy to get on with but she would call me 'Poppet' She frequently called into the branch without appointment and would say to my secretary, 'Is Poppet free?'

She was sometimes a little indiscrete about Princess Margaret when the princess was still alive; giving details of early morning phone calls between the two of them, and she would end with, 'But you won't tell anyone, will you Poppet?' I never did and don't intend to do so now, but I gather that to this day, 23 years since I retired, some of the Malton branch female staff when chatting together still call me 'Poppet'.

Another woman customer caused me some concern – and not only because her borrowing was nearly always in excess of what it should have been. After this customer had made a few unsuccessful and not very concealed suggestions that there could be other ways to deal with her borrowing I asked Anne Guest, my personal secretary, to keep peering through the spyhole in the door to my room and to keep coming into the room on some pretext or other if she thought the customer was trying to get too friendly. Anne kept popping in and out when this woman was with me; she watered the flowers and plants twice during each visit; emptied the waste paper bin a few times; came in and asked if we wanted coffee, told me the next customer was waiting, and so on.

Luckily, after a number of interruptions the customer seemed to get the message although, even after I had retired, I needed to give evidence at Leeds Crown Court as the bank made a move to get its money back from her and she incorrectly claimed that I had given her inappropriate advice. Her case collapsed completely when I produced the retirement leaving card she had sent me which completely demolished her defence in court.

The weeks fled and retirement was now coming nearer at quite a pace. It was time to arrange a retirement party. I considered various venues but when the offer to use Castle Howard was offered, I felt there could be no better venue to say goodbye to the bank, to the branch and to my staff and customers. Castle Howard held – and still does and always will – so many happy memories of the time we lived at Great Barugh and of my days at Malton branch.

We settled for Friday, 9th September 1994, which coincided with my very last day at work. Ian Martin organised things from the Castle Howard end; we suggested how we wanted things and as usual he came up trumps.

We had 108 guests there; bank staff with whom I had worked over my 39 years in the bank, but also friends from Great Barugh, all Malton branch staff, some customers, my successor John Weatherall and his wife, and Regional Director Doug Ross and his wife.

*Above: Castle Howard*
*Below: Eileen and I, with me clutching notes ready for my speech*

That afternoon, the branch staff had provided me with a carriage clock and a special bottle of vintage wine which they had purchased through Ian from the cellars at Castle Howard. When handing this precious bottle to me at the branch, my secretary Anne, apologised that 'I wasn't able to get all the cobwebs and dust off the bottle but I did give it a good scrub!'

At the Castle Howard event we started off with a champagne reception in the Great Hall. There I gave a farewell speech thanking the branch staff for their support and everyone for attending. I also made reference to football, as the bank was sponsoring the Premier league and many of the top brass seemed to be football crazy. All this was woven into a quasi–biblical–cum–football based theme, as at one time, and mentioned earlier, working together in local head office at York (the forerunner of regional office at Leeds) was director Noel <u>Pharaoh</u>, and members of staff Mike <u>Saul</u>, Mike <u>Moses,</u> and John <u>Angell</u>. Mike Hanlon had also worked there and to complement the four he had been nicknamed <u>'God'</u>.

*Above: Me giving my speech*

Regional director Doug Ross responded and presented me with a watch and a book of signatures from past and present colleagues in the region and Keith Dickinson, then chairman of the manager's club, presented me with an engraved tankard. We then moved on to supper in the Grecian room after which Ian Martin gave a very humorous speech, then Sarah Beth Briggs, later to become Ian's wife, and a renowned classical pianist, gave a short piano recital. Sadly, the evening came to a close far too quickly and the trusty Ford Granada, on auto-pilot, took us safely back home to Old Church House.

*Above: Supper in the Grecian Room*

The evening had been all we had hoped for – a wonderful send off for Eileen and myself and a thank you and goodbye to many of the colleagues and staff with whom I had worked over the previous 39 years in the bank. I had tried to contact all of those I had worked with but, sadly, some had died and some lived too far away to travel but I feel the 108 of us there had a great evening.

And, of course, we still meet many of them at the Bank's pensioners' club quarterly lunch meetings.

Above: *Ian Martin speaking after supper*

By this time we had bought a home in Newby on the northern outskirts of my home town Scarborough, as my elderly parents were needing more help. We still hadn't sold Old Church House at Great Barugh so hadn't then moved.

Had circumstances been different we would both have wished to stay in Great Barugh but the hamlet was in the middle of nowhere being seven miles from each of Malton, Kirbymoorside and Pickering. There was no village shop and little public transport and we were conscious that, in the case of illness the village was rather remote. We would also have been reliant on still being able to drive. Another factor was that some of the friends who were all part of the same group in the village had, or were planning to move on, so the camaraderie in the village was gradually diluting and not what it had been. Finally, in retirement there would not have been the closeness of the branch, the staff and the customers.

The 7 years we lived at Old Church House; the 7 years in Great Barugh; the 7 years I was responsible for Barclays' Malton branch; the 7 years I was proud and privileged to work with the branch staff – all these things together just seemed so right and gelled into one almost perfect whole: as if it had all been pre-planned.

That then was Malton. Whilst the work at the bank had been very challenging and at times stressful; it had also been very satisfying, successful and, I felt, worthwhile.

Nevertheless the strain which had been slowly building up, would, unknown to me, manifest itself just a few months later....

\*

# CHAPTER 15

# 'Damn protocol!!'
# 1994 to 1996

> **1994: Brief Timeline**
>
> Brian Johnston, the BBC cricket commentator, dies aged 81; Jayne Torvill and Christopher Dean win the British ice-dancing championship; The Duchess of Kent joins the Roman Catholic Church; The Prince of Wales retires from competitive polo at the age of 45. British Aerospace sells its 80% stake in Rover to BMW, leaving Britain without an independent volume carmaker; British Coal confirms the closure of four more pits, a move which will claim some 3,000 jobs; Three men are jailed in connection with the IRA bombings of Warrington gasworks 11 months ago; Forensic tests reveal that MP Stephen Milligan died of asphyxiation; Honda sells its 20% stake of the Rover Group, allowing BMW to take full control; 24 February – Police in Gloucester begin excavations at 25 Cromwell Street, the home of 52-year-old builder Fred West; The IRA launch three successive mortar attacks on Heathrow Airport; Women's Royal Air Force fully merged into Royal Air Force; Rosemary West, 40-year-old wife of suspected serial killer Fred West, is charged with three of the murders her husband stands accused of; The Channel Tunnel, a 32 mile long rail tunnel beneath the English Channel at the Strait of Dover, officially opened; Film *Four Weddings and a Funeral* released in the UK.

I knew I would miss the bank and the staff. I did, of course, very much; but initially retirement was just like being on holiday which kept getting extended. Officially I was on holiday leave until the end of September, and we travelled to Saint Émilion for the Ban des Vendages – the celebration of the harvesting of the new crop of grapes, to meet other members of the Jurade de Saint-Émilion.

I had bought the trusty Ford Granada Scorpio from the bank on retirement and we drove down to Poole, then caught the ferry to St Malo and drove from there down to Saint Émilion. We were all meeting up at a small hotel on the Friday with events having been arranged at various Chateaux and vineyards until the Monday morning when everyone broke up to make their way home.

*Saint Émilion*

Saint-Émilion's history goes back to prehistoric times and it is a UNESCO World Heritage Site, with fascinating Romanesque churches and ruins stretching all along steep and narrow streets.

The Romans planted vineyards in what was to become Saint-Émilion as early as the 2nd century. In the 4th century, the Latin poet Ausonius lauded the fruit of the bountiful vine. The town was named after the monk Émilion, a travelling confessor, who settled in a hermitage carved into the rock there in the 8th century. It was the monks who followed him that started up the commercial wine production in the area.

These long weekends the Jurade held in Saint Émilion were hectic but extremely enjoyable. After visiting vineyards on the Friday afternoon, a luncheon was attended on the Saturday by Jurade members of all nationalities although each country's group had their own tables. The lunch extended to five courses with maybe eight Saint Émilion wines to water down the excellent food throughout the meal. The wines had been donated by the vineyards and the cheapest were produced for the early courses – but 'cheapest' is an understatement as even they would have cost at least £25 a bottle back home. And this was over 20 years ago. By the end of the meal we were drinking the likes of Cheval Blanc – a misnomer if there ever was one, as it is a St Émilion red and only one of four wines to gain the 'Première Cru classé' classification.

The Sunday morning was taken up with a church service in Saint Émilion Cathédrale, to give thanks for the new wine harvest.

After the service, all the Jurats, (members of the Jurade's governing body) in their colourful red and white cloaks climbed the stairs of the historic Saint Émilion Tour du Roi to the open air roof and celebrated the new vintage by throwing their red hats into the air. As they did so they all shouted, 'St Émilion. Halleluja!'

On the last day – the Monday morning – we had a brunch at one then small privately owned vineyard – Chateau Puy–Razac. This was open air and we sat on benches at long trestle tables whilst our hostess cooked everything imaginable. However, the gardener was responsible for cooking steaks over vine branches on an outside barbecue and 'rare' seemed to be the only way he could cook them. We English often like our steaks reasonably well done whereas our French cousins prefer them rare.

The family dog was nicknamed 'the bionic dog' as he had been in a bad road accident some years earlier and some skilful vet had saved his life by putting him back together with numerous pieces of metal. The dog seemed happy enough and not in pain but he did have a somewhat unbalanced gait as he ran.

It became very obvious that the dog enjoyed steak the French way – very rare – so around 2 dozen Brits were feeding him under the table so we could all leave clean plates.

*Above: The Monday brunch event at Chateau Puy–Razac, St Emilion. Behind where the photographer would have been standing was the charcoal barbecue where the steaks were cooked over vine leaves. I am front right and Ian Martin 2nd left.*

Whilst most of the party had to leave to fly home for work, we could, and did, take our time as we were driving. We stopped in Normandy and had a couple of nights in La Rochelle, in western France, a seaport on the Bay of Biscay. The seafront was particularly enjoyable and picturesque and had numerous small restaurants to choose from. There were no amusement arcades and Scarborough could well do to follow its example.

*Above: La Rochelle – at night*

Eventually we arrived at St. Malo for our ferry back to Poole, then the long car journey back home.

After we had returned home we decided that, against agent's advice, we should move to the Scarborough house we had bought, even though Old Church House had still not sold. The respected estate agent customer from my Malton days stressed that, occupied and furnished, Old Church House would sell more easily and for a better price. There was, he said, (and this hadn't been told us by the agent we bought from 7 years earlier) difficulty in selling property in the village because of lack of amenities and its distance from the nearest towns.

However, Eileen was not feeling well and she said if we didn't move soon her health would deteriorate. My parents were also needing more help and during the summer the route to and from Scarborough was time consuming with frequent traffic jams around Kirby Misperton, so, somewhat reluctantly we arranged to move to the house we had bought in Newby, on the northern outskirts of Scarborough. We called the house 'Farthings'.

The house had been built a few years previously for a

bank customer who then wanted to buy an old vicarage to modernise but to do so he needed to sell the Scalby Road house. It was well designed and laid out and also had a floored attic with Velux windows which would have made a perfect workshop or office.

There were small gardens back and front.

In the early days I went through there regularly with my tool box to do necessary jobs, keep the garden tidy and so on. We also had carpets and curtains fitted throughout prior to us moving.

The house itself was double glazed and would have been ideal – but for the traffic noise. We had moved from a small village where traffic was occasional, but outside Farthings, it was constant. Not only that, but there were cross roads nearby and car brakes squealed almost continually as they braked as they approached the cross roads. Most of this was muted from inside the house but there was no pleasure in gardening or sitting out in the garden.

Mentioned in an earlier chapter was the fact that health problems were possibly looming for me before retirement. I had got breathless at Malton walking from the bank's car park up a slight incline to the branch itself and those symptoms, added to what I was later told was delayed stress, eventually erupted.

In 1995, fourteen months after retiring, I was Lions' district secretary and deputy district governor. The annual district convention was to take place in Darlington in November, which was partly my responsibility to organise.

We arrived at the Darlington hotel and once everyone had booked in, a social evening had been organised for the first evening with a buffet and a railway theme, (remember it was Darlington of George Stephenson and 'Rocket' fame) Everyone had been given a train ticket to give them entry!

The main conference was to take place the following day, the 18th November 1995 and all my paperwork for this annual meeting was carefully prepared and stacked. That night I awoke in bed around 2.00am with a very tight pain across my chest. It certainly wasn't indigestion and I recalled I had not felt as well as normal that evening.

I hoped it would go away but it didn't so I woke Eileen and said, 'I think I'm having a heart attack.' She was incredulous and said I couldn't be but I was insistent so she tried to ring reception to get an ambulance. She picked up the room phone, there was no signal and the whole unit then fell off the wall. The hotel was in the middle of refurbishment and the phone had been disconnected.

Eileen put on a dressing gown and went down to reception. She says that on the counter was a singing Father Christmas but no human staff. She was getting concerned but eventually the night porter appeared and he had been getting our conference room ready for the following day.

He called for an ambulance and in the meantime Eileen took my briefcase to Richard Lukey, the assistant secretary who was with his wife in the room next door.

'Sorry Richard; David's going to hospital so you'll have to run the meeting tomorrow. Here are the papers.'

What a baptism of fire for Richard.

The ambulance arrived and took me to Darlington Memorial hospital – very slowly. The roads were very icy and slippery.

In hospital, various tests were carried out and I was put in the cardiac unit – and somewhat appropriately into a bed previously donated by Darlington Lions Club whose members had planned the Convention I had been attending. 36 hours later it was confirmed from test results that I had had a heart attack.

I thought back to my Malton days and recalled that I frequently got short of breath and that was probably the start of my problem.

While I was in hospital Eileen moved out of the hotel into her sister Heather's house which was fortunately in Darlington. But before doing so she had a word with Richard Lukey.

'We swopped our two cars for a new automatic Saab last week and I've never driven it!' she said. She had had a little Fiat Uno automatic and whilst it got her wherever she wanted to be, she was a timid driver and was concerned about driving the new Saab back to Scarborough. Richard got a few Lions members together and they had her driving to and fro and round the hotel car park until she felt comfortable.

She then stayed with her sister in Darlington until I was released from hospital, probably 10 days later and she successfully and smoothly drove us both home to Scarborough – right through a football crowd in the middle of Middlesbrough heading for a match.

One severe initial side-effect of a heart attack I discovered was a considerable lack of confidence in the recovery period, tied to spasms of extreme tiredness which could come on very suddenly.

After returning to Scarborough from Darlington hospital I visited my doctor who didn't exactly give me encouragement when he exclaimed, 'You must be my youngest patient ever, to have had a heart attack!' I was then 57.

Scarborough hospital did more tests and enrolled me into a cardiac patient class which helped my recovery and brought back my confidence. One aspect of this course was to do physical exercises, to prove you still could do them, as the feeling is always there – at least in the early stages - that the least little bit of exercise can trigger another attack.

Another aspect was for the cardiac nurse to visit you at home and discuss your progress. One of these visits was quite amusing. Clare, the nurse asked if I had an Angina spray in case angina chest pain occurred. I had and I produced it. She then went on to relate that a very young heart patient - just 18 - had been asking for replacement sprays on a very regular basis. This was very unusual as each spray unit has around 200 metered doses and there was no way he could have used all these by the time he was asking for a replacement. Clare had asked him what he was doing with the sprays and he had replied, 'all my mates borrow mine!'

She mentioned that this was dangerous if they had not been prescribed them, in which case they would have had their own sprays.

'Ahh,' he said, 'you don't understand. It only takes one squirt of the spray to get an almost immediate erection so the sprays are in great demand!'

Following on from the heart attack I put my hopes of becoming Lions' District Governor on the back burner.

The heart attack had been on 18th November 1995. Recovery was going well when, late in December 1995 I received an invitation *'to attend an exhibition and presentation of work produced by businesses supported by The Prince's Youth Business Trust in the presence of His Royal Highness The Prince of Wales, to be held on Friday, January 12th 1996 at 9.45am at the Merchant Adventurer's Hall, Fossgate York.'*

I had been an adviser for the Princes' Trust for a few years, meeting and guiding young people whom the trust had helped financially. The role was to get get these – mostly young – entrepreneurs established in self-employment and in sound business principles.

My doctor told me I would be fit enough to go – but by train. As only advisors were invited, Eileen was not included but she came to York with me, saw me to the Merchant Adventurer's Hall and we met later for lunch before returning by train to Scarborough

At the Merchant Adventurer's Hall we were told that Prince Charles would arrive in 10 minutes time and would be directed to two far corners of the room where Yorkshire business leaders had been gathered to meet him. We business advisers were asked to form two lines through which he would walk to get to the two big-wig corners and we were told before he arrived, that protocol dictated that we did not speak to Prince Charles unless we were first spoken to.

All business advisers were sent a Christmas card from him – normally a reproduction of one of his own water colours – and, as he quickly moved up our line of invitees towards the VIPs at the top of the room, I thought, 'Hang on. Protocol? Damn protocol! I'm lucky to be alive. I've survived a heart attack,' so as he passed me I called out, 'Thank you very much for the Christmas card Sir'. He stopped slightly ahead, did a double-take, turned and retraced his steps to me and smiled warmly. 'Glad you got it,' he said, and chatted amiably for a few minutes.

I am so grateful for all you have achieved over the last twelve months. This comes with my warmest best wishes for Christmas and the New Year.

*Above: One of the Christmas Cards sent to each Business Trust Adviser each year by Prince Charles.*

I had not met him previously but by this small action he shot up inestimably in my opinion. He could, so very easily, have ignored my comment and moved on to the 'big-wig' corners and to the important business people who were much more likely to be in a position to fund his charitable trusts; rather than we, much lesser mortals, who merely regularly gave a few hours of our time to pass on guidance and expertise to some of the start-up firms he was assisting. Thank you Sir.

Back at the Scalby Road house we initially took the view that we had 'made our bed and must lie on it' and we would possibly become accustomed to the traffic noise which so upset us.

And so we did initially, then after my heart attack, and with my doctor's blessing, we decided later that year on taking the advice of friends who had just returned from a Nile cruise.

This would be something different for both of us so we started looking at brochures. The holiday we picked consisted of a week's Nile cruise from Aswan to Luxor. For the second week we had the choice of staying in one of a number of hotels and we liked the look of one on its own 180 acre island in the middle of the Nile, about 4 km from Luxor. So we booked, and went in May 1996. That island, then called Crocodile Island but subsequently renamed Kings' Island, was an oasis of peace and quiet. There was no traffic on the island – unless you counted the staff moving round on bicycles, or the silent battery powered golf buggies which were used to move supplies round the island or to take or collect guests from their rooms. At the time of our early visits all rooms were single storey and were spread around the island with the main restaurants, reception, shops and so on, being situated centrally. The rest consisted of swimming pools, garden areas, abundant flora and fauna and wonderful views of the tourist boats and river traffic going up, and down, the Nile. The island was also a bird sanctuary.

The island, the facilities and particularly the staff and the management were all so much to our liking that over following 20 years we visited the island 30 times, our most recent visit being in 2016. Recent visits were a little in doubt because of the political situation in Egypt, although we have always found Luxor much safer than Scarborough on a Saturday evening.

The following extract comes from a chapter I included in my book *'Why Should England Tremble'* and includes details of that first visit:

*'On our first visit to Egypt a Nile cruise between Aswan and Luxor took up the first week. Early on, one of the passengers was quickly nicknamed 'Hyacinth Bouquet' because of her pretentious mannerisms and actions. She was a dead ringer for actress Patricia Routledge's character who starred in the popular British TV show 'Keeping up Appearances'. On one occasion, on a visit to the West Bank from our Nile cruise boat RA II, – which, incidentally, was built in Hull – 'Hyacinth' insisted on visiting a tomb, access to which consisted of numerous steps and very steep slopes downwards which eventually took you at least 100 feet below ground. Once down there Hyacinth gave a regal moan, extended an arm, gave an exaggerated twist of her wrist and announced to one and all that back home she had just been diagnosed with a serious heart defect and 'maybe I really shouldn't have visited this tomb!'*

*Three male passengers eventually helped get her back to the surface.*

*On another occasion 'Hyacinth' stood at the bow of our vessel RAII, in the pose adopted by actress Kate Winslett in the film 'Titanic'. She had one hand on the flag pole at the front of the vessel, the other extended into the air, her palm facing upwards and her fingers spread. She wore a large brimmed garden party hat on her head, and with her chiffon finery blowing in the breeze, she instructed her husband how to take her photograph....*

*During the first week we saw and explored many antiquities and as the last night of the actual cruise approached we were told that this would comprise an impressive fancy dress affair where all guests were expected to dress up. Of course, there was a shop on board selling suitable costumes!*

*After dinner we all moved to the top deck ballroom and bar for entertainment. The one really memorable act was the belly dancer – but not for reasons you might expect. The poor girl was obviously heavily pregnant and this alone gave an unwieldy gait to her performance. Not only that but her tights were badly laddered and, worse still, she gave the impression that she just didn't want to be there! After she had left the stage to mild but polite applause the compere asked if anyone in the audience would like to try to belly dance.*

*One girl did volunteer. She appeared to be at least an amateur dancer and probably professional and she danced very impressively in her chiffon cocktail dress which was far more alluring then the costume worn by the official dancer. That British girl redeemed what could have been a very disappointing last night at what had been a memorable Nile cruise.*

*After the 7 day cruise we disembarked at Luxor and were transferred to a garden paradise, the Jolie Ville Hotel, about 4km from the town.*

*The hotel is situated on its own island of around 180 acres. In those days everything from rooms to reception and restaurants was single storey, although more recent extensions have created a few two storey properties on the island....*

A further extract about a later visit follows:

*It is 6.00am as I write this chapter in the sunshine on the patio outside our room. We are on our 23rd visit to a wonderful hotel on its own island in middle of the Nile, near*

Luxor, Egypt and we have been visiting for the last 18 years – sometimes more than once and on a few occasions, also at Christmas.

At the end of each day the view of blood red sunsets visible from the island's Sunset Terrace, with Feluccas criss–crossing the Nile in silhouette as the sun sets over the West Bank, must be one of the most evocative and memorable experiences ever.

The hotel is the Maritim Jolie Ville Hotel, Luxor. We call it our second home and staff members still work on the island who remember us from our first visit.

The management and staff, headed by General Manager Urs Umbricht from Switzerland, are excellent, many going well beyond the call of duty to make a guest's stay memorable. Herr Umbricht is not at all the sort of General Manager you might expect. He is very energetic, active, open; approachable, friendly, enthusiastic, and even somewhat boisterous in his manner. But in this environment and taking into account the size of the island these very positive traits make him the perfect man for this job. His effervescent energy gives out a real buzz which radiates throughout the whole island to the benefit of all guests, managers and staff.

His leadership is superb and is reflected throughout the island – immaculate gardens, spotless public areas, paths and guest rooms, swimming pools you could drink from, superb well prepared food from various restaurants, and very well trained, happy and friendly staff throughout who speak extremely well of him. To many he is almost like a God.

Around 1988 – 5 years after the island hotel opened, a young Egyptian waiter called Okasha was given charge of drink and food served around the then single swimming pool. Okasha still undertakes that role.

Shortly after taking over, he thought that to serve traditional English afternoon tea could be a useful addition to the hotel's services. Cucumber sandwiches round the pool might be a bit over the top; but could a cup of English tea, or coffee and a piece of cake be popular? It proved to be so.

At 3 o'clock every afternoon, Okasha, or one of his staff if it is his day off, trundle out the very same tea trolley they have used for the last 25 years.

On it is coffee, tea and a variety of cakes and to attract attention. Okasha and his staff call out 'Coffee, Tea, Cake', as they push the trolley round the pool side and surrounding area. However, over the years the three words have been rolled into one so what you actually hear is 'Coffeeteacake'.

You might think from the above comments that this is such a wonderful hotel that nothing ever goes wrong. As in all businesses, it does, but it is how things are dealt with that makes the difference. On our most recent stay we had a call from a receptionist telling us we had outstayed our welcome and were only booked for 7 days which had expired that lunchtime. My wife was unwell at the time but we knew that we had booked and paid for 2 weeks. And so it proved, with a clerical error eventually being pinpointed as being the problem.

Eating in La Fleur Restaurant that evening, Urs Umbricht, then General Manager came in to the restaurant and did a double take on seeing us. His brain must have gone into overdrive as he said, 'I am delighted you have decided to have your last meal in the hotel.' Even his personal print–out of comings and goings had wrongly indicated we should have flown home that afternoon.

The following evening he came into the restaurant again. 'Welcome back!' he said, and we all laughed.

Anecdotes about the Island and the hotel staff are of a gentle nature as it is a peaceful and tranquil sort of place.

For instance, on a Christmas visit, the mainly Muslim staff had gone to great lengths to decorate the hotel and 'Father Christmas' even rode round the island on a camel distributing presents. By Boxing Day all decorations had been removed. There is no 12th Night in Luxor!

On Christmas Day the staff you meet greet you with 'Happy Christmas Sir', (or Madam), – but they always added the ubiquitous 'Inshallah' [If God wishes].
'Happy Christmas Sir. Inshallah'. Think that one out!
On our recent visit and in one of the restaurants, an obviously young, newly trained waiter was putting everything he had learned at college into practise in a very correct, dedicated but somewhat diffident manner.
'How long have you worked here?' I asked.
'One day sir!'
Each day afterwards he came up and said quietly to us, 'It's 2 days, now sir', and so on.
A now senior waiter but who was a trainee at the time of this anecdote, many years ago, carefully took the wine bottle to refill our wine glasses – and poured wine into my half full water glass. From the horrified expression on his face you would have thought he had committed a hanging offence. We laughed, he relaxed and laughed, and he reminds us of the episode on each visit.
Later, back home, we were at a dinner where a humorous grace was said. It always reminds me of the island, that waiter and the water and wine episode:

'O Lord above, Oh God divine.
Thou turnest water into wine.
Have mercy on we mortal men,
That we might turn it back again!'

On the island was a 5 year old camel called Rameses. His keeper, Mohamed, takes him round the island and he'll give rides to visitors. I said to the keeper I'd like to take a photo of Rameses.
'Go ahead', he said.

'But first, ask him to smile.' I felt completely barmy asking a camel to smile; but I did – and he turned his head towards me and actually smiled.

Rameses, the smiling camel

For many years the only easy way to get to the West Bank where most of the tombs and temples are located, was by way of a ferry about 5km north beyond Luxor. It got very congested so the authorities decided to build a new road bridge across the Nile. Over different visits we watched from the hotel as the bridge grew in the distance – it was only around 1 km south of the island.

There was much excitement in Luxor when it was announced that Britain's Princess Anne was to open the new bridge, especially when there was gossip that she might stay on the island.

Well before the opening date and to deal with the expected additional traffic, the single carriageway from Luxor to the bridge was made into a dual carriageway. As the new section was being built the locals of course continued to use the old road.

*But so attached were they to their old road that even when the new dual carriageway was officially opened with a central reservation containing trees and flowers, they refused to use the dual carriageway for many months, preferring to use the old road in both directions and leaving the new section completely empty.*

*On one visit to the island we decided to book a Balloon flight. We were collected from the hotel at some unearthly hour – around 5am – and taken to a massive forecourt in front of Hapsetshut's temple where a few years later on 17th November 1997, 62 people, mostly tourists, were murdered by terrorists.*

*In this area, tables had been set up with refreshments and the balloon was slowly being inflated.*

*Around 12 of us then climbed into the basket – there was no door – with instructions 'don't get near to the burner!' and the balloon took off into the early morning sunshine. The pilot introduced himself;*

*'I am a Swiss balloon pilot and very experienced. I normally fly in the Swiss Alps. In Luxor we are normally restricted to 500 feet by air traffic control but I wish to fly higher.'*

*He had a radio link to air traffic control at the nearby military airport and kept asking for permission to fly above 500 feet. Each time the reply came back, 'Denied'.*

*Eventually he got permission to fly to 1000 feet and he started 'bumping' the balloon up the mountain face on the other side of which lies The Valley of the Kings. He would let the balloon gently blow towards the mountain until it nudged it, before giving it a burst of gas which took us higher. The procedure was then repeated until we soared over the top of the mountain and dropped down slightly on the other side towards the valley far below. He then tried to reach control to get permission to go even higher but by this time and within the mountain range, we had lost radio contact. After about forty minutes he said,*

'We haven't much gas left. Can anyone see a road?' No-one could as we were in the middle of a mountain range and all we could see was the valley floor well below us.

So he started bumping the balloon down a different mountain face in the same way we had climbed originally. Into the face, turn off the gas, drop but this time by scraping the mountain face.

Around 100 feet from the dried up riverbed below he yelled to his young assistant 'get out with the rope!' The young man was more than reluctant and looked terrified but the demand in the pilot's voice eventually persuaded him that he might be better off out of the balloon, rather than in it. He jumped and landed on the very steep, very loose shale mountain face. There was no way he could safely climb down and he effectively rolled and skidded down in the shale to the valley floor, still clutching the balloon's tethering rope. When he got down, of course, there was nowhere to tie the rope so he heaved at a great rock to stop the still partly inflated balloon from taking off again.

We had come down in one of 5 dried up river beds but the pilot hadn't Satellite Navigation in those days and his map didn't indicate which river bed we might be in. They were spread out like fingers, with mountain ranges in between each.

Apart from there being no sheep it reminded me of the poem called 'Michael' by William Wordsworth:

'No habitation there is seen; but such
As journey thither find themselves alone
With a few sheep, with rocks and stones, and kites
That overhead are sailing in the sky.
It is in truth an utter solitude.'

'Don't worry,' said the pilot, after we had all scrambled out of the balloon. 'We have a walk of about two miles to get out to the open. There the minibus will collect us.' So far, so good. But I was recovering from a heart attack I'd had a few months previously and the heat was well over 100 degrees. Eileen and I had hats with us and we were the only couple to have water – we were all supposed to be on a short balloon ride which was to have been followed by breakfast in the desert. We stumbled across the river bed, picked our way over Wordsworth's 'rocks and stones' – although I don't think he had the Egyptian desert in mind when penning his poem – and eventually came out into the open as the pilot had promised. And it had probably been nearer a mile than the two he mentioned.

There, on the horizon, were our rescuers looking like matchstick men and there were the two rescue minibuses. But they couldn't get any nearer to us because of Wordsworth's 'rocks and stones', with a few boulders thrown in for good measure. We continued walking and the rescuers made their way towards us with water. We met somewhere around the middle.

Once we got to the rescue minibuses we were taken for breakfast – in the desert!

We enquired about the promised certificates of our adventure which, by now, had taken around 2 hours. The pilot promised he would drop them into the hotel, but when he did so, each certificate merely said, 'Balloon flight certificate – 20 minutes'. We queried this as we had been in the air for around an hour. His reply?

'I cannot put an hour as I'd lose my job – for using too much gas!!'

We still have those certificates.

We arrived home, back to Scarborough, safely but somewhat sadly, at leaving such wonderful sunshine and people.

On retiring I had been adamant that I would not let my

grey matter congeal. I had been a member of Lions Clubs International for almost 40 years and as well as club offices I had also taken a few at zone then district level, eventually rising to district secretary and deputy district governor. The ultimate would have been a year as District Governor, responsible for, and having to visit each club in an area roughly defined by drawing a line from Filey, just below Scarborough, across to Liverpool, on the west coast, then including everything north of the line, including Scotland and all the islands. But as mentioned earlier after my heart attack I thought all the travelling might not be sensible so didn't go further.

Other interests at that time involved me being on the committee for many years of the Friends of Theatre-in-the-Round – later to be The Stephen Joseph Theatre, in Scarborough. I was also treasurer of the local branch of the British Heart Foundation, and a business advisor for Prince Charles' Business Trust.

Shortly after returning home from our first trip to Egypt, I was asked to become a Governor of East Ayton County Primary School. It was a successful school, mainly rural, a few miles outside Scarborough, and well run with talented teachers and happy, well-adjusted children who were keen to learn.

After our first visit to Egypt and when we were back in the Scarborough house, we came to the conclusion – in fact I think we came to the conclusion while we stayed on the Island – that buying the Scalby Road house had been a big mistake. We had carpeted and curtained it and put money into improvements. However, we reluctantly made the decision that when the time was right we had to move. We stayed there for around 18 months by which time the health of both my parents had deteriorated. Father was not very mobile and mother's memory had started to slip so they felt it was time they moved into a residential home.

Veronica England, wife of close friend Bob who was still

in practice as a solicitor at that time, was matron of a residential home at Thornton Dale about 12 miles from Scarborough which had the reputation of being one of the best homes in the area. It also had the benefit of having two wings – one residential and the other nursing.

At the time my parents moved into the residential part, dad was the doddery one as he couldn't walk far. They were allocated what amounted to a wonderful self-contained flat on the first floor with its own lift to the ground floor. Possibly it had been intended originally as owner's accommodation. After only a few days there we received a phone call saying mother was in hospital as she had broken her hip.

The story emerged that dad had wanted to use the bathroom and mother pushed him there in a wheelchair. She hadn't used one before or realised the brake needed applying, so the wheelchair tipped over leaving them both on the floor with dad and the wheelchair on top of mother. The break was plated and after recovering, she and dad lived happily together in the home.

On one of our holidays my parents had been commenting that they ought to update their wills despite the fact that the sale monies from the Throxenby Grove family house – meagre by today's standards – were being rapidly swallowed by care home costs.

Their own solicitor had died some years previously so we arranged for friend and solicitor Bob England to visit while we were away. When we returned, Veronica told us the story. Bob had visited, prepared new wills and then called to get them signed. He had then asked if he should take the old wills for destruction or would my parents prefer to deal with them? They asked how he would destroy them and he said 'by burning'. He didn't apparently explain that he hired the use of a furnace to burn confidential papers.

They decided to destroy them themselves after Bob left,

and apparently they had torn them into tiny pieces, then put them in a glass ashtray – dad was an avid pipe smoker – then set them on fire. This turned into a small inferno, the glass ashtray broke with the heat, the burning pieces fell onto the carpet and that burst into flames. Certainly the fire alarm went off and from memory I think the fire brigade had attended as well.

Veronica stressed that my parents had pleaded that she wouldn't tell us of their exploits so when we visited them we merely asked 'Have you been good?' 'VERY good', they both chorused in unison with smiles on their faces.

Another amusing anecdote was when Veronica England casually commented to us in conversation that drinking glasses in the home seemed to be disappearing at an alarming rate.

Next time we visited my parents we noticed mother, with a tea towel, carefully drying drinking glasses having first washed them in the bathroom wash basin.

I passed some comment on the lines that she didn't need to wash them as the staff would do that when they collected the glasses. 'Oh no,' she said, 'I keep them all tidy in the cupboard.'

And she opened the large wardrobe door, and there, taking up the entire top shelf, about three glasses high and four deep, was row upon row of drinking glasses!

Eventually mother's memory started failing, she became ill and was moved to the nursing wing of the home. Dad couldn't understand why he couldn't visit her but she was at the end of her life and died shortly afterwards aged 90.

Veronica told us that the doctor had said that if dad survived for around six weeks after mother died, he had a chance of living another year or two. However, it was not to be.

We visited one afternoon, six weeks and a day after mother's death and he looked well and as if he was slowly coming to terms with his loss. However, as we were leaving, he called me over and insisted on shaking my hand and hugging me.

'Thank you for everything', he said. He had never been demonstrative and the hug, in particular, was most unlike him. I told him to take care as we'd be visiting again in a few days' time and we arrived back home about 5.00pm.

At around 6 o'clock the phone rang. He had died peacefully, aged 92.

*

# CHAPTER 16

# 'A German shell is buried in your wall...'
# 1996 to 2010

> **1996: Brief Timeline**
>
> In France, President Jacques Chirac declares a 'definitive end' to France's nuclear testing; The Irish Republican Army (IRA) is unhappy about its political wing, or party, Sinn Féin, not being included in settlement talks with Britain; A 17–month ceasefire ends with an IRA one–ton bomb explosion in London's Canary Wharf District, killing 2, injuring 39 and collapsing a six–story building; In Scotland an unemployed shopkeeper, Thomas Hamilton, walks into a grammar school, kills sixteen students and one teacher and then himself; The city of Sarajevo is united again when city authorities take control of the last district held by Serbs; Saddam Hussein accepts the UN's offer of food in exchange for his selling oil on the world market; Göran Kropp of Sweden reaches the Mount Everest summit alone without bottled oxygen or Sherpa support; In Britain, Prince Charles and Princess Diana formally divorce at the High Court of Justice; Peace talks begin in Northern Ireland without Sinn Féin; An IRA bomb in a busy shopping area in Manchester injures 200 people; The first successfully cloned mammal, Dolly the sheep, is born at the Roslin Institute in Midlothian, Scotland; Prince Charles and Princess Diana formally divorce at the High Court of Justice; In Ireland, the last of the Magdalen Asylums is closed. These were places for women that the Roman Catholic Church considered 'fallen'; The Taliban take control of the city of Kabul; Candidates opposed to President Milosevic won elections in 13 Serbian cities in November.

Having met one Prince of Wales, we were soon to become involved in another, as my parents moving to the residential home at Thornton–le–Dale had meant we were free to move elsewhere within the town.

We decided that a flat might make more sense for us than a house at that stage in our lives and in 1997 the Prince of Wales Hotel on Esplanade seemed to be an attractive option as it had views over Scarborough's South Bay and had recently been converted into apartments.

We met the developer who seemed reasonable and very fair and he told us that options had been taken on most of the remaining properties but there remained two three bedroomed apartments available, No. 54 on the ground floor and no 56 on the first floor. We decided upon No. 56 and he gave us sample books from which we could choose the entire flat's wallpaper and carpeting. We could also have access to enable us to have built in furniture installed, whilst we found a buyer for the Scalby Road house.

We had met a few other buyers who were completing purchases around the same time and most seemed to be very friendly, genial people.

The apartments themselves were well designed and spacious and with the added advantage of sea views, and Esplanade being a much quieter road than Scalby Road, all seemed to auger well.

We moved and had not been in long when we had a knock on the door. It was one of the owners saying he, and two others, were concerned about the developer 'sitting' on required maintenance jobs so would I be prepared to attend a meeting in his flat?

I agreed and at the meeting it became obvious that out of the 26 owners, these 3 (later 4) felt aggrieved by actions they felt the developer should have taken and they wanted firm action to be taken.

At that time the developer hadn't been in control long as it transpired that he had bought the block of 26 part completed flats from the Official Receiver as the previous firm of developers who had done most of the work had gone into liquidation. The whole block was on the corner of Esplanade and Prince of Wales Terrace. The first phase had been to convert the Prince of Wales Terrace frontage into flats, but when the original developers got to the Esplanade frontage they discovered that part of the foundations were under pressure. This meant demolishing the whole Esplanade frontage, putting in new foundations, then completely rebuilding. This, the previous developers had done but some of the hidden work was later found to be shoddy.

The three owners whom I met, had wanted to take a very firm line with the new developer and obviously crossed swords with him as he said if they didn't toe the line he would put DHSS tenants into the unoccupied flats to bring in rental income for his company.

Falling out with the developer at that stage was, in my opinion, the worst action which they could have taken. He then still owned the freehold but when a certain percentage of flats had been sold it would be passed to all the owners via a new management company. Leaseholders would then be in a strong position owning both leasehold and freehold.

This minority obviously had their own agenda and weren't concerned about the views of the majority as they then refused to pay any service charges.

More ill feeling soon arose and the developer started to withdraw some maintenance services for which he was then responsible but towards which those few leaseholders refused to pay. As he was not getting full payment this was understandable.

However, this affected all residents so a meeting was called and it was agreed to withhold service charges but to add these to an Administration account out of which we would pay for necessary services ourselves. The minority still refused to pay but claimed that the administrators – leaseholders elected by, and acting for all owners – were not looking after their particular interests so appealed to a Landlord and Tenant Tribunal. It was convened and held but refused to act, as the minority's wishes were outside the tribunal's remit.

That decision caused more friction which was exacerbated when heavy mouldings to the frontage of the building, (it had had to be rebuilt to give the same visual appearance as the original hotel) fell into the street, only narrowly missing a passing car.

The minority had, of course, been asked to join the administration but had continually refused, and they also refused to pay their shares of service charge for which they were responsible.

A solicitor I had complete faith in and had known many years, was employed by the administration and eventually the case was taken to arbitration which led to the developer, the then freeholder, agreeing to pay to the administration an agreed amount which would enable a proportion of necessary repairs to be completed. He also agreed to pass over the freehold. Some of the cost which had been classified as 'routine maintenance' was to be borne by the 26 leaseholders and whilst this was in accordance with the terms of the leases, the dissenters were not happy and again refused to pay.

As scaffolding would be needed for both the work which had been deemed to be the responsibility of the developer and also that deemed to be the responsibility of the leaseholders it was agreed by the majority that a complete renovation be carried out with leaseholders paying the shortfall, in the proportions stated in individual leases.

By mid-2002, Carter Jonas, a reputable, well-known firm of surveyors, drew up a renovation plan in phases. However, when scaffolding had been erected they found additional necessary work as the exterior mouldings, which had been added by the previous developer to replicate the original appearance of the building, had been fixed with ferrous mountings. The mouldings had not been properly sealed to the main structure so rain had percolated and rusted the fittings. This, in turn, made these fittings unsafe and they needed replacing.

An extraordinary general meeting was held and a majority of owners agreed that work must proceed. The administration needed to be confident that they had sufficient funds to pay for the work to be carried out so all 26 owners were invoiced with their proportions. All but five paid promptly. As five refused, this meant that the remaining twenty-one had to make up the shortfall in the hope and expectation that this would be received at a later date.

The work continued but no payments were received so the administrators had little alternative but to take the 4 defendants to court. The case was transferred from Scarborough County Court to Leeds and on behalf of the administrators, of which I was a member, I was due to be cross examined by the four defendants who acted for themselves. The hearing took place in June 2004 but another heart attack had intervened a few weeks earlier and my cardiologist refused to let me attend.

Administration chairman, Barry Ibbeson, took my place and to cut a long story short, the amounts including costs and interest, awarded to the Management company by the court against each of the 4 defendants, were in excess of the amounts the administration had actually claimed from them.

From shortly after that very first meeting with three of the four leaseholders, I had been involved either as chairman, secretary or treasurer of the administration, and later of the management company. The stress was intense and most of the very frequent letters from the four defendants, with which the administrators, and later the management company, were bombarded on an almost daily basis, went far beyond the remit of polite business correspondence. I was professionally advised that many, which I still hold on file, were without doubt, defamatory.

Whatever advice the 4 defendants had received had let them down badly as, somewhat ironically, had they been properly advised they would have been told at the outset that no judge had any power to alter the terms of the lease, except in very unusual and specific circumstances which did not apply in this case. Yet, in effect, that is exactly what they were expecting the Judge to do.

Healthwise, since the first heart attack in Darlington in November 1996, I had felt that I was only firing on two cylinders. Stress caused by the action of the dissenters had not helped. However I had coped for 10 years until Good Friday, 9th April 2004, when I felt a gradual tightening of my chest over a 2 day period. Being a weekend and Bank holiday to boot, there was no doctor's surgery so, reluctantly, I rang the emergency services.

They admonished me for not ringing straight away, especially as I had had a heart attack previously, and an ambulance was with me within a few minutes.

A hospital examination and various tests proved I had had a second heart attack. 'Ah well', said a local cardiologist. 'You've already had nearly 10 years extra you might not have had!'

I was initially a patient at Scarborough hospital, then around 3 months after the attack I was called in for a treadmill test. The nurse said there 'seems to be some abnormality with your heart.' This appeared to be something of an understatement and became especially pertinent when I could only cope with the treadmill test for 20 seconds before the staff had to slide a chair under me to save me from collapsing.

I was told that I needed an angiogram to assess what treatment my abnormality needed. I asked how long that would take. '12 months', I was told. 'But privately?' I asked. 'I have insurance.' The answer was not reassuring. '11 months, as we would use national health equipment in Hull'.

The bank then let retirees take private health insurance

into retirement with them, and, after the bank pension, that must have been the best benefit they could possibly have provided. So I phoned the bank's insurers who were extremely helpful. They arranged an angiogram at Leeds BUPA hospital and within 10 days I was referred to a very friendly, helpful and dedicated Irish cardiologist, Jim McLenachan. He arranged to examine me and carry out an angiogram on the same day to save two visits. After doing the tests and procedures he called into my room and advised me that I needed at least a triple and possibly a quadruple bypass as soon as possible. It was also likely that I needed at least repair to and possibly replacement of my aortic valve. He explained that medication might help for a short time, and angioplasty, where stents are inserted into the blocked arteries, might help – but again for only a short time as the position and extent of my blockages meant they would be difficult to stent.

To quote son–in–law Mark Waddon's expression on a much later occasion, it was a 'no–brainer' and I told Jim McLenachan that I felt the only option was to have whatever surgery was necessary, and as soon as possible.

He smiled and agreed. He explained that they worked in teams and he would refer me to surgeon Chris Munsch from Leeds of whom he spoke very highly. With holidays, courses and operating theatre slots all to be considered it looked as if it could be a month before Chris Munsch could operate.

Two days later he telephoned me at home and asked if there was any chance of me getting to the BUPA hospital in Leeds 2 days later. He had managed to swop an operating slot with a colleague. He would see me and assess me on entry then operate the following day.

This was extremely positive news. It meant there was little time to worry and Chris Munsch and his team gave me open heart surgery on September 16$^{th}$ 2004 year. When I came round after the operation he said, 'I was only able to bypass three heart arteries as the fourth fed into one of the others. Oh, and by the way, I didn't need to replace your aortic valve as when I removed the clamps, allowing blood to flow through your new arteries, the heart immediately started to come back to life'.

He had explained that he had to be in London for a conference the day after the operation but he said, 'Don't worry. I'll keep in touch with the doctors to check your progress.' Not only did he do that but he returned that evening from London to see how I was getting on which I thought was a very generous gesture. He then travelled back to London the following day.

Chris Munsch told me to allow a full year for recovery; to gradually build up walking to 3 miles a day, and, most importantly, to try to be positive. He suggested that during the early days of my recovery I should assess how I felt each Monday morning, and compare this to the previous Monday. I did this and invariably I felt better, and this small action in itself proved therapeutic and increased my confidence.

Before leaving he smiled and asked how long the local NHS hospital had said it would take before I could even have an angiogram to establish what was wrong. '12 months,' I replied.

He smiled and said gently, 'It's already been 5 months since your last heart attack. Your heart wouldn't have lasted another 7 months. And the 12 months would only have been to have an angiogram to find out what was wrong. You'd have still needed an operation but you'd have been dead well before then.'

One evening when I was in intensive care after the operation, and asleep, my heart started beating very quickly and I had a weird experience. I was dreaming of being home at Prince of Wales Apartments. In the dream the Emperor Grandfather clock I had built at home from a kit, showed it was 9.05pm and I went to look out of the window before drawing the curtains and switching on the light. As I touched the brass standard lamp I received a large electric shock and woke up from the dream with a start. I then heard what I thought was a heavenly choir and really thought I had moved on to another place.

A doctor in a white coat was standing by the bed as I woke and asked how I was feeling. Apparently staff had been monitoring me as I slept and the doctor told me my heart had been fibrillating, but this was normal after open heart surgery. However, he said my heart had corrected itself 'a couple of minutes ago'. The ward clock showed it was 9.07pm. I told him about the dream and the electric shock and, as far as we could tell, the shock in the dream had occurred at the very moment that my heart had corrected itself. That was an extremely strange experience and I have found no one who can explain how the dream appeared to be in real time, with the 'electric shock', coinciding with the time with the heart righted itself.

I then asked the doctor whether I had died and I mentioned the heavenly choir. 'No' he said smiling. You were nowhere near dying. The choir was some of the night staff starting early rehearsals for their Christmas concert!'

The operation Chris Munsch and his team had given me was certainly a life saver and I shall be eternally grateful to both him, Jim McLenachan their respective teams; and the BUPA (now Spire) hospital in Leeds. Together they gave me back my life and, as I write this memoir I have already had a bonus of over 22 years – since that first heart attack in Darlington.

Moving back to Prince of Wales Apartments and whilst we had a lot of friends there, the atmosphere and unnecessary ill feeling shown by the very small minority, which didn't fully ease after the court case in 2004, had its effect and I am certain it was at least part to blame for my second heart attack.

A lot of unpaid work by both myself and other administrators, (who all then became directors of our management company when the freehold was passed to us) had gone into getting the building into the state it should have been when we all bought our apartments. But there were 26 owners so as well as looking after our own interests we were also acting for them – some elderly and part infirm – who would not have been able to fight their own corners in the dispute. In that respect, and also the fact that the building was in a far better condition when we left than when we had bought; all the hassle and unjustified unpleasantness we had to endure must have been worth it.

Had the dissenters, or even some of them, agreed to become administrators, at least a consensus could have been reached at meetings with some give and take. However they steadfastly refused, with one reportedly saying, somewhat crudely, 'I want to stay outside and p*ss into the tent.' I think that sums up what we were up against and how he and his co-conspirators worked continually for a couple of years.

In the next chapter I mention meeting the then soon-to-be Lord Chief Justice. Had we met him a chapter earlier we might have been able to bring this present chapter to an end much sooner!

One day when leaving the outer front door of Prince of Wales Apartments, Eileen saw three men poking at the frontage of the building with a screwdriver and looking very excited.

'Can I help you?' she said. 'I live here.'

They explained they were WWI experts and did she know the town had been shelled by the German Imperial Fleet?

She confirmed she did. They then asked if she knew that this particular building had been shelled in that bombardment. Again she confirmed that she did.

'Well, look here,' the spokesman said excitedly, pointing at the wall. 'There's rust here which is from part of a shell's casing buried in this wall.'

'Really?' replied Eileen. 'I'm terribly sorry to have to disagree but this part of the property was completely rebuilt only 5 years ago.'

Three faces dropped and three very disappointed WWI 'experts' went on their way to look for more shell damage.

Another interest at this time was a local Residential home called Combe Hay, situated on the outskirts of Scarborough. I was asked to join the board of trustees and agreed to do so. It was, and still is, a wonderful home, extremely well run with good food and facilities for those who choose to live there, and with excellent staff, care facilities and gardens.

After a few years I was asked to take over as chairman of trustees and was pleased to do so, only resigning a few years later when health problems arose.

In 2005 we decided on a holiday in Madeira. We had been there before and knew the island and appreciated the mild climate. Also it was only a few months after my heart bypass and whilst my doctor supported us going to Madeira; Luxor, Egypt and 'our second home' might have risked my recovery a little.

Whilst in Madeira, we had a phone call from our daughter Susan – who by that time had become 'Sulyn' to virtually everyone as she had coined her two forenames 'Susan' and 'Lynne' to satisfy the theatrical Equity card requirements.

She told us that she, and Mark her boyfriend had decided to marry. We were, of course, delighted for them. However, she went on to say that they had decided to marry the following March in America on her birthday, the 3rd March. The bad news (for us) was that they didn't want parents there – both Eileen and myself, and Margaret, Mark's widowed mother. This came as a great disappointment to me although I tried not to show it at the time. Sulyn was our only child and I was to have no opportunity of giving her away, or to see her get married. They obviously had their own reasons but I would have dearly loved to have been there – even as a bystander – on March 3rd 2006 which was also her 42nd birthday.

They decided on Las Vegas where Phoebe has lived for many years and Phoebe and her family looked after them royally and made sure they saw all the sights.

Thank you Phoebe!

The following year we stayed in a small historic hotel full of character in Ravello, above Amalfi, in Italy. We had been to an excellent open–air performance by the London Philharmonic Orchestra – at the annual open air Ravello Festival at the Villa Rufolo. Every year for the weeks of the Festival a stage is built which cantilevers out from the almost sheer cliff face.

*The cantilevered stage for the Festival at Villa Rufolo, Ravello in Italy*

We were having a late meal on the hotel terrace after a superb performance one night and we got into conversation with another couple from England sitting at an adjacent table who were also enthusing about the performance. Professions came into the discussion and I said I was in banking.

We exchanged names and all of us laughed at Igor's surname, 'Judge' when he said he was involved in the law. We had an interesting conversation and 3 years later we realised we had met the man who had by then become the new Lord Chief Justice. We had been proud to meet him and have a pleasant discussion – but in a private rather than professional capacity!

*'Igor Judge, Baron Judge PC QC (born 19 May 1941) is a former English judge and was Lord Chief Justice of England and Wales, the head of the judiciary from 2008 to 2013. He was previously President of the Queen's Bench Division, at the time a newly created post assuming responsibilities transferred from the office of Lord Chief Justice.*

*He was born in Malta and educated at St Edward's College, Cottonera, in Malta, from 1947 to 1954 and The Oratory School in Woodcote in Oxfordshire from 1954 to 1959. He was awarded an Open Exhibition to study History and Law at Magdalene College, Cambridge in 1959, and he graduated BA in 1962.*

*He was called to the bar (Middle Temple) in 1963 and became a Recorder in 1976 and Queen's Counsel in 1979. From 1980 to 1986, he served on the Professional Conduct Committee of the Bar Council. In 1987, he was elected Leader of the Midland Circuit.*

*On 10 October 1988, Judge was appointed a Justice of the High Court, assigned to the Queen's Bench Division, and awarded the customary knighthood. He was appointed a Lord Justice of Appeal, a judge of the Court of Appeal, on 4 June 1996, becoming a Privy Counsellor.*

*He was appointed as the first President of the Queen's Bench Division on 3 October 2005, when that post was split from that of Lord Chief Justice. In addition to that role, Judge was appointed Head of Criminal Justice in January 2007.*

*Judge replaced Lord Phillips as Lord Chief Justice on 1 October 2008. The same day, he was created a life peer as Baron Judge, of Draycote in the county of Warwickshire, and he was introduced in the House of Lords five days later.*

*In 2007 Lord Judge was awarded an honorary doctorate from Nottingham Trent University, and in 2010 was made an Honorary Fellow of Aberystwyth University as well as Kingston University. On 20 June 2012 he received an honorary doctorate from Cambridge. He retired as Lord Chief Justice at the end of September 2013. He was Treasurer to the Middle Temple for the year 2014.'*

\*

Earlier in this memoir, I briefly mentioned my longstanding interest in Theatre in the Round. It was brought to Scarborough Library Concert Hall from the USA by the late Stephen Joseph and the theatre opened on 15th July 1955 – now over 60 years ago. It was later to move from the Library Concert Hall to the old Scarborough High School for Boys building off Valley Bridge. Later still on 30th April 1996, it moved to the Odeon building in the centre of town where its name changed to the Stephen Joseph Theatre in memory of its founder.

The move of venue and opening of The Stephen Joseph theatre, was celebrated by the launch of a new musical, 'By Jeeves', written by Alan Ayckbourn and Andrew Lloyd Webber. The opening of the new theatre was celebrated by a reception and buffet for invited guests, of which Eileen and I happened to be two.

*'In 1996, Lloyd Webber and Ayckbourn decided to revisit the show, Jeeves, jettisoning most of the score and the*

*entire original book. Retitled 'By Jeeves' (so as to dispel all previous associations with the original production), the character of Roderick Spode and his fascistic intentions were eliminated from the plot. The character list was whittled down from 22 to 10, and the original orchestrations also underwent a reduction to a little band. Only three songs from the original show remained lyrically intact: "Banjo Boy", "Half a Moment" and "Travel Hopefully". The other songs and musical interludes were mostly new or reworked compositions by Lloyd Webber.*

*'By Jeeves opened on 1 May 1996 at the Stephen Joseph Theatre in Scarborough, North Yorkshire, an English seaside resort. Audience reaction was generally enthusiastic so the show moved on 2 July 1996 to London for a 12-week season at the fairly intimate Duke of York's Theatre. The show turned out to be more popular than first thought, and the run was extended to February 1997 when it moved to The Lyric Theatre in Shaftesbury Avenue.*

*'Steven Pacey played Bertie Wooster and Malcolm Sinclair played his valet Jeeves. The Musical Director was Kate Young. The cast recording has an unusual format, taking a track between every song where Bertie and Jeeves humorously summarize the plot. Pacey was nominated for an Olivier Award for Best Actor in a Musical, and By Jeeves also received nominations for Outstanding New Production and Best Costume Designer.*

*The show had its U.S. premiere on 12 November 1996, at the Goodspeed Opera House in Connecticut. U.S. actor John Scherer took the part of Bertie, and Richard Kline played Jeeves. The show was specially recorded and released on VHS and DVD where British actor Martin Jarvis took over from Richard Kline as Jeeves. It also had a brief run on Broadway at the Helen Hayes Theatre, from 28 October 2001 (in previews October 16) to 30 December 2001, for 73 performances. Directed by Ayckbourn, the cast featured Stephen Pacey (Bertie) and Martin Jarvis (Jeeves) (who received the Theatre World Award).'*

But I am getting well ahead of myself and in July 1955, just after I had left Scarborough Boys High School, and the same month that the theatre opened, a friend, Julian Knowles invited me to some of those very early performances at the Library Theatre. His parents ran a small hotel and in exchange for displaying a poster for each production, they received two complimentary tickets. They always said they were far too busy looking after their guests to go to the theatre so their tickets found their way to us.

Many years later in 1976 a Stephen Joseph Theatre in the Round Friends' organisation was formed and over the years I took on the role of chairman, treasurer or as a member of the committee on a number of occasions. From the library the theatre moved to the building in the valley, where years before the Boys' High school had been situated.

The days when the theatre was located in the valley are memorable as the then bar and bistro were located in two class rooms in which I had been taught whilst at the High school; the men's' toilets were in what had been the headmaster's study and the Round stage area was in what had been the old school hall.

My first foray on to the Friends' committee was in the 1970's when accountant Geoff Heselton was Friends' chairman and we met in Keith McFarlane, the finance officer's office, behind the Box Office at the Westwood theatre.

The committee decided a regular news sheet would be of benefit to members and the job I was given was that of 'magazine editor'. It sounds grand but initially consisted of a couple of foolscap sheets of paper letting Friends know what was happening. When I had prepared a draft, Mary 'Lolly' James, Alan Ayckbourn's Mother, who had become a very close friend to Eileen and myself and had a professional writing background as well as being a published author, became my unofficial proof reader.

Photocopiers were primitive, expensive, and not readily available and I remember Geoff suggesting I approach a local church to borrow their 'duplicating machine'. This, in itself was archaic even by the then mid 1970's standards, and it was necessary to cut a wax based stencil on a typewriter by typing without a ribbon. The main problem was to see what you had typed! A carbon, and paper beneath the wax stencil provided a copy but you could only read this once it had been taken out of the typewriter. Errors then had to be corrected by painting over the appropriate part of the stencil with a pink fluorescent sealer. Then, it was necessary to type the correct version over the previous error – if you could find the correct place!

For the next stage it was necessary to dress in one's oldest gardening or car servicing clothes. Once the stencil had been cut it had to be carefully wrapped around a drum on the duplicating machine; thick oozy ink had then to be squeezed on to a platform and spread out smoothly with a roller. If too much ink was applied it had a habit of spurting everywhere. And it did not wash out of clothes in the weekly wash! Then, by turning a handle, copies appeared one at a time. As the ink was still wet they had to be laid out separately all over the room until they dried. Happy days!!

I resigned from the Friends committee in 1982 when the bank moved me to Driffield but Eileen and I still supported the theatre and attended nearly all performances. My association with the SJT then re-started, but professionally, as Russ Allen, a rather colourful publicity manager employed by the theatre at the time, fell foul of the theatre's then bankers in a rather dramatic and public way. This led to headlines in the Scarborough Evening News, 'Theatre told to find new bankers...' The following day I took a phone call from Keith McFarlane, the theatre's accountant whom I knew well, 'I don't suppose you'd like to take on another bank account?' I was more than happy to do so, and as far as I know that association with Barclays Bank extends to this day.

I retired from the bank in 1994 and a little later we moved back to Scarborough. An appeal had been posted on the theatre's Friends' notice board seeking a new treasurer from the next AGM. I volunteered but couldn't attend that AGM as I'd had my first heart attack in the meantime; nevertheless, I was elected. After acting as treasurer, I was voted in as chairman, a position I held for 3 years. This period was particularly exciting as it covered the move from Westwood to the new purpose built theatre in what had been the Odeon cinema. (I notice that the electricity substation set into the Westborough wall of the theatre is still called 'Odeon' sub–station!)

A few years later in 2001, then chairman of the Friends Roy Field, decided to step down and I was asked to take his place. I was somewhat diffident, having already carried out the role and not wishing to tread on the toes of others. However, I was voted in at the AGM.

Up until then the Friends had maintained their own funds from membership fees and fundraising events, and had then made donations to the theatre for specific items for which the theatre had asked. Framed programmes of every production put on by the theatre were displayed on the walls and spring to mind, as does funding the building of the wine bar (now the cloak room!) in the Odeon building, and Christmas decorations.

Instead, and to encourage the committee to do more fund raising, we decided to pass all the Friends' membership income to the theatre at the end of each year and to meet committee expenses out of additional fundraising with any balance from that also going to the theatre. We also aimed to increase Friends' membership numbers which, in turn would increase monies for the theatre each year. After a short time membership peaked at over 1100 and our annual average donation to the SJT to £16,000.

These changes enabled the theatre to anticipate these monies each year and helped their budgeting. Additional fundraising income came from such things as garden parties we held at Wykeham Abbey; a summer draw we held every year when we sold tickets in the theatre and also sent them out in Friends' and theatre mailings, then drew the winners at the end of the season; a champagne reception and dinner at Castle Howard; a live, open–air performance of The Tempest in the garden at Hackness Hall (it poured down!); and Gala Evenings when the cast of a show would join us in the theatre restaurant after a performance for a meal and to mingle.

We calculated that the total we had donated from the very small beginnings of the Friends to that time was in the region of £300,000.

In 2006 when the Friends was the only SJT support organisation, I had a big disappointment when I was chairman. Eileen and I had gone to London to celebrate our joint birthdays on 18th June and as part of our trip we had booked for the show *Mack and Mabel* then appearing at the Criterion theatre. In fact, the show was due to close a few weeks after our visit. Starring were David Soul and Janie Dee. Janie had appeared at the Stephen Joseph Theatre in Scarborough in leading roles on a number of occasions and had also brought her one woman shows to the theatre and these performances were usually packed out. We had arranged to meet Janie after the performance and she took us to a local pub the cast used where the red wine flowed!

We complimented her on the show and said something along the lines, 'Wouldn't it be wonderful if we could have a show like this at the SJT?'

One idea led to another and by the time we left for our hotel Janie had offered to approach the cast to see whether sufficient members could (and would) put on a concert performance of *Mack & Mabel* at the Stephen Joseph Theatre in Scarborough. The theatre is a registered charity so the cast would be unpaid apart from basic expenses and the performances would take place over a weekend; possibly a Friday evening, with both a matinee and evening performance on the Saturday, and possibly a Sunday matinee if ticket sales were buoyant. The performances would need to take place within a very few weeks of the show ending in London as cast members could have other roles waiting for them.

We left the pub as dawn was breaking. Over the next few days Janie was to approach the cast – and a big condition had to be that star David Soul was prepared to take part and that the Mack and Mabel producers were prepared to release the show for a concert version in aid of charity.

I would approach the SJT to seek provisional agreement that the theatre would participate, and to make sure there would be no clash with other booked productions over the same weekend.

We returned home to Scarborough a few days later and had a phone call from Janie. As far as the cast and producers were concerned it was 'on' and David Soul very much wanted to be part of it. The Friends' committee members were all excited.

I arranged to see the theatre's then administration director who, as Friends' chairman, I usually met at least once a month on routine Friends and SJT matters.

I stated my case but he poured very cold water on the proposal and threw every objection under the sun at us – most of which had already been discussed, investigated and overcome. He possibly had his reasons but certainly didn't share them with me.

That was a great personal disappointment to me and the Friends committee. I had worked in finance all my life, and I was confident such performances would have been not only viable, but profitable for the theatre. At its best it could have made a substantial sum for the Stephen

Joseph Theatre and raised the high esteem of the theatre even further.

With hindsight, I really should have taken it further to the theatre's board to seek their agreement but, sadly, the West End production of Mack and Mabel in Scarborough was not to be.

Whatsonstage.com reported at the time:

*'Olivier Award winner Janie Dee will join David Soul in the Watermill Theatre revival of 1974 musical Mack and Mabel as it embarks on a UK tour in the New Year ahead of a planned West End transfer [to the Criterion].*

*The tour opens at the Theatre Royal Bath on 24 January 2006 before continuing, until 25 March 2006, to seven further venues.*

*Out of the silent movie era and the heady heights of 1920s Hollywood, Mack and Mabel tells the love story of two of its greatest legends: director Mack Sennett, 'the King of comedy', and his star, comedienne Mabel Normand.*

*Together they bring magic to the silver screen. Yet ambition, dalliance and the impending threat of changing times make for a tempestuous relationship. The score includes 'Look What Happened to Mabel', 'I Won't Send Roses', 'Time Heals Everything' 'Hundreds of Girls' and 'Tap Your Troubles Away'.*

*Soul – the former Starsky and Hutch TV heartthrob who was last seen in the West End as the American chat show host in Jerry Springer – The Opera – will reprise his role as Mack. He played the part in the production's original eight-week season at the Watermill in Newbury this summer, when he was described as 'the best Mack I've ever seen' by the musical's octogenarian composer Jerry Herman (the man behind Hello Dolly, Mame and La Cage Aux Folles).*

*Dee takes the part of Mabel, played in Newbury by Anna-Jane Casey in a TMA Award-winning performance. Dee's many musical credits include Cats, Carousel (for which she won her first Olivier), My One and Only, Oklahoma! The Sound of Music and South Pacific. She's also been seen in the plays Between the Lines, Design for*

*Living, Betrayal, Much Ado About Nothing* and, in 2000, Alan Ayckbourn's *Comic Potential* for which she won Best Actress accolades at the Laurence Olivier, Evening Standard and Critics' Circle Awards before the comedy's New York transfer.

We continued to live at Prince of Wales apartments and by this time I had resigned from Scarborough Lions Club. Much earlier, after my first heart attack I had backed out from going further in the hierarchy of the charitable movement because of my health, and I resigned a few years later when I felt a friend whom I had introduced as a member and who was then President, was getting a raw deal through no fault of his own.

In 2007 we decided it was time to move house again. We looked at various properties and initially were keen on a newly modernised bungalow on the north side of the town but the survey report left a lot to be desired and the owners were not prepared to reduce the price to part meet these shortcomings.

Then, one Friday night in the local paper we saw a flat advertised only a few hundred yards from the Prince of Wales. Montrosa, a residential home for older people, had occupied part of the site with the other part being its garden.

The Montrosa management had had a new property built backing on to the old site and the developers then took over the old property and converted it into flats. Next door, in what had been the old Montrosa garden, they had built a new block of flats, with both being connected by a glazed central entrance, staircase and atrium in which a lift had been installed.

Our Prince of Wales flat had been on the market and we had a buyer standing by. We had earlier queried the availability of flats at Christine House with our estate agent but he said demand was high and most flats changed hands without getting as far as being advertised.

Yet here was Flat 8, the top floor flat, being newly advertised. We visited it twice that weekend, and again on the Monday, then made an offer on the Tuesday and a deal was struck.

8 Christine House is ideal for us. Roomy for a modern flat with two bedrooms and two bathrooms, a decent sized lounge and kitchen, and a somewhat quirky character because of its top floor position just beneath the roof, it meets our needs superbly.

Why do health problems always seem to happen at weekends or bank holidays when there are no doctors' surgeries open?

I had been going to the bathroom quite a few times each night but in May 2010 I suddenly found it was impossible to urinate and as my bladder filled, discomfort, then acute pain set in. I phoned the surgery which was closed but a recorded message referred me to an emergency unit at Scarborough hospital to which my surgery subscribed out of hours.

This unit replied very quickly, asked a few questions and asked if I could get to hospital straight away. I could and I did. I wasn't waiting more than a few minutes when a doctor took me into a room and told me that the only remedy in such a situation was for him to insert a catheter into my penis to empty the bladder and relieve the pain. Whilst a bit uncomfortable, it all happened quickly and the end result was like a tidal wave breaching a dam. I had to keep the catheter in place until the problem was fully sorted.

A later hospital appointment showed that I had an enlarged prostate which was causing the problem and I would need an operation. A biopsy would also be needed to make sure the prostate was not cancerous.

The bank's health insurance scheme again came to the rescue and on 26th May 2010 Mr JR Wilson at York Nuffield Hospital operated and gave me a resection of the prostate. Afterwards I woke up to find a large plastic drum at the end of the bed and discovered I now had two catheters in place. Apparently one was to keep my bladder supplied with saline and the other to allow it to flush away.

These catheters were removed before I left hospital when a male nurse came into my room and said I could leave as 'all readings were normal'. I took this to mean that they had found no cancer so was not concerned over coming weeks and it was not until mid-June when I received a letter from Mr Wilson confirming that he had just received the biopsy results which were clear. Phew!

\*

# CHAPTER 17

# Mark's 'No-Brainer'
# 2008–2015

---

**2008: Brief Timeline**

Monarch: Elizabeth II; Prime Minister: Gordon Brown (Labour); Four men were jailed for 15 years each for their part in the 2006 Securitas raid, the UK's biggest cash robbery; A jury at Ipswich Crown Court found Steve Wright, 49, guilty of murdering five prostitutes during late 2006; Northern Rock was nationalised by the British government; An earthquake with an epicentre in Lincolnshire was felt across most of the country; The inquest into the death of Diana, Princess of Wales recorded a verdict of accidental death; The Conservative candidate Boris Johnson defeated the incumbent Labour candidate in the London Mayoral election; The FA Cup Final took place at Wembley Stadium between Portsmouth and Cardiff City with Portsmouth winning 1–0; Construction work began on the Olympic Stadium being built for the 2012 games; A highlight of the London Motor Show was Vauxhall's launch of its new Insignia that replaced the Vectra; Barry George was acquitted of the murder of Jill Dando; Great Britain competed at the Olympics in Beijing; An episode of *The Russell Brand Show* aired, featuring a series of prank phone calls to the actor Andrew Sachs by comedians Russell Brand and Jonathan Ross, leading to a media row ; Woolworths announced their 807 UK stores will close by 5 January 2009, putting some 27,000 people out of work; MFI ceases trading, closing all 111 of its stores and leaving its 1,400 workforce redundant.

---

The following circuitous route will explain how my writing and publishing interests came about.

I had always wanted to write – probably from my grandfather's much earlier involvement as an author.

A good deal of writing and detailed analysis was necessary whilst working for the bank, but this was mainly in report form to a formal set style and format.

When I retired and started to put pen to paper – or fingers to keyboard - for the first few years I found writing difficult as bank 'guidelines' kept intervening and produced very stilted results.

However, I persevered and my style gradually improved.

When we lived at Great Barugh, two friends in Malton were members of the Old Scarborians' Association – something I had never joined. Members were ex-pupils and ex-masters of the old Scarborough High School for Boys and the Association held a lunch in London and a Scarborough Christmas dinner each year. At that time there was also an annual lunch in the Midlands area.

With friends and members Mike Elvy and Peter Bell I went to a number of these Old Scarborian events and became a member. Then, when Eileen and I retired back to Scarborough I joined the committee which was based in the town and from 1999 took over the annual newsletter which was circulated to members. Gradually I expanded this to a proper A5 booklet which I edited and produced twice a year. Content rolled in from members and gradually this publication increased from around 4 to 64 pages.

The Association had been run by two older members who were wanting to step back, but who had kept the Association alive for many years. So a new committee was appointed with each member having a specific responsibility. This new committee was vibrant and expansion was possible because of the then availability of home computers, printers and so on. Membership grew rapidly even though the school had closed in the 1970s on comprehensive schools becoming the 'in' thing and most grammar schools having been absorbed into the new doctrine.

In 2006 I was elected President of the Association for two years, and after I stepped down from that role I was appointed an honorary life vice president.

London lunches have been held at first class venues: The House of Lords, the House of Commons, Mosimanns, The East India club, and the RAF club a number of times – to name but just a few.

The Old Scarborians Christmas dinner was held for many years at the Palm Court hotel in Scarborough but when the Rugby Club relocated to new and substantial premises, superbly designed by Old Scarborian member Howard Acklam, we moved our meetings and Christmas dinners there and the events have grown in popularity with around 100 members now attending the dinner.

Member and friend Maurice Johnson was at that time UK sales director for Gruyère cheese – a large Swiss company. He supported and subsidised many Old Scarborians' London lunches, which were normally held on a Saturday, and on the Friday evenings he took me, together with another friend to such upmarket restaurants as the Ritz Hotel and Mosimanns restaurant; places in normal circumstances I would never have been able to visit.

Editing and contributing to the Old Scarborians Association magazine from 1999 helped me break away from the bank's writing style and further help came from the Stephen Joseph Theatre Friends. There, I prepared and published magazines twice a year which we then sent out to all members.

Whilst living at Prince of Wales apartments, I had heard brief details of how the hotel had been involved in WWII and how Scarborough had been anything but a backwater during those wartime years. So, when we moved to Christine House I started to research what had actually happened at what had been the Prince of Wales Hotel during the war. This led to my first book *'God Bless the Prince of Wales'*, extracts from which appear earlier.

By that time a new member had joined the Stephen Joseph Friends committee. She was called Ren Yaldren, had recently moved to the area and later became the secretary, then later still the chairman of the Friends. Ren is highly intelligent, thinks on her feet, and can have quite strong views. She was a real asset to the organisation and came up with many positive ideas, especially when she became chairman. After Ren attended her first committee meeting someone said to me in the bar afterwards, 'Crikey! She's effervescent, feisty and sparky!' It was not a bad description!

A few months later a competition called Local Heroes was launched in the town by the Scarborough Museums Trust. The idea was that 12 people be nominated – one each, by different individuals or organisations. The promotion was intended to find the person who was felt to have made the largest contribution to Scarborough over the years.

Amongst many other organisations the organisers wrote to the Friends' committee seeking a nomination from them which would have involved the committee preparing and giving a presentation at the town hall about the person being nominated and the reasons they were thought worthy to appear in the final dozen.

Ren suggested that Stephen Joseph be the Friends' nomination. Stephen had died early but he had seen theatre in the round in America and had brought it to Scarborough. His protégé was a very young Alan Ayckbourn.

For some reason the then Friends' chairman felt we should not take part so Ren asked if she could nominate Stephen Joseph in a personal capacity. This was agreed so Ren subsequently sent in her personal nomination for Stephen Joseph and with the help of her husband Roger, she prepared an illustrated presentation which she delivered before a judging panel in the town hall.

Two members of the SJT theatre staff had been at Ren's presentation and mentioned to Heather Ayckbourn how professional her presentation had been.

All presentations were videoed and were exhibited in the Rotunda Museum and Heather, who opened this exhibition in the Rotunda, had obtained a copy of the CD of Ren's presentation which she showed to Alan who thought it could provide the basis for a booklet about Stephen Joseph which could be sold through the theatre's shop and which he could also distribute to visiting actors, and the annual Theatre School whose members frequently asked about Stephen Joseph's background.

The judges placed Harry W. Smith first in the competition. He was a very deserving winner and, as an early Scarborough Borough Surveyor, he had done an exceptional job in improving the town's gardens – to both north and south bays, introducing the North Bay miniature railway, designing and bringing to fruition Peasholm Park and the Northstead Manor Gardens; the south bay open air bathing pool, the south bay chalets, the Clock Cafe and much more when tourism was on the rise in the early 20th century.

Ren's presentation about Stephen Joseph in 'Local Heroes' came second out of the 12 presentations and was highly commended. This was an extremely creditable result for her and, of course, the late Stephen Joseph. Later, Ren was approached to discuss the possibility of writing a booklet about Stephen Joseph based on her presentation and the suggestion was made that if the Friends could fund the production costs this would be a valuable donation to the theatre.

The same person who objected to the Friends' involvement in the presentation appeared a little miffed at the success of the presentation and Ren having been asked to write the booklet, but he commented that it wasn't a big job and could be completed on 'a couple of sheets of A4'.

However, the committee agreed to pay for the printing of the booklet which Ren would prepare from all the material she had compiled.

At this point I came out of the wings and onto the stage as I already edited and published the Friends' magazine in booklet form so I offered that if Ren prepared the manuscript and got together the necessary photographs, I would willingly look after the technical side and turn it into a professionally produced booklet.

This long preamble really led to the start of Farthings Publishing although we didn't appreciate it at that time. First had come the magazine I had helped produce in the 3rd form at the High School with English master Gerald Hinchliffe; then had come the very early hand duplicated SJT Friends' newsletter; this was later followed by proper Friends' A5 magazines a few times a year. Around the same time I was producing the Old Scarborians' Association magazines twice a year, and then came the Stephen Joseph booklet. These were my first efforts at publishing – with the latter being a joint effort with Ren.

In 2008 the theatre decided to set up its own support group called The Circle which was to be administered by the theatre rather than the independent committee which ran the Friends, although we were assured the Friends organisation would continue. The Circle started as an organisation intended for business members. Then, a couple of years later in 2010 the theatre decided to merge the Friends into the Circle (we had over 1,000 members against their 50 or so) with the theatre taking over full responsibility for the combined group which would continue to be called the Circle. This was to be the end of the Friends.

The Friends reluctantly went along with this and it was agreed at our next AGM as it was what the theatre wanted – but the committee did have their reservations...

Back to publishing and one thing led to another. I had tried unsuccessfully to get my first book, *'God Bless the Prince of Wales'* about Scarborough in WWII, published. Yes, the book had its faults and I would probably do things differently if I was starting it now, but it was my first book and did repay its print costs and is still selling slowly today, some 8 years later.

Before writing it I had advertised in an RAF magazine for memories from ex aircrew who had trained at the Prince of Wales hotel during wartime (it was then 11 Initial Training Wing RAF) and I received over 70 replies. Most contained information which I included in the book and when it was published I had 70 potential customers ready to defray the costs involved in getting the book to print stage. Many also bought more than 1 copy.

Ren, who has excellent writing skills, had been very supportive and helpful while I was writing the book and trying to find a publisher. She had also written a book of poetry at that stage so we both said, 'If we can successfully publish a book for the theatre why don't we publish our own books ourselves?'

Roger, Ren's husband then came into the discussion and said he had been listening to the radio and mention was made of an international firm called Lulu which used modern automated, digital technology to help authors get their own books into print. The greatest advantage was that this firm would print from a single copy upwards at an average cost of around £5 for a single book. This opened up a complete new market as, until then, substantial orders had to be placed to justify print costs.

We tried Lulu for our own books. There was a very steep learning curve in those early days, but Lulu was, and remains, very professional. We have used them ever since and this reduces the expensive technology we would had to otherwise have had to invest in, which would have made Farthings not viable.

I remember vividly the sheer excitement when the first proof copy of *God Bless the Prince of Wales* arrived in the post. That is, until I opened the book. In those days I hadn't realised about all the technicalities needed - particularly to 'lock' text and photographs. The book appeared with text running over the face of most photographs. However, I sorted this out and learned a lot from the experience and books we publish these days are professional and indistinguishable from books produced by the large publishing houses and available in any bookshop.

Years before, Eileen and I had used Farthings as a house name, probably because of its banking connotation, then I had designed a few websites as an interest and used the name 'Farthings Web Design' so Ren and I adapted that and used 'Farthings Publishing' for our own books.

*As the two of us appear on Farthings Web site and on our visiting cards.*

A year or so later I researched and wrote *'National Service, Elvis & Me!'* and again appealed to ex-national service men, many of whom contributed and who were delighted to be able to buy a copy showing their contribution.

My own books over the last 10 years have been: *'God Bless the Prince of Wales'*; *'National Service, Elvis & Me!'*; *'Berby & Fuz'*; *'Why Should England Tremble?'*; *'The Clock Café Story'*; *'Scarborough Snippets'*; *'Don Robinson – Story of a High Flier'*; and now this present marathon, *'I've started so I'll finish…'*

Ren wrote, *'A Mixed Bouquet'*; *'The Alpha and the Omega'*, and *'Maurice Johnson – A Man of many parts'*. Her own biography is in progress, *'It's Heavy so it must be good!'* together with a book about Jack the Ripper visiting the town and carrying out his vile trade amongst the alleyways off Foreshore in Scarborough.

Under the Farthings banner we published our own books and we then started to get enquiries asking us to consider publishing for friends. This slowly expanded to friends of friends and these days we often have a book in progress most of the time – either our own – or for others.

When friend Maurice Johnson was nearing his 80th birthday he told us he wanted his life story writing so he could have 80 copies to hand out to the 80 guests at his party. We asked him for his manuscript and he stared blankly at us, then admitted his story was in his head. Ren then arranged to meet him on a number of occasions to interview him and to get his story on tape which she then typed and we produced his book *'Maurice Johnson – A Man of many parts'*.

Maurice's birthday party was a great success held in the restaurant of the Stephen Joseph Theatre – incidentally in the same building where Maurice was interviewed for his first job as a trainee cinema manager many years earlier.

Maurice remains very active and over the years has become a close friend. Whilst, in 2009 I visited Phoebe and her family in Las Vegas for 3 weeks and they gave me a wonderful time; during the following 6 years he and I have had a number of holidays together, usually around September time. These have included, Cornwall; Germany (to visit our old national service camps); Kent (for the WWII airfields and museums); Berlin; Belgium and France, (for the old battle fields); Cumbria, the Lake District and surrounding area and, more recently Munich, Germany.

All were very enjoyable but, for me America and Berlin were extra special and will be covered in more detail later on in this book.

Going back to Farthings, Ren is a trained interviewer, professional typist, is computer literate and is a psychologist to boot, so she interviews anyone who hasn't a manuscript but who has 'a book in their head'. She then types it up from a recording and I take then it over to deal with all the formatting and technical 'putting together' work which has become my speciality. We each work from our respective homes, but we meet once a week for a full day where we combine the various parts of a book on which we have each been working separately.

Farthings Publishing operates very much in a niche market as there are only the two of us, so sales and distribution of other people's books is not practical and remains the responsibility of each author. We also charge to get a book to first proof copy stage, but from that stage there is no obligation on an author to buy any copies.

If they choose to do so, they can have from one copy upwards with discounts on a rising scale. Many books are wanted for families, small clubs and organisations, schools or just by new, and not so new authors. One author, Malcolm Smith writing as Malcolm Bruce, recently completed his 6$^{th}$ excellent book in a series about the fictional Sheader family. All were published by Farthings. Thank you Malcolm!

We do advertise books we publish, online through the likes of www.Lulu.com and www.Amazon.co.uk, but as they print direct from files we provide, neither Farthings, nor the author, has the expense or hassle of having to send them actual books for general sale, which might or might not sell. Any sales royalties are then passed on to us periodically and we pass these on to the author.

Farthings will never make us rich because of the cost of the technology we need to use, but with both of us in retirement it keeps our grey matter active and we enjoy working together and merging our different skills to produce books of a professional standard.

For their 2013 centenary we researched, wrote and published a booklet called 'The Clock Cafe Story'. Clock Cafe stands on the cliff side to the south of Scarborough Spa and the views of the old town, the harbour, beach and sea from its terrace are magnificent. We donated the cost of our work and the first 100 books to the cafe as sales were in aid of their charity The Little Foot Trust, in which Jackie Link, the cafe owner is involved.

These copies quickly sold so the cafe bought reprints from us and they are now on their 9th reprint of 100 copies which an excellent local printer prints and binds for us, at cost, to help the charity.

By 2011 I had been suffering for some time with acute pain in my left knee joint. X–rays showed that a complete replacement knee was necessary.

This time it was Neil Hunt at the Nuffield Hospital, York who carried out the replacement, and after having physiotherapy for about a month after leaving hospital, I was walking comfortably without a stick although the knee did at first tend to get very stiff on long car journeys...

\*

This leads us on to Eileen's health which had been good apart from her suffering long standing food allergies and more recently asthma and arthritis, all of which she learnt to cope with admirably. But from the start of 2011 there became a build–up of symptoms which worried me to the level that I started to keep a note of them.

Her handwriting had always been clear and distinct but it started to vary over short periods of time. All of a sudden she would write like a five year old using joined up capitals. The next day her writing would be perfectly normal but a day later would then become almost illegible. Yes, the arthritis didn't help but... It went on my list...

Time started to mean nothing to her and she would start to get ready for something we had agreed to go to, a matter of minutes before we were due to be there. She then started leaving tea towels, and odd papers on top of the halogen electric cooker hob. This was usually switched off but on two or three occasions it was still on, or cooling. These went on my list...

She occasionally stumbled and fell and sometimes her voice changed, almost to that of a little girl. Other strange things started to happen and my concern increased.

In 2010 we were spending a holiday in Scotland with Phoebe who had flown over from her home in America. We had travelled by train to Manchester, collected Phoebe from her flight and then we had all flown from Manchester to Inverness. During the week we were to meet up with cousin Jean Bucknall (nee Taylor) and her husband Peter.

Eileen seemed a bit unsteady on her feet and somewhat slow and confused, although she said that apart from not being able to rush, she was fine.

All these symptoms were later traced to a severe medical condition which was subsequently treated very successfully, but they give the background to the following story.

On our last day in Elgin, at 4.00am the hotel fire alarm sounded and we all had to wait outside in the rain. The hotel restaurant was next door and whilst we could have sheltered inside no staff member had a key. It seemed to take forever for 2 fire engines to arrive – possibly from Inverness some 36 miles away. The officers quickly assessed it was a false alarm but we could not return to our rooms until the fire system itself, and all rooms, had been checked. The hotel staff did a roll call and it seemed 4 couples were missing. They were eventually found in their beds with their heads under the covers. How on earth they could have stayed in bed with the alarms ringing constantly and stridently I shall never know. Eventually we were told we could return to our rooms and Eileen hurriedly finished her packing before our 5.00am departure for the airport for our early flight to

Manchester.

When we got to Inverness airport, security was very tight and a few flights were leaving around the same time. Because of the fire alarm confusion, Eileen had put her make-up, shampoo, hairspray and all other paraphernalia women need to take with them, in her hand luggage and not in the hold luggage or the stipulated transparent plastic bag. Security went into overdrive. When I mentioned Eileen was not well and would by then be the last one to board, the security officer said the flight wouldn't go without her – providing they didn't detain her! I was not allowed to wait with her and was told to board. I did so reluctantly and eventually she ambled across the airport forecourt to the plane as if on a gentle walk in the garden. She climbed the steps and the plane doors were just about to be closed when she said in a loud voice, 'Where's my coat?'

She had apparently left it in the security section of the departure lounge. I offered to go but the stewardess called over an engineer and asked him to fetch it. I went to the door and apologised to the stewardess. 'Don't worry', she said, 'we're used to little old ladies forgetting things!' The coat eventually arrived, the doors were closed and we departed from Inverness to Manchester.

From Manchester we had booked a direct train to Scarborough – the last station on the line. Phoebe and I got off in Scarborough and unloaded all our luggage but where was Eileen? We waited patiently then we heard a loud 'click' which sounded very much like the train doors locking. We then saw the driver wandering off for his break. Then we saw Eileen in the carriage and mimed to her to ask what she was doing.

She mimed back, 'I'm putting my coat on!' But as all the doors had been locked, she couldn't then get off the train and the driver had gone off to the canteen. Eventually we found a cleaner who rescued her and guided her right through to the front of the train and got her out through the driver's door!

Back home and one day a few weeks later Eileen wandered through the flat with a box of dirty laundry casting individual pieces on the floor as she walked, as if she was scattering corn in biblical times.

I phoned our doctor and found he was on holiday but a partner promised to visit after surgery that evening. The lady doctor called and talked with Eileen and listened to the various symptoms I had been keeping a note of, then said that she was concerned and a case meeting would be held on the following Monday when our doctor returned.

They decided she needed an urgent MRI scan and this was taken at Scarborough Hospital.

The next morning I had a phone call from Hull Infirmary. Could I possibly get Eileen there for 3.00pm that afternoon? The Hull doctor who phoned explained that the Scarborough scan was of poor quality and Scarborough had sent it to Hull's neurological department for a second opinion. Hull decided to take their own scan, hence the call for me to get her through to Hull. Her scan was scheduled for first thing the following morning and a bed had been reserved for her overnight.

I drove her to Hull despite the fact that I was recovering from my left knee replacement. How lucky it was that our car had an automatic gearbox and I had been given the all clear to drive, even though when we reached the hospital I had to walk round the car a few times to get feeling back into my leg.

We were very fortunate that the head neurological surgeon, with a very wide and excellent reputation, Mr Chittoor Rajaraman, took Eileen under his wing and called a family conference on the Thursday after the scan was taken.

Daughter Sulyn was there with her husband Mark and there was Eileen and myself. Mr Rajaraman had a screen on the wall showing the scan of Eileen's brain. He described the left and right hand sides of the brain on the screen and pointed out one side as being normal. This contained a sausage shaped mass whereas the other side was much smaller and contained what looked more like a worm. He told us both sides should be the same size. Then he pointed out a large oval shadow to one side and said this indicated that Eileen had a tumour about the size of a hen's egg. That was the bad news. The better news was that the tumour was located between the skull and the membrane covering the brain, so it was not actually growing within the brain itself. However, it was putting extreme pressure on the brain and had reduced the size of the actual brain on that side of the head, thus leading to the smaller worm shape he had pointed out a little earlier. The tumour, and the pressure it was causing had led to the various symptoms she had been having which had appeared on my notes. From its present size he estimated that it had been growing for around 12 years but as it would only have grown a few millimetres a year it had only recently reached the size where it caused pressure and thus symptoms, such as we had noticed and which I had listed.

He said they could operate but there were risks and he needed a decision. Son-in-law Mark piped up and said that it was a 'no–brainer' – maybe not a very appropriate choice of words in the circumstances!

Eileen, who I have never known to chair a meeting before, then banged on the table.

'Let me call this meeting to order. It's my brain we're talking about and I want to speak. I feel we must proceed and ask Mr Rajaraman to do all he can to cure me. Now, can we vote on it?' And we did.

The surgeon said he could operate within a week and that Eileen could return home in the meantime. 'No!' she said. 'If I get home I won't want to come back here.' So she stayed in hospital until the operation had been completed and her recovery was assured.

The medical team decided that on Monday 1st August 2011 they would give Eileen an angiogram to give access the roots of the growth near the brain, via an artery leading from the groin. Then they would cut the roots to stop the blood supply to the tumour and they would then cauterise the blood supply to the roots which should have the effect of starving the tumour of blood and thereby reducing pressure which could have damaged the brain when the top of the skull was removed.

The following day the main operation would be undertaken whereby a circular section of Eileen's skull would be cut and hinged forward so the tumour could be removed.

Eileen had the impression that all her hair would be removed for the operation even though Mr Rajaraman said this was not the case. She was most insistent that she had maintained her hair style for many years and was very concerned about losing her hair. Mr Rajaraman was very patient and explained that she would not lose all her hair. He would cut a horseshoe shape of hair away, no more than half an inch in width and this would enable him to cut a section of the scalp which would hinge down so he could access the brain and perform the operation.

Eileen still had a job getting her head round this and was convinced that all her hair would go.

After the operation which went extremely well but took around 7 hours I was told not to visit for a couple of days as she would be confused and might not recognise me.

When I did visit she had a bright blue streak in her remaining hair and I had to restrain myself from laughing in relief.

How it appeared I do not know; nurses assured me it was not medical treatment but would say no more although some of them smiled. I might be entirely wrong but suspect that it was a joke from the staff who were conscious that Eileen had been so concerned about losing her hair.

The rest is history. I was told that the operation would prevent any further deterioration but it was unlikely that the existing symptoms would all disappear as that side of the brain would remain smaller even though there would now be no pressure on it.

However, looking back the operation was highly successful and Mr Rajaraman and his team did a remarkable job. They managed to remove all of the tumour, and when the biopsy results arrived it was non-malignant.

For the first 18 months she had to have MRI scans each 6 months but these showed no recurrence of the problem and after 18 months Mr Rajaraman said she was fine and he was signing her off.

Now, some six years later, she has made a remarkable recovery and we were indeed fortunate to have had such a talented medical team looking after her.

Eileen's health improved rapidly but in 2012, she fell in the kitchen. She couldn't move so it was another hospital job and it transpired that she had broken the top of her thigh bone. I shall never forget the description – apparently entirely medically correct – that she greeted me with when I visited her in hospital. She said, 'They've given me a dynamic screw!'

She made a good recovery from that operation and, healthwise has been fit since then apart from existing asthma, arthritis and grain allergies.

While she was recovering Maurice and I had a holiday booked to visit Germany which was already paid for so Sulyn suggested that Eileen stay with her and Mark in Bury and it relieved me to know Eileen wouldn't be on her own whilst I was away.

Sulyn and Mark had 4 cats and one in particular, then called Dave (I've never ever heard a more inappropriate name for a cat!) took to Eileen and spent lots of time on her knee. He was a Norwegian Forest cat, large with lots of very soft fur, and Sulyn mentioned that he was really a loner and the other cats did not get on well with him.

That Christmas we were invited to Bury and 'Dave' took to me, spending a lot of his time on my knees.

I said later to Sulyn that we couldn't cope with a cat at that stage but if they ever decided 'Dave' should move to another home could we have first refusal?

Later that year they planned to get another pedigree cat and asked if we really would take 'Dave', on the basis that if he didn't settle they would take him back. We could and we did and overnight 'Dave' became 'Oskar' – rather a more appropriate name we felt for a Norwegian Forest cat.

Oskar didn't take long to acclimatise as a flat cat (Flat in the sense that we live in a flat) and he has become a friendly, loyal and contented member of the family.

\*

# CHAPTER 18

# The Stars & Stripes, Berlin, and a Celebration
# 2009 – 2013

### 2009: Brief Timeline

A light aircraft crashed into overhead power cables on the West Coast Main Line near the village of Little Haywood in Staffordshire killing the three occupants of the aircraft; Cold weather consisting of snow and freezing temperatures caused widespread disruption across the UK; Marks and Spencer announced they were to close 25 of their Simply Food stores and cut 1,230 jobs; New car sales for 2008 were reported to have fallen to a 12-year low of just over 2,100,000; The Bank of England cut its base interest rate to 1.5%; At the 66th Golden Globe Awards, British actress Kate Winslet won Best Actress (Motion Picture Drama) and Best Supporting Actress (Motion Picture); Approval was granted for the building of the controversial third runway and sixth terminal at Heathrow Airport; Jonathan Ross returned to television after serving a three-month suspension from the BBC following the row over prank telephone calls made to Andrew Sachs; The Halifax reported a rise in house prices of 1.9% in January; The Bank of England reduced the base rate of interest by 0.5% to 1.0%; The Yorkshire Ripper is released from Broadmoor Hospital to face a life sentence, for killing 13 women and attempting to kill 7 more.

Eileen and I had last visited America in 1976 to visit Phoebe and her family who have lived there for many years. That holiday had coincided with the United States Bicentennial, a series of celebrations and observances during 1976 that paid tribute to the historical events leading up to the creation of the United States of America as an independent republic. It was a central event in memory of the American Revolution. The Bicentennial culminated on Sunday, July 4, 1976, with the 200th anniversary of the adoption of the Declaration of Independence.

That visit is mentioned in an earlier chapter. Since then Phoebe has regularly visited the UK and spent a week or so in Scarborough but since the earlier visit I had never revisited America. Phoebe suggested it was time we got together as brother and sister and suggested I visit her for a 3 week holiday based on her home in Las Vegas.

Before I left, Eileen looked a little askance at the size of my suitcase and said, 'Aren't you coming back?' I assured her that of course I was – it was merely that the scheduled airline allowed larger suitcases than on tourist flights and I wasn't sure what laundry arrangements would be like whilst we were travelling within America. Whilst there had been no thought in my head of not returning, this was not to say there was not a little subtle pressure from Phoebe. One day she suggested we visit various new housing developments. With moving home number of times within the UK because of bank moves, these had always been an interest of mine and she had obviously been round these Las Vegas developments a few times before. She had lost her husband Brian a few years earlier and was maybe considering a move herself. One property in particular to which she appeared attracted had three levels – a joint utility area in the basement, then effectively, two self–contained flats – one on the ground floor and an upper floor unit. She passed some comment at the time that it could be ideal for people similar to us.

But this visit was well into the holiday, so let me start at the beginning from a diary I kept at the time.

I landed at Las Vegas on Tuesday, September 8th and after immigration checks Phoebe was waiting for me. After the flight she drove us to her home up in the hills very much on the outskirts, via the Las Vegas strip so I see all the lights. Being aged 50 or above was one of the conditions of living in 'Siena' although younger relatives of owners were permitted to visit.

On Thursday the 10th September, we made an early start to Zion Canyon which we then explored in a tour bus. We stayed at the Zion Park Inn before moving on the next day to Bryce Canyon Grand Hotel in Utah. We toured the Canyon and on the Saturday travelled to Cameron through Kanab then Fredona (both in Utah which is Mormon country which made me remember that somewhere beneath or within a mountain was stored a copy of our family tree, along with, no doubt, millions of others). We passed through Marble Canyon and had an overnight at Cameron Trading Post Hotel Lodge, in the Hopi building owned by that tribe.

Phoebe is very much into bird watching and as she or I drove, she would call out the names of the many birds we saw. A list is given later in this chapter for anyone who might be interested.

We then moved on to Grand Canyon staying there for 7 hours. It was much more commercial than the Grand Canyon I remembered from 1976 and we could not find Moqui Lodge in which Eileen, Susan and I had stayed on our earlier visit.

We asked, but no one seemed to have heard of it. On getting home I googled it and found it had closed in 2001 and been demolished so that gave me my answer. It had been a magnificent building and I recall a tree growing within it and through the roof.

We stayed overnight in Cameron then drove to Flagstaff along route 66, then on to Kingman and Hoover Dam with its new bridge in the course of erection; then to Lake Mead. From there we went on to Boulder, built originally for the workers on the original Dam, then back to Las Vegas.

We spent the next day leisurely in shopping outlets and

then at night we walked in Freemont Street for an amazing light, music and picture show projected on to the curved roof of the street. This again was a big change, as on our 1976 visit Freemont Street had just been another street open to the sky and adjacent to The Strip.

The following day we visited the Atomic Testing Museum and experienced an explosion at Ground Zero in the Ground Zero theatre. I particularly enjoyed this visit as I had been researching the Las Vegas atomic testing site for my book, *National Service, Elvis and Me!* and the original artefacts in the museum made a lot more sense of my research.

Wednesday morning was spent at the outdoor pool at Siena and in the evening we had dinner with my nephew Mark and his daughter Emily at their home. After dinner we went to the Venetian hotel and travelled in a gondola through mock canals imitating the Venice scene.

*Left: Photo of an atomic explosion taken from the Nevada test site*

The following day was then spent leisurely, with lunch at the Siena Golf Club and getting ready for the following day's early flight to San Francisco.

San Francisco Cable Car

Sunday saw us on Alcatraz, the old convict island. Then, back on the mainland we had lunch at Fog harbour and saw many seals on Pier 39.

I had a bad fall on the pier when I walked into the end of a large timber block around a foot square and many yards long, used to prevent traffic driving off the pier into the harbour. We took a taxi back to the hotel via Lombard and Nob Hill; then in the evening we saw an excellent performance of Brief Encounter at a local theatre. Incidentally the company was the Knee High Company – from Cornwall, England.

On Monday 21st we went to Fisherman's Wharf, had lunch at a restaurant called Boudins then we rode the cable car from the terminus to Market Street. It clanked and seemed to travel at breakneck speed, absolutely full of passengers – just as we have seen so many times in American films.

On Tuesday 22nd we packed, then left the luggage at

the San Francisco hotel until leaving time and took a bus to Ocean beach where we paddled in the Pacific Ocean and saw the Golden Gate Bridge. For some reason, possibly because of the name, I had expected the bridge to be gold in colour. It was painted with red lead and in that respect was a disappointment. The Humber Bridge appears much more elegant, but it is, of course, much newer.

Back we went for our luggage and found the hotel had supplied a black Lincoln Continental courtesy car to the airport. We arrived back in Las Vegas around 8.00pm.

On Wednesday 23rd we had an overnight stay in the sumptuous Bellagio hotel, Las Vegas. We used the hotel pool, had coffee, ice cream and, at night ate in their 'Olives' Restaurant. It had very attractive décor but seating seemed very crowded with tables very close together and the meal was not up to the standard of many UK restaurants I have visited, including Tuscany Too in Scarborough, although the meal cost at least twice the price.

We then watched the 'dancing waters' at the front of the hotel – massive fountains which danced to music and attracted crowds of sightseers.

On Saturday 24th we checked out of the Bellagio and went back to Phoebe's home.

In the evening we went to the Rio Hotel where Phoebe had planned a surprise and obtained tickets for 'Ride in the Sky' which was literally just that. Carnival floats were suspended from rails close to the ceiling, about 50 feet high, and the route zig-zagged through the hotel and casino. Show girls occupied the front float and around 5 floats followed containing guests who, like Phoebe, had obtained tickets in advance.

We had a marvellous bird's eye view of the casino, the gamblers at the gaming tables and those putting dimes into slot machines. We had been provided with bundles of necklaces, and mementoes which we were told to throw down to the waiting crowds below.

Left:
Myself and Phoebe adorned with necklaces similar to the ones we threw to the crowds below.

Right:
Show in the Sky advert

On Sunday 27th Mark entertained us to a fabulous meal at the Red Rock Country Club. It was situated in a beautiful setting amongst the hills and as well as Phoebe and Mark, Mark's daughter Emily was also there.

The following day was our last full day together and we again spent it at the Siena pool then moved on to the home of Dena and Steve. (Phoebe's daughter and son-in law) for a pool party.

And on Tuesday 29th September 2009 the holiday was over and it was back to Manchester by Delta, via Atlanta.

It had been a superb holiday into which we had packed a great deal. Thank you Phoebe!

---

*Birds seen on my American visit:*
*Anna's humming bird; Berdins; Brewers blackbird; Crackle blackbird; Black chinned humming bird; Black Phoebe; Canada Geese; Common Night hawk; Coopers hawk; Coots; Costa's humming bird; Green Heron; House finches; House sparrows; Scrub Jay; Grey Jay; Stella's Jay; Kildear; Mallards; Mocking birds; Morning doves; Mountain bluebird; Pigeons (galore!); Ravens; Road runners; Sharkfinned hawk; Swallows; Turkey vulture; Vestper sparrow; White Crowned sparrows.*

---

\*

Earlier I mentioned my friend Maurice Johnson. He had regularly gone on holiday around September time with a friend of his, Geoff Nalton, who, sadly, had died in February 2006, so Maurice and I agreed to have an occasional trip away for a few days.

Going back to my schooldays at Scarborough High School for Boys, German master 'Bonn' Clarke had always urged us to visit Germany in later years and, in particular to visit 'Unter den Linden', a very wide tree lined boulevard in Berlin, the capital of Germany.

I intended to take Bonn's advice as Berlin was our

destination in 2012; a massive city of around 345 square miles and with a population of around 3.5million. We had booked at the Adina Apartment Hotel, each room of which had its own small kitchen, cooker, hob, and dishwasher. Family rooms even had washing machines.

*Unter den Linden, Berlin*

The hotel was excellently situated for sightseeing and the following extract gives information about the city's history:

'Berlin is located in north eastern Germany on the banks of Rivers Spree and Havel. Due to its location in the European Plain, Berlin is influenced by a temperate seasonal climate. Around one-third of the city's area is composed of forests, parks, gardens, rivers and lakes.

First documented in the 13th century, Berlin became the capital of the Margraviate of Brandenburg (1417–1701), the Kingdom of Prussia (1701–1918), the German Empire

(1871–1918), the Weimar Republic (1919–1933) and the Third Reich (1933–1945). Berlin in the 1920s was the third largest municipality in the world. After World War II, the city was divided; East Berlin became the capital of East Germany while West Berlin became a de facto West German exclave, surrounded by the Berlin Wall (1961–1989). Following German reunification in 1990, Berlin was once more designated as the capital of all Germany.

Berlin is a world city of culture, politics, media, and science. Its economy is based on high-tech firms and the service sector, encompassing a diverse range of creative industries, research facilities, media corporations, and convention venues. The city serves as a continental hub for air and rail traffic and has a highly complex public transportation network. The metropolis is a popular tourist destination. Modern Berlin is home to renowned universities, orchestras, museums, entertainment venues, and is host to many sporting events. Its urban setting has made it a sought-after location for international film productions. The city is well known for its festivals, diverse architecture, nightlife, contemporary arts, and a high quality of living. Over the last decade Berlin has seen the emergence of a cosmopolitan entrepreneurial scene.

During the Weimar era, Berlin underwent political unrest due to economic uncertainties, but also became a renowned centre of the Roaring Twenties. Albert Einstein rose to public prominence during his years in Berlin, being awarded the Nobel Prize for Physics in 1921.

In 1933, Adolf Hitler and the Nazi Party came to power. After the end of the war in Europe in 1945, Berlin received large numbers of refugees from the Eastern provinces. The victorious powers divided the city into four sectors, analogous to the occupation zones into which Germany was divided. The sectors of the Western Allies (the United States, the United Kingdom and France) formed West Berlin, while the Soviet sector formed East Berlin.

All four Allies shared administrative responsibilities for

Berlin. However, in 1948, when the Western Allies extended the currency reform in the Western zones of Germany to the three western sectors of Berlin, the Soviet Union imposed a blockade on the access routes to and from West Berlin, which lay entirely inside Soviet–controlled territory. The Berlin airlift, conducted by the three western Allies, overcame this blockade by supplying food and other supplies to the city from June 1948 to May 1949. In 1949, the Federal Republic of Germany was founded in West Germany and eventually included all of the American, British, and French zones, excluding those three countries' zones in Berlin, while the Marxist–Leninist German Democratic Republic was proclaimed in East Germany. West Berlin officially remained an occupied city, but it politically was aligned with the Federal Republic of Germany despite West Berlin's geographic isolation. Airline service to West Berlin was granted only to American, British, and French airlines.'

## The Berlin Wall

'During the early years of the Cold War, West Berlin was a geographical loophole through which thousands of East Germans fled to the democratic West. In response, the Communist East German authorities built a wall that totally encircled West Berlin. The first version was thrown up overnight, on 13 August 1961.

The Berlin Wall was a barrier that divided Berlin from 1961 to 1989. Constructed by the East German Democratic Republic (GDR), starting on 13 August 1961, the wall completely cut off (by land) West Berlin from surrounding .15

Over the next few weeks, euphoric people and souvenir hunters chipped away parts of the wall; the governments later used industrial equipment to remove most of what was left.

Contrary to popular belief the wall's actual demolition did not begin until the summer of 1990 and was not *completed until 1992. The fall of the Berlin Wall paved the way for German reunification, which was formally concluded on 3 October 1990.'*

From the Adina Hotel we decided to visit the Brandenburg Gate and had been told it was only a train stop away from nearby railway station Hackescher Markt. A train pulled into the station with, what we thought was our destination showing and on we hopped. It seemed to be a long distance train and was a double decker with travellers stepping down a couple of steps into the ground floor or up a few steps for the upper deck.

It didn't seem to be stopping at all and when the conductress came to examine our passes we asked how long it would take. She consulted her ticket machine, looked at her watch and said, 'about one hour 20'.

*The Brandenburg Gate*

We explained we had been told that the Brandenburg gate was only one stop away and she then told us we were on the train to Brandenburg some miles away. We would have to alight at the next stop and retrace our steps. This we did and we eventually did find the magnificent Brandenburg Gate. It was well worth the 20 mile or so detour we had taken.

We decided to spend our first evening meal at an attractive looking Italian restaurant called 'Olives' not far from the hotel. Again it was very busy but a waiter, who we later found out to be the proprietor, found us a table and made sure we were looked after.

The second evening we went back to Olives but hadn't booked. It was very busy but there he was at the door waiting and he said, 'I thought you'd be back. I've kept a table for you'. After the meal he brought us complimentary Limoncellos and explained they came from his mother's small vineyard in Italy.

'Olives' became a regular for us. There was also an excellent ice cream parlour at Hackescher Markt station which sold every flavour of ice cream imaginable.

Later we tried unsuccessfully to book tickets for the Berliner Philharmoniker orchestra conducted by Simon Rattle, but, not unexpectedly, it was fully booked.

One memorable trip – for the wrong reasons – was to Spandau to see the gaol where Rudolf Hess had been imprisoned after WWII. We went by the U-bahn (subway) to Rudow and got off at Zitadelle which we were told was the nearest stop to the prison. We then had a walk from the station and were told to pass a large garage and motor tyre complex and Spandau was a little further on, on the opposite side of the road. We did find it eventually and paid our entrance fee and to be fair to the scrupulously correct Germans there was a small notice saying that whilst this was Spandau prison it was not the prison in which Rudolf Hess and the German High Command had been imprisoned after WWII.

We thought that was probably a safeguard to prevent

trouble from Nazi sympathisers and we went ahead and had a very informative visit and realised that after WWII the British had run the prison for some time.

Only much later did we realise that the notice was 100% correct. There had been two Spandau prisons and the one in which Hess had been imprisoned was demolished shortly after his death – for the very reasons we had thought the notice was incorrect – to prevent trouble from Nazi sympathisers. There was also a sting in the tail for us. The original site of the prison had been on Wilhelmstrasse, Spandau, where the motor repair and tyre complex which we had passed on our arrival now stands.

*Above: The actual Spandau Prison, in Wilhelmstrasse, where Rudolf Hess was imprisoned and died. It was demolished directly after his death.*

We made arrangements through our hotel to visit the Reichstag Dome at Platz der Republik 1, Berlin, but needed to book in advance, with passports being a security requirement.

As well as being gutted by fire, the former home of German democracy was further damaged during Allied bombing of Berlin in World War II. It was left in this run-down state until the 1960s, when it was opened as a conference centre. The Reichstag was the site of the German reunification ceremonies at midnight on October 2nd, 1990.

Then in 1992 UK firm Foster and Partners won a commission in 1992 to transform the building into the new home for the unified German Parliament. The Foster team's design focused on making the processes of government more transparent.

*Above: The new German Parliament building – the Reichstag building in Berlin designed by Foster & Partners*

Foster's dome is a gleaming metal and glass structure with a ramp that spirals up a to a roof terrace with 360-degree views over central Berlin. The dome overlooks the debating chamber for the Bundestag and a central mirrored cone draws light into the plenary chamber. The design also preserves remnants of the buildings' colourful past, including graffiti left by the Red Army in 1945.

Foster was awarded the Pritzker Prize in 1999 for his work on the building, which has become one of the top tourist destinations in Berlin.

There are magnificent views of the city from the viewing platforms at the top of the dome.

*Above: The glass dome of the Reichstag building with the spiral path by which you reach the top of the dome. The mirrored cone is in the centre and sightseers can be seen walking up and down the spiral viewing platforms.*

Another day we went up the Berlin TV tower – 368 metres high with more magnificent views and took a bus trip round Berlin and saw part of what remains of the Wall, Einstein's café, and Checkpoint Charlie. The latter crossing point between what was the East and the West is re-enacted by German actors who take the part of American troops.

An interesting thing we learnt was that whilst East Berlin had trams, the west never did and the same remains the case to this day. So, if you see, or use a tram, you are in what was East Berlin. One day we took a No. 12 tram from Hackscher Markt to its destination – Berliner Allee. This area had all been part of East Berlin and whilst buildings had been painted and spruced up it was still obvious that the architecture of the many blocks of flats didn't match that in what had been the western part of the city.

Another interesting discovery was that the route and positioning of the Wall is commemorated by lines of small coloured paving blocks which indicate clearly and continuously where the Wall used to stand.

The following day we visited the Holocaust museum, the Brandenburg Gate (again), and Unter den Linden as well as a few of the large, leafy parks in and around the city

The next day, Friday, we took a trip to Potsdam by train and once there we took an open bus tour and visited Frederik I's Palace Sanssouci. This tour also included the Glienicke Bridge where it was somewhat atmospheric to stand in the place where, on February 10th 1962, U2 pilot, Frances Gary Powers was exchanged for Soviet KGB Colonel Vilyam Fisher, known as 'Rudolf Abel'

*'Powers was recruited by the CIA for his outstanding record in single engine jet aircraft. By 1960, Powers was already a veteran of many covert aerial reconnaissance missions. U–2 pilots flew espionage missions using an aircraft that could reach altitudes above 70,000 feet, making it invulnerable to Soviet anti–aircraft weapons of the time. The U–2 was equipped with a state–of–the–art camera designed to take high–resolution photos from the edge of the stratosphere over hostile countries, including the Soviet Union. U–2 missions systematically photographed military installations and other important sites. Soviet intelligence had been aware of encroaching U–2 flights since 1956 but lacked effective countermeasures until 1960. On 1 May Powers' U–2, which departed from a military airbase in Peshawar, Pakistan was shot down by*

an S–75 Dvina (SA–2 Guideline) surface–to–air missile over Sverdlovsk. Powers was unable to activate the plane's self–destruct mechanism before he bailed out and was captured. Powers' U–2 plane was hit by the first missile fired. A total of eight were launched; one of them hit a MiG–19 jet fighter which was sent to intercept the U–2 but could not reach a high enough altitude. Another Soviet aircraft, a newly manufactured Su–9 in transit flight, also attempted to intercept Powers' U–2. The unarmed Su–9 was directed to ram the U–2 but missed because of the large differences in speed.

What CIA officials did not realize was that the plane crashed almost fully intact, and the Soviets recovered its equipment. Powers was interrogated extensively by the KGB for months before he made a confession and a public apology for his part in espionage. The incident set back talks between Khrushchev and Eisenhower. On August 17, 1960, Powers was convicted of espionage against the Soviet Union and was sentenced to a total of ten years, three years in imprisonment followed by seven years of hard labour. He was held in Vladimir Central Prison, 100 miles east of Moscow. The prison contains a small museum with an exhibit on Powers, who allegedly developed a good rapport with Russian prisoners there. Some pieces of the plane and Powers' uniform are on display at the Monino Airbase museum near Moscow. On February 10, 1962, Powers was exchanged, along with American student Frederic Pryor, in a well–publicized spy swap at the Glienicke Bridge in Berlin. The exchange was for Soviet KGB Colonel Vilyam Fisher, known as 'Rudolf Abel', who had been caught by the FBI and tried and jailed for espionage'.

Our holiday was drawing to a close but before we left Berlin we took a morning boat trip down the river Spree through Berlin. We then walked through the Tiergarten to see the Russian memorial to 2,000 soldiers killed in the Battle of Berlin whose bodies are buried there.

In the afternoon we packed, ready to return to the UK the following day.

Berlin is certainly a city to which I would like to return.

*

In March 2013 Eileen and I held our Golden Wedding Anniversary. We discussed whether we should have a party but decided we would prefer to go with family to our favourite holiday spot, King's Island in Luxor, Egypt, which is much mentioned elsewhere in this book.

There we spent three weeks in what we, the management and the staff call 'our second home'. Sulyn and Mark joined us for first two weeks and my sister Phoebe joined us for the second two, flying over from Las Vegas, where she has lived for many years. It was a good enjoyable family get together in the comfort of the island; with its excellent restaurants and food, first class staff, and superb weather.

*

# CHAPTER 19

# 'Bodgit and Scarper'
# 2015

Hobbies and interests over the years have been numerous – possibly because I am a Gemini. I gained an interest in short wave radio from my uncle Percy (call sign G8KU), and built the miniature radio mentioned much earlier which I converted from a hearing aid. This was at the time when portable radios were the size of a briefcase. I also built a very early electronic calculator in 1973, which still works, but would be a blessing to anyone with shares in a battery company; and I built a black and white, valved television set long before transistors became the norm and before colour sets were available. When I had added the components, finished all the soldering and switched it on, it actually worked first time but the picture was 'inside out' on the cathode ray tube, which simply meant a 2 minute job to swap four wires around.

When I moved to the Malton branch of Barclays bank I decided to have some 'me' time (which didn't last for long!) and I built a grandfather clock which still ticks away the hours.

I have had a few small company directorships over the years although these are now down to one – and between 2013 and 2016 I was President of the Barclays Bank Pensioners Club – York Section, having earlier been Chairman of the club in 2006–7.

I have already mentioned that I am involved in the Old Scarborians' Association – which consists of ex–pupils and masters from the long defunct Boys' High School, and that brings back to mind an editorial I wrote in May 2001 for the Association's magazine Summer Times:

> 'Relaxing on a sunbed in Luxor on the banks of the Nile, there was little breeze to cool the 100 degree heat, and I was grateful for the iced drink by my side.
> I was reading a thriller by Robert Goddard. A paragraph caught my eye and I thought how appropriately it related to members of the Old Scarborians Association.
> I hope Robert Goddard won't minding me quoting from his book 'Beyond Recall':

> 'Living in the past. It's always said pejoratively, as if the past is necessarily inferior to the future, or at any rate less important; nobody's ever condemned for looking forward, only back. But the truth is that we do live in the past, whether we like it or not. That's where our life takes shape. Somewhere ahead, however near or far, is the end. But behind, shrouded in clouds of forgetting, lies the beginning.'

The editorial continued:
> 'For most of us, the real beginning we remember was our schooldays, and, was the Association not to exist, those memories would already be shrouded in 'clouds of forgetting'. Through the Association flows friendship and recollections of years long ago.
> For very few of our present members the beginning was Scarborough Municipal School; for the majority it was Scarborough High School for Boys, either at the buildings in Westwood, or, for younger members, at Woodlands, Scarborough.
> But, important though these buildings were, our beginnings were not in the fabric, but in the very soul of the school; nourished and nurtured as it was in our time by such talented Headmasters as HW Marsden and Alec Gardiner; and by the generally excellent members of staff whom were hand–picked and brought to the school.
> This Association is like a cherished jigsaw puzzle where,

*in much younger days, the pieces were scattered to the four winds as we left school and embarked on our individual careers.*

*Now mature, and through the Association, we are trying to reassemble the puzzle and find the lost pieces. Never again can the full picture be reproduced. Ex–pupils and many members of staff have died along the way; some have elected not to join us; some probably do not know that we still exist.*

*But we all now try in our own ways, to make the jigsaw picture as complete a whole as possible. By being members of the Association, we renew, refresh, and make new friendships with those of our contemporaries we may not otherwise have seen for the majority of a lifetime.*

*The school does not now exist. Potential membership is finite and only by seeking new members from old boys can we extend the life of the Association.*

*From my sunbed in Luxor, I raise my glass to the two stalwarts who were instrumental in keeping the Association alive for very many years when it would otherwise surely have withered and died. I refer to two Honorary Life Vice Presidents, Geoff Nalton and Frank Bamforth.*

*We owe to both of them a large debt of gratitude. Without them, and their determination and vision, there wouldn't now be a strong and vibrant Old Scarborians Association.*

*And without them the memories and friendships from our schooldays, which we are able to share and enjoy, would, in Robert Goddard's words, 'be shrouded in clouds of forgetting'.*

(Geoff Nalton, involved at Dunkirk during the war, died in February 2006 and Frank Bamforth was well into his 90's, when he died in June 2017)

\*

The following has become the chapter heading for this

particular section. By way of background Old Scarborian member Jim Goodman approached me in 2011 and said he had a friend who wanted a book publishing.

He mentioned that there was an early morning radio programme on BBC Radio York called *'Early Birds'* to which various listeners from all over the country, and in fact the world, contributed, on air.

One of these contributors whom Jim mentioned was called Bryan D. Overall, and Jim told me Bryan had written a book of odes about those taking part in the radio programme and about various aspects of the programme. Bryan wanted his book publishing in a small way.

I gave Jim, our Farthings Publishing business card and web site address to pass on to his friend and suggested Bryan contact me direct. Before long a reply came from Bryan, a retired British police officer who was, by then, living in Cyprus.

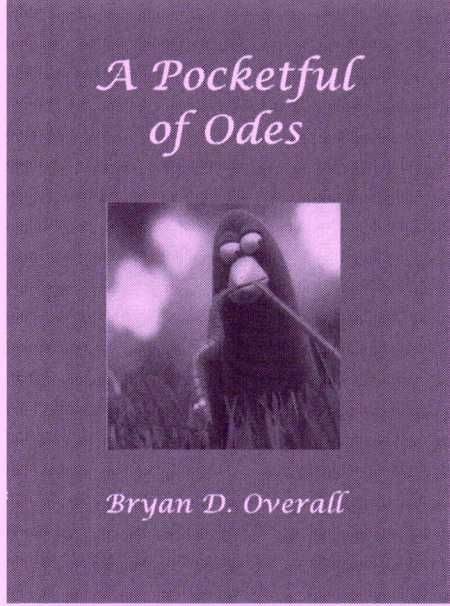

Bryan subsequently contacted me, we discussed his book, and a few weeks later, *'A Pocketful of Odes'*, was born. The cover depicts a cartoon bird eating a cartoon worm to reflect the radio show which was called *'The Early Birds'* and it is said that the early bird catches the worm.

It transpired that before his retirement, Bryan and his wife Linda had visited Cyprus frequently on holiday; just as Eileen and I had visited King's Island in Luxor. On Bryan's retirement they had decided to move to Paphos in Cyprus where they lived in a house built by 'George', a

Cypriot builder whom they had known for many years.

At this stage the four of us hadn't met, but Jim, who had originally put us in touch, suggested the 5 of us should meet up for lunch. That became the first of a number of lunches we all enjoyed.

Eileen and I, and Bryan and Linda, gradually got to know each other better and we mentioned that we liked to holiday in Luxor at a hotel called Jolie Ville on an 180 acre island in the Nile called Kings' Island. They mentioned that they had also enjoyed holidays there.

One thing led to another over the following months and the four of us decided to make a joint visit to Luxor. Although the temperature was unusually hot in mid-October 2015 when we visited, we all had a wonderful time on the Island, getting to know each other, eating together and taking trips on the Nile by Felucca, or motor boat when the wind was too weak for Feluccas to sail.

One memorable evening was a visit to the Son et Lumiere performance at Karnak Temple. Eileen and I had seen it in the late 1990s but had thought because of dropping visitor numbers to Luxor partly caused by the lack of direct airline flights from UK regional airports, the evenings had been cancelled.

Bryan is nothing if not inquisitive and he likes to ferret things out. It's probably his police background and there is definitely a book in there somewhere!

One afternoon he appeared and said that if we wanted to see the Son et Lumiere in English at Karnak Temple the following evening, a mini bus would pick us up at 7.15pm.

It did – but at 6.15pm – as there had been some misunderstanding about times and the driver almost flew to Karnak to get us there in time. In fact the accompanying guide said, 'You like to fly?' as the bus bounced over road speed humps and nearly took off.

Earlier, Bryan had told me that after retiring from the police in 1999, and when he and Linda had moved into their house in Cyprus, he had asked 'George the Builder' about having a carport erected on the side of the house.

George was extremely busy at that time and couldn't build houses fast enough to meet the growing 'ex-Pat' demand so, having witnessed some of Bryan's DIY skills, he encouraged Bryan to 'do it himself'.

Bryan did, and made such a success of the car port that other owners approached him to do small jobs. Then friends of friends approached him and he decided to form 'Bodgit and Scarper', effectively a home maintenance-cum-do-it-yourself business, although it was Bryan who was 'doing it'. He had T shirts and baseball caps made, sporting the firm's name *'Bodgit and Scarper. We* **never** *live up to our name',* and these were given to all his customers.

*Karnak Temple*

On one trip to Luxor, Bryan even discovered a *Bodgit and Scarper* cap perched on an ancient building at Karnak Temple which was being repaired at the time. His small firm's fame had spread far and wide.

Reluctantly, in January 2012, Bryan and Linda had to leave Cyprus and return to their home in the UK and it was then that we actually met face-to-face and our friendship really began.

On our last night in Luxor we had arranged a felucca

boat ride on the Nile. The setting sun over the Nile is always a memorable sight.

All was well as we set off and there was a very gentle breeze which enabled us to gently glide on the Nile and get some wonderful photos of the sunset. Returning, we ran out of wind so Mahmoud, the boatman, used a long punting pole to gradually propel us nearer to the island and landing stage. However, at one point the pole was obviously not long enough to reach a deep part of the Nile. It seemed we were temporarily stuck. We were within hailing distance of the landing stage so Mahmoud shouted to a colleague who was preparing to come to rescue us in a motor boat.

Meanwhile, two Egyptians in a tiny rowing boat they were using to fish; hardly large enough for the two of them; realised what was happening and rowed over.

They unwound a seemingly very thin piece of rope from the front of the felucca and secured it to the tiny rowing boat. The oarsman pulled strongly and gradually the tiny fishing boat pulled the comparatively massive felucca a few yards until we were clear of the deep dip in the river bed and Mahmoud was again able to punt us back home.

It was the end of a memorable holiday, and the real start of a friendship with Bryan and Linda which I am sure will last for years to come.

And, Bryan's 'other book' mentioned a few pages earlier? It's apparently a novel which features Luxor, skulduggery, the Secret Service, tomb antiques and... Castor Oil!!

As this book draws to a close, five particular strands have proved very important to me since I retired: family, of course; the Old Scarborians Association; writing and publishing through our micro firm Farthings Publishing; the Stephen Joseph Theatre and our favourite holiday island in the middle of the river Nile – original Crocodile

Island but more recently renamed King's Island.

We made out 'last trip' to the island in October 2016 but the pull of the island and of the Nile, is so strong that we hope to visit again in October 2017.

Health will be the decider, but if it happens, it will be our 31st visit.

*Sunset over the West bank of the Nile*

# ENDPIECE

Looking back over many years, I have enjoyed, and continue to enjoy a good life.

Whilst I try to keep relatively active and I usually swim three times a week, I am slowing down a little and have cut out various committees and responsibilities to concentrate on books; reading, writing and publishing – the latter in a very small way. Turning pages of text into a professionally finished, bookshop quality book, is, I always find, extremely challenging, stimulating and satisfying.

Three regrets over my lifetime have been, first, that Sulyn and Mark chose to marry quietly in Las Vegas without even parents having the opportunity of attending or me being able to give her away. This is not criticism in any way as it was their right and their decision. It is merely disappointment on my part at missing such an important, one–off event.

The second is that we have only the one daughter, Sulyn, and no son. Without a son, our line of the Fowler family dating back to 1541 and probably earlier, will die with me. Another child for us, either girl or boy, was not to be and I know Sulyn would have dearly liked to have a brother or sister.

And third, whilst Sulyn always has been, and will always remain a treasure, she and Mark have no children of their own, so we have no grandchildren.

Health during my working years was generally good, and although since retirement I have had various health ailments, luckily all of these seem to have been satisfactorily resolved. The best benefit the bank provided from my retirement and after the pension, was definitely private health insurance - although that is not intended to knock the National Health Service which has reacted admirably to emergencies.

Health over the last few months has been a matter of 'ups and downs'.

In 2016 Eileen and I went to Luxor with Bryan and Linda in October. I had a fall on the Island, the full consequences of which, thankfully, did not become apparent until we had returned home.

Initially I was treated for sciatica but my physiotherapist became concerned that my symptoms were not improving and suggested I seek an MRI scan. At the time I had also been getting breathless and had little energy but I was putting it all down to the fall.

My doctor referred me to a spine specialist and surgeon in York, Mr Kenan Deniz who arranged the MRI scan and was disturbed to find from it that I had stenosis of the spine in two places. Technically this was described as *'Severe L3/4 and L4/5 canal stenosis causing neurogenic claudication'*. This is translated as being two holes at belt level in the tube which carries the nerves within the spine.

We discussed his assessment and he said he could and would operate, but from symptoms he had seen he was not convinced my heart was strong enough to withstand a major operation and he advised me to first have my heart checked out. My own doctor then carried out blood tests and an ECG, which showed 'abnormalities'. The results were sent to Scarborough Hospital where an appointment followed for a 'routine' heart scan. The scan itself seemed to take a lot longer than the half hour we had been advised and when a doctor entered the room I asked if we were free to go home.

'I'm sorry but you're not going anywhere,' he said. 'You could drop down dead at any time. Your heart beat is dangerously low and we're keeping you in hospital as an emergency and will give you a pacemaker tomorrow.'

The following day, Wednesday 29th March 2017, a pacemaker was plumbed in to the left hand side of my chest just below the collar bone, by Dr Justin Ghosh. A local, rather than general anaesthetic was used and it was interesting to know what was happening and to be able to talk as it proceeded – with no pain or discomfort whatsoever.

I asked Dr Ghosh how many pacemakers he had fitted and his 'rough estimate' was between 700 and 800.

When I was wheeled back to the ward where Eileen was waiting she exclaimed, 'Crikey! You've got back your colour and your Egyptian suntan!' And so I had. In 90 minutes.

Almost instantaneously my energy levels rose and breathlessness and tiredness dropped to the much lower levels they had been at some months earlier.

My sincere thanks go to both Mr Deniz and Dr Ghosh whose respective talents proved to me that miracles can, and do happen.

With the heart now working properly, the back pain has eased and while it is still there, certainly at this stage I don't feel I wish to risk a major spine operation as I know of people who have ended up paralysed from the waist down.

*

And finally, as I was completing this marathon, I decided to drive to Newby and to 3 Throxenby Grove, which still holds many happy memories of the years during which Phoebe and I were growing up and where this long and rambling story started.

As I approached, dusk was falling and outside number 3, the street lamp was alight. That very same street lamp - albeit now electric and not gas - which had cast its friendly, welcoming, golden glow 78 years ago, when mother had brought Phoebe home from the nursing home and I had been waiting on the doorstep for her with my father, aunt Alice and Patch the family dog.

It seems very appropriate to me that, as that old street lamp was involved at the start of *'I've started, so I'll finish'*, so should it be, at the end.

*I've finished!!*

*David Fowler*

Scarborough
September 2017

****

Printed in Great Britain
by Amazon